The New Rules
of Personal Investing

The

NEW RULES

of PERSONAL

INVESTING

The Experts'
Guide to
Prospering
in a Changing
Economy

Financial Correspondents of
The New York Times

Edited by ALLEN R. MYERSON

TIMES BOOKS

Henry Holt and Company • New York

Times Books
Henry Holt and Company, LLC
Publishers since 1866
115 West 18th Street
New York, New York 10011

Henry Holt® is a registered trademark of
Henry Holt and Company, LLC.

Library of Congress Cataloging-in-Publication Data

The new rules of personal investing : the experts' guide to prospering
in a changing economy / by financial correspondents of the
New York times ; edited by Allen R. Myerson.—1st ed.

     p. cm.
  Includes index.
  ISBN 0-8050-7273-X
    1. Finance, Personal. 2. Investments. I. Myerson, Allen R.
    II. New York times.

 HG179 .N446 2002
 332.6—dc21

                          2001054404

First published in hardcover in 2002 by Times Books

First Paperback Edition 2003

Designed by Victoria Hartman
Illustrations designed by Pat Lyons

Printed in the United States of America
10 9 8 7 6 5 4 3 2 1

Contents

Introduction: The New Rules, and the Older Ones

GRETCHEN MORGENSON

The old investing adage still holds true today: Dollars do better when they are accompanied by sense.

Unfortunately for many investors, both beginner and practiced, commonsense investment advice has been hard to come by in recent years. That is why this book was conceived.

Even as Americans put more and more of their investment dollars to work in the stock market during the 1990s, well-grounded and informed guidance about investment strategies was drowned out by hot tips and hype. One of the defining characteristics of the mania for stocks at the turn of the millennium was that while sources of investment advice exploded—investing Web sites, cable television shows, market newsletters and the like—the quality of information actually declined. All that guidance did little to prevent millions of investors from losing billions of dollars as technology stocks plunged in 2000.

With this in mind, the editors and reporters of the *New York Times* set out to write *The New Rules of Personal Investing*, a book that provides a clear, comprehensive and unbiased source of financial advice and information that you can rely on now and in years to come. In addition to giving an overview of strategies and investing styles that can help you achieve your financial goals, *The New Rules of Personal Investing*, dispelling the myths that circulated during the recent stock market frenzy, will help you sift through the post–bull market wreckage for investment truths. Our goal is to put current conditions in the financial markets into a longer-term perspective, to keep you on the path to prosperity and away from pitfalls.

The fact is, some investing rules written during the mania need to be discarded while other, more venerable strategies need to be relearned.

During the unusually long and enriching bull market of the 1990s, many investors began to believe that successful investing was a cinch. Investment advisers were jettisoned for do-it-yourself schemes. Buy-and-hold strategies that had served investors well for decades seemed positively banal and were replaced by rapid-fire trading. It was a natural response to four consecutive years of 20 percent returns or more.

But the ease with which investors coined these profits hid the fact that the overall market was growing increasingly perilous. So even as the stock market looked more alluring to investors, the risk in many people's portfolios was rocketing.

During the Internet craze, for example, investors junked the venerable notion that companies ought to be able to turn a profit before their stocks merited purchase. For a wild period during 2000, the more money a company lost, the better its stock performed. The more profitable a company was, the less attractive its shares.

But this perverse investing style quickly caved in. Investors who had thought that profits didn't matter suddenly learned how wrongheaded they were. Internet stocks plunged, in some cases losing almost all their value. Dead dotcoms became commonplace. Unfortunately, when the music stopped, few investors were able to get off the dance floor.

Another cold fact that recently confronted investors is that the nation's financial markets can be held hostage by terrorists. The September 11 attacks on the World Trade Center towers and the Pentagon destroyed investors' optimism in the near-term future of the country. And investors without optimism are much more likely to put their money in a mattress than into a company's stock.

The lesson that investors can draw from the market turmoil is this: Even though the financial terrain appears to be constantly changing, some rules remain steadfast winners. Knowing how to value companies based on the cash they produce, for example, is far superior to analysts' habit during the Internet frenzy of valuing them based on the number of people visiting their Web sites. And contrary to the recent belief in putting everything into stocks, adding some bonds can be immensely profitable, the right place even for more aggressive players.

The throngs who bid the buy-and-hold strategy good-bye in the late 1990s should reacquaint themselves with this strategy as well. In 1999, investors held stocks for just over eight months on average, according to Sanford C. Bernstein, a brokerage firm in New York. A decade earlier, investors typically held shares for two years. The trading frenzy even infected the staid mutual fund world: investors at the end of the twentieth century held funds on average for less than four years. In 1990, the average holding period had been eleven years.

Rapid-fire traders quickly learned that transaction costs have a way of eating up the returns of even the most high-flying stocks. And when shares began to fall, the costs exacerbated the traders' already distressing losses.

Americans are now so involved in the stock market that, at the end of the century, the value of their equity portfolios had sailed past the value of their homes. Many people receive stock as part of their compensation. Most intend to supplement their Social Security and pension funds with gains generated in the stock market. At the turn of the century, stocks have become America's pastime.

But investing successfully is not like spending a day at the ballpark. It is harder work, and it carries higher stakes. *The New Rules of Personal Investing* aims to help you achieve your investing goals and therefore your life dreams.

In chapter 1, "From Depressed to Delirious: Understanding Today's Market," Floyd Norris explores how in just one generation the American investor went from holding the stock market in deep suspicion to embracing it full force. Easier trading and access to information, the explosive growth of mutual funds and the long bull market all swept even the smallest investor up into the mania for stocks.

Chapter 2, "Investing for the Ages: Long-Term Strategies," helps you assess the risks worth taking and gives advice on how to put together an appropriate mix of stocks, bonds and money market funds based on how far along in life and savings you are. Kurt Eichenwald examines how to save for a home purchase, a child's college education and retirement. It shows the risks of playing things too safe, and the huge benefits of starting to save while young. What should a young person put away in a retirement account, and how should this differ from what someone in the middle of life or later chooses? "Investing for the Ages" answers such questions.

In addition to reacquainting themselves with some of the old rules, investors have a host of new principles that they must consider as well. A prime example of a worthwhile new rule pertains to the search for trustworthy information sources about a company. The Internet is an essential new tool, with company documents available online and several reliable Web sites on investing. But investors who act on chat room tips without doing a great deal of further research are imperiling their portfolios. In chapter 3, "Stocks: How (and How Not) to Invest Directly," Leslie Eaton explains where you can go for the best information on companies, and how to apply it in picking stocks.

Another of the old, reliable rules that some investors need to relearn is how to structure a diversified portfolio through the use of mutual funds. During the late 1990s, funds seemed positively boring to investors excited by the ability to trade shares via computer. Technology stocks were the rockets that propelled the stock market skyward as many investors dumped other shares in their rush to profit. Yet with the benefit of hindsight, mutual funds with a broad array of holdings proved to be much less risky than a portfolio stuffed with stock market darlings. In chapter 4, "Mutual Funds: Leaving It to the

Pros," Danny Hakim helps you get back to the basics of finding the best, low-cost portfolio managers. But new principles also apply in the venerable world of mutual funds, so the chapter also advises you on how to make the most of some of the newer investment vehicles. Exchange traded funds, for example, are a completely new phenomenon that began in the late 1990s, and here you learn how they differ from traditional mutual funds and what benefits and drawbacks they can bring to your investing portfolio.

In chapter 5, "Bonds and Bond Funds: Why They Belong in Your Portfolio," Robert D. Hershey Jr. helps investors renew their appreciation for an entire area of the financial markets that was viewed as stolid and sluggish while stocks were racing. But boring can be beautiful, as evidenced by the fact that bonds outpaced stocks in 2000 and at least through much of 2001. Clearly, going back to basics can help you reduce your risks and even out your returns. But the bond market is far more opaque than the stock market, so investors must do a lot of investigating to decide whether to buy bonds outright or invest in a fund. Which bonds are safest and which are more like shares of stock and therefore risky? Chapter 5 helps you assess credit quality and consider how the economic outlook should affect your bond holdings.

Investing overseas is another area where conventional wisdom has changed. For years, putting eggs in foreign baskets was a fine way to diversify. But in recent years it has become evident that the globalization of business makes it tougher to diversify by investing abroad. In fact, economies and markets around the world are much more likely to work in tandem today than ever before. Choosing the right foreign stocks, or stock funds, can still help improve your performance, but currency risk, differing accounting practices and the relative lack of financial information complicate overseas investments. In chapter 6, "International Investments: The New Landscape," Jonathan Fuerbringer helps you overcome these obstacles.

Given Congress's maddening propensity to change the United States tax code, there will always be new rules for how to invest with taxes in mind. In chapter 7, "Taxes: How to Protect Your Gains,"

David Cay Johnston explains, in plain English, how taxes can harm investment returns and how to keep your taxes down without sacrificing returns. Are individual stocks superior to mutual funds for avoiding taxes? How can you be sure you aren't getting ripped off by a mutual fund manager who is grossly inefficient in minimizing your taxes? What can you do to stay clear of the alternative minimum tax trap? Chapter 7 provides these critical answers for protecting your future.

Finally, chapter 8, "Let the Investor Beware: Traps, Scams and Myths," advises investors on how to steer clear of common investing pitfalls and avoid falling victim to frauds. Although the Internet has helped make Wall Street more accessible for even the smallest investor, it has been a great boon for swindlers, promoting the spread of questionable new practices that can harm those who are too trusting or unaware. This chapter discusses what deceptions to watch out for, especially on the Internet, and explains how to shield yourself from poor service and trade execution in online brokerage accounts. Among the modern-day touts you should regard with skepticism are the many Wall Street analysts who act more like salesmen than objective advisers. With legal protections for investors fairly weak, the markets are truly an area where customers must stay on their guard.

In short, *The New Rules of Personal Investing* gives you the analysis and advice you need to demystify the financial markets today. This is not, however, a book full of faddish tips that will be out of date soon after it rolls off the press. Rather, it gives you guidance on how to think wisely about the market as a whole, advice that will have a longer life and deeper application than the proverbial list of ten stocks to buy now.

Written by the most authoritative markets team in journalism, *The New Rules of Personal Investing* tells you what lessons from the past still work and what conventional wisdom is dead wrong. For investors who want to reach a happy ending, it is crucial to have solid footing at the start.

The New Rules
of Personal Investing

1.

From Depressed to Delirious: Understanding Today's Market

FLOYD NORRIS

In the early twenty-first century, American investors are confident that stocks are and will be excellent long-term investments.

To gauge whether that belief is reasonable, it is useful to see how we got to this point by tracing the history of investing over the past seventy-five years. During this period investor enthusiasm rose and fell while the world changed. Regulation forced investors to be more cautious after the 1920s and innovation made it possible for them to be far less cautious after the 1970s.

The extent to which that lack of caution has colored today's market is one of the most important unanswered questions. It clearly helped investors make phenomenal profits before the Nasdaq market crumbled in 2000—and, equally clearly, it led to huge losses in 2001.

By mid-2001, investor caution was higher than it recently had been, but still relatively low by historic standards. Investors are still inclined to pay high prices for expected growth, a strategy that takes on two types of risk: that growth will not materialize, or that investors will later be unwilling to pay such high multiples of profits even if it does.

The Death of Equities

Our tale begins in the 1920s, when stocks were hot and a larger proportion of the public than ever before grew interested in Wall Street. It was an era in which the most prominent economist of the time could proclaim that stocks were destined to trade at a permanently high plateau, and in which tales of ordinary people who grew rich through investment caught the imagination of many.

The beliefs of that era were largely forgotten in the coming decades, or, if not forgotten, then heaped with scorn. The Depression that followed the crash was the defining event in the lives of those who lived through it, and colored investing attitudes for the next quarter century.

The prevalent view was simple and, in the context of the times, quite obvious. The crash of 1929 had been caused by speculation run wild that drove stock prices up to unprecedented and unsustainable levels. And the crash in turn had caused the Depression that followed it.

Few historians now think it was as simple as all that. It is clear that the Federal Reserve used its monetary policy tools very badly, both during the speculative bubble that preceded the crash and in the later depression. The Smoot-Hawley tariff passed in 1930, designed to protect domestic business by keeping out imports, helped to spark similar actions in other countries and worsened the situation considerably.

For our purposes, however, what investors saw was the reality. They saw that stocks were inherently very risky. Amid the ruins after the crash, who could quarrel with that?

In the 1920s the theory had emerged that stocks were the best long-term investment. "Only in the 1920s," noted Ron Chernow, a financial historian, "did retail brokerage houses and securities affiliates of commercial banks tout stocks as safe bets for the middle class."

They did that because the demand was there, for a variety of reasons. One was the publication in 1925 of *Common Stocks as Long-Term Investments* by Edgar L. Smith, a money manager who had traced stock prices back to the Civil War. He concluded that stocks were better investments than bonds over the long run, although he conceded that if one got into stocks at a cyclical peak, it could take as long as fifteen years to catch up.

The book created a sensation in financial circles. Irving Fisher, the most noted American economist of that era, cited the work as evidence "that the market overrates the safety of 'safe' securities and pays too much for them." Bonds could not maintain purchasing power in inflationary times, he said. "In steadiness of real income, or purchasing power, a list of diversified common stocks surpasses bonds."

Today, those arguments sound obvious to millions of investors. "Smith's conclusion was right, not only historically but prospectively," wrote Jeremy J. Siegel, a professor at the University of Pennsylvania's Wharton School, in his 1994 book, *Stocks for the Long Run*. That book, from which many of the historical comments in this chapter are taken, had a similar influence in the 1990s.

There were a couple of caveats in the theory that the brokers did not emphasize, and that the investors of the 1920s did not give much attention to. One was the assumption that all dividends would be reinvested; that is, that no income from investments was needed to live. There was also an assumption that taxes on investment profits would somehow be paid from other income. Both tended to overstate real returns.

As investors grew more confident, the 1920s became an era of maximum leverage. Even mutual funds, which debuted during the decade, were used for wild speculation. Some funds would borrow money to buy shares in other funds, which in turn had borrowed money to buy stocks. Brokerage firms encouraged investors to put as little as 10 percent down when they bought stock or fund shares. With just a 10 percent rise in the price of a stock, a speculator could double his money. There was a flip side to that, of course, which became vividly apparent when the crash arrived.

"Wall Street was a street of vanished hopes, of curiously silent apprehension and of a sort of paralyzed hypnosis yesterday," the *New York Times* reported on October 30, 1929, after the worst day of the crash. "Men and women crowded the brokerage offices, even those who have been long since wiped out, and followed the figures on the tape. Little groups gathered here and there to discuss the falling prices in hushed and awed tones. They were participating in the making of financial history. It was the consensus of bankers and brokers alike that no such scenes will ever again be witnessed by this generation. To most of those who have been in the market it is all the more awe-inspiring because their financial history is limited to bull markets."

In an editorial, the *Times* was harshly critical of the "orgy of speculation" in stocks that preceded the crash and sneered at "those newly invented conceptions of finance" that had been used to justify such high stock prices. But it was otherwise sanguine, forecasting that the Federal Reserve would keep the economy on an even keel. It was wrong.

The heaviest speculation in the late 1920s had been in broadcasting stocks. The new communications medium of radio was seen as ushering in a new era of instant communications and continued growth. The most popular stock of the era was the Radio Corporation of America, later known as RCA but then known simply as Radio.

The investors in RCA were right in their business forecast. Radio was a revolutionary technology and RCA was destined to be one of the dominant players. But the stock nonetheless fell more than 90 percent from its 1929 peak to the Depression bottom, and it was decades before it recovered.

During the Depression, Congress passed laws providing federal regulation of the markets by the newly created Securities and Exchange Commission. The Federal Reserve Board was given the duty of setting limits—called margin requirements—on how much money could be borrowed to buy stock. During the next forty years, the Fed raised the requirement when it thought speculation was getting out of control, and lowered it when markets seemed to be less heated.

Other reforms also were made, which one day would be important. The law for the first time banned corporate insiders from trading while they knew material information not disclosed to the general public. Companies had to publish financial reports and file them with the S.E.C. for all to read, if they chose to do so.

There had been many well-publicized "pools" during the 1920s, in which insiders pushed up share prices and then tried to sell to gullible outsiders. Then, many investors reacted by trying to profit from the pool—buying when rumors spread that a pool was starting to operate and then selling before the price was allowed to fall back. After the crash, such activities were blamed by many for their losses, and the new law constrained them.

The new laws had little impact on the public in the 1930s. Few people had the money to speculate, and even fewer had the desire. But the rules would mean something when later bull markets arrived, assuring there would be less leverage available and that investors would have far more information about the financial condition of companies. (By the end of the century, however, financial innovations made it possible to gamble on the stock market with even more abandon than was shown by the wildest swingers of the 1920s.)

Edgar Smith's theories were first ridiculed, then rebutted, then forgotten.

"Common stocks, as such, are not superior to bonds as long-term investments," wrote Lawrence Chamberlain, an investment banker, in 1931, "because primarily they are not investments at all. They are speculations."

In their 1934 book, *Security Analysis*, which became a classic read by generations of investors, Benjamin Graham, a money manager, and David Dodd, a Columbia University professor, were not scornful of stocks as such, just of overpriced ones: "The 'new era' doctrine— that 'good' stocks (or 'blue chips') were sound investments regardless of how high the price paid for them—was at the bottom only a means of rationalizing under the title of 'investment' the well-nigh universal capitulation to the gambling fever."

It was a combination of those two views that would dominate public thinking about investments for many years.

In fact, there had not been that many stock traders in the 1920s in any case, probably about 1.5 million at the peak in 1929. Many Americans no doubt took a certain pleasure from the stories of rich swells being ruined, although that pleasure vanished as it became clear that the Depression would engulf everyone, not just those who had benefited from the roaring market.

During the Depression, hatred of Wall Street grew. As the financial community tried to stem the flow of hostile legislation, its principal public spokesman was Richard Whitney, the president of the New York Stock Exchange.

No one seemed to be more a pillar of the establishment than Whitney, whose own firm had specialized in bonds, not stocks, and whose brother was a partner of J. P. Morgan. But Whitney was not what he seemed. His firm had speculated in stocks and lost huge amounts, which Whitney recovered by embezzling from clients and various stock exchange funds. When he was eventually exposed, it appeared that the establishment had tried to cover up for him, further tarnishing Wall Street's image. Whitney went to prison, and suddenly it became much easier for the S.E.C., under the dynamic leadership of William O. Douglas, a future Supreme Court justice, to force reforms on the N.Y.S.E.

During World War II, interest rates were low and profits for many companies were strong. But share prices remained depressed. There was a widespread expectation that the Depression would return when the war was over and the soldiers began looking for civilian jobs. Even when that forecast did not materialize, many remained skittish about risking money in the stock market.

"In 1949, it was still considered racy stuff when J. P. Morgan & Company, for the first time, bought common stocks for portfolios managed by its trust department," wrote Ron Chernow in *The Death of the Banker*, a marvelous short book on the declining ability of banks to dominate the financial world.

Corporate pension funds began to spread after World War II, as tax-law changes encouraged them and unions bargained for them. They were invested strictly in safe securities, which meant bonds. After all, one should not gamble with the money being set aside for old age. "When General Motors permitted 50 percent of its pension-fund money to go straight into stocks," wrote Chernow, "well, this seemed positively licentious to some straitlaced trust men, as if a parade of drunken Mardi Gras revelers had suddenly burst into their monastic realm." No one would have dreamed that a president would someday push for legislation to invest Social Security money in stocks.

During the 1950s, the hostility to stocks began to soften. The United States was the dominant economy in the world, and its most feared enemy, the Soviet Union, preached the Communist gospel, a fact that if nothing else tended to moot criticism of the capitalist citadel that had been so roundly scorned twenty years earlier.

Memories of just how risky the stock market could be were still alive, of course, but the reality was that it did not seem to be very risky, at least not then. The economy fell into recessions in 1953, 1957 and 1960, but the stock market did reasonably well, year after year.

One measure of just how skeptical investors are toward stocks is the difference between what companies pay in dividends on their shares and what they pay in interest on their bonds. Before the late 1920s, it was common for the dividend rate—expressed as a percentage of the stock's price—to be higher than the interest rate on the bonds. That seemed perfectly reasonable to most investors. Stocks were inherently riskier than bonds, and companies had the right to reduce or eliminate the dividend. Surely shareholders had the right to be compensated for the higher risk.

In the fever of 1929, stock dividend yields fell below those of bonds even for high-quality companies, and investors were willing to buy companies that did not pay dividends, expecting to get rich off capital gains when they resold the stock. After the Depression set in, investors vowed never again to be so incautious.

It was not until the mid-1950s, a time of continued economic growth and steady stock market rallies, that two events took place that seemed momentous, and—to those with memories of the Depression—scary. The Dow Jones Industrial Average, the best-known market indicator, surpassed its 1929 high. And the dividend on stocks fell below bond yields.

There were warnings of impending doom. John Kenneth Galbraith, the Harvard economist and author of a best-selling book on the 1929 crash, testified before a congressional hearing that there were parallels to 1929 and that another crash was possible. The stock market fell as his views were reported on the wires.

"A flood of mail, by far the heaviest of my lifetime, descended on Cambridge," Galbraith recalled in his memoirs. "It was denunciatory, defamatory, physically menacing or pious, the latter being from correspondents who said they were praying for my death or dismemberment." A right-wing senator denounced Galbraith as sympathetic to Communism.

A majority of the Senate Banking Committee was worried, however. It called for more regulation in a report that saw signs of dangerous speculation. "When preoccupation with the stock market results in widespread distortion of perspective, the stock market may become a potential threat to the stability of the economy," warned the committee majority.

In fact, there was little danger of excessive speculation in those days. The American economy was growing and those who remembered the Depression were still holding down stock prices.

Moreover, most Americans were not interested in the stock market. It was still relatively rare for a person to own stocks, and mutual funds were still in their infancy. The preeminent financial asset was a bank account, usually in the form of a passbook savings account.

By the 1960s, however, depression memories were fading, and the economy was booming. A recession ended in February 1961, beginning what was to become the longest period of expansion in American history, which was not to end until December 1969. (That record would in turn be broken by the recovery that began in 1991 and continued until 2000.)

As the economy gained strength in the 1960s, the stock market began to rise. In January 1966, the Dow Jones Industrial Average challenged 1,000 for the first time ever. But the highest closing level it could reach was 994.20. It would be more than six years before the Dow managed to close above 1,000, and not until 1982 would it pass 1,000 for the final time.

The late 1960s saw the beginning of many of the financial attitudes that came back during the great bull market of the 1990s. For the first time, managers of risky mutual funds became media stars. New issues were hot, and technology stocks became darlings. Some funds got rich purchasing so-called letter stocks—securities that were not yet registered with the S.E.C. and that therefore could not be traded. They were sold at a discount to the market price of the same company's registered securities, but could be valued at the same price. When the prices of the registered shares cratered, however, the funds could not quickly sell the stocks, and fund investors lost large amounts of money.

(Things do repeat themselves. In early 2000, at the peak of the fever for small technology stocks, the Janus Funds scored what was widely viewed as a coup. By putting up almost $1 billion, it was able to buy an entire secondary issued from Healtheon/Web MD, a hot Internet stock play, at $62 a share, a 12 percent discount from the market price. By November, when Janus managed to get the shares registered, making them saleable to other investors, Healtheon shares were trading for about $10.)

In 1968, at the height of investor interest in the stock market, about 39 percent of individuals' financial assets were in the stock market, and 26 percent of all their assets, including homes and other property, were in the stock market. Those were records that would stand for three decades, until the late 1990s. The late 1960s new issue boom is worth looking at for the ways it parallels, and the ways it differs from, later such booms.

While there are always new issues coming to market, the willingness of investors to buy them varies greatly from time to time. Times of highest hostility to new issues generally provide the best bargains, but even then most new issues do not prove to be good long-term investments.

That fact should surprise no one. A new offering is the ultimate insider trade. Companies go public when their managements decide it is a good time to sell and determine that public financing is the cheapest way for the company to raise cash. The buyers are sure to know less about the company than do the sellers. In times when investors are generally hostile, young companies must turn to other sources for financing, and only the best companies are likely to go public.

In the late 1960s, investors flocked to new offerings, many of which doubled during the first day despite the fact they had little if any operating history. Technology was hot, and many claimed to have plans to become big players in some area of technology that few investors understood. In that regard, it is starkly reminiscent of the late 1990s.

But it was very different in at least one major respect. In a report dated January 1969, Merrill Lynch warned, rightly as it turned out, that there was "considerable risk" in buying such issues—which, it piously pointed out, it and other leading brokerage firms would never sell.

"We require that a company have substantial earnings, that its growth record extend over several years, that the company be important to its industry, and that the price to be paid for the shares be reasonable in relation to actual and projected earnings," Merrill advised its customers. That was an attitude that did not endure. The most overpriced of the most recent group of new issues came from the most prestigious underwriters.

The great 1950s–1960s bull market stumbled to an end. The Dow peaked in early 1973 at 1,051, and the "Nifty 50" stocks—growth companies such as Xerox, the copier company, and Avon, the door-to-door cosmetic company—peaked later in that year. That was the first great Wall Street love affair with growth stocks since the 1920s. They became known as "one decision" stocks on the theory that an investor needed only to decide to buy them, not to decide whether to ever sell them.

Those stocks held up longer than other stocks, and the money managers who had embraced them did better than other managers, which brought more money in for them to manage. That money went into the same stocks, which made them even better performers, and brought in more money.

It was a virtuous circle while it lasted, but it could not survive the 1973–74 bear market, which was accompanied by a severe recession brought on in part by the surge in oil prices that followed the 1973 Arab-Israeli war. The Dow fell 45 percent, its worst fall since the Great Depression. The Nifty 50 stocks did even worse. Those who pay very high prices for shares in companies they expect to grow rapidly are taking on a double dose of risks: the overall market could fall, rendering high price-earnings ratios obsolete, and even if the market does not collapse, the companies could fail to live up to the growth expectations.

Little noticed at the time was another index that fell much farther than the Dow. The Nasdaq composite index plunged 60 percent. That index was made up of all the stocks traded on the Nasdaq market, which had begun in 1971. The over-the-counter market had always operated by telephone, making it difficult to find prices. The new Nasdaq market allowed for quotes to be disseminated electronically, although phone calls were still required to actually make a trade. The growth of the Nasdaq market into a major competitor to the New York Stock Exchange was under way, and with it would come widespread acceptance that stocks could be worth buying even if they did not meet the more stringent listing standards of the N.Y.S.E.

That recession ended, and stocks recovered to some extent, but they did not get back to the levels from which they had fallen. A lot else was going on in the world that seemed ominous to investors. Inflation was rising and so were interest rates. Americans concluded that stocks were not nearly as good investments as real assets, whether commodities or real estate. Gold and oil soared in the late 1970s and few doubted those trends would continue. In 1979 *Business Week* magazine published a cover story entitled "The Death of Equities," concluding that in an era of inflation stocks were likely to remain bad investments.

"This 'death of equity' can no longer be seen as something a stock market rally—however strong—will check," the article stated. "It has persisted for more than ten years through market rallies, business cycles, recession, recoveries and booms." It advised that the American economy should regard the death of equities as a "near permanent condition, reversible some day, but not soon." It added that "experience has taught investors that inflation will lead to an economic downturn that will wreck corporate profitability and stock prices." Far more attractive were such alternative investments as gold, real estate and even artwork.

"Today," concluded the article, "the old attitude of buying solid stocks as a cornerstone for one's life savings and retirement has simply disappeared. Says a young U.S. executive: 'Have you been to an American stockholders' meeting lately? They're all old fogies. The stock market is not where the action's at.'"

The Birth of the Bull Market

The inflation of the 1970s and early 1980s had major effects on American savings habits. The bank passbook account at first could not increase its interest rate enough to keep up with market interest rates because of Federal Reserve regulations. That led to the growth of money market mutual funds, and to increased interest in bond market funds. It helped a generation of Americans grow more comfortable taking on additional risk.

Other things were going on as well. In the late 1970s, the accounting regulators began to look carefully at the way corporations accounted for their pension obligations, and began to push for new accounting standards that would force companies to face up to their obligations, and record them on their financial statements. Many companies were in no position to do that. Their pension funds had stocks that were trading below the levels of the mid-1960s and bonds that were depressed because rising interest rates were driving down the market price of existing bonds.

By the time the accounting rules were changed in the early 1980s, companies were looking for a way to avoid the risk to earnings that was inherent in maintaining pension funds with guaranteed benefits. They began to look for alternatives, and defined contribution plans began to look more attractive.

In a defined benefit plan—most notably 401(k)s, named after a section of the tax law—the company contributes a specified percentage of an employee's salary, which is then placed in investments over which the employee has some control. Companies were thrilled to be unloading the investment risk onto the employees. If a traditional pension fund makes investments that do not pay off, the company must make up the difference to be sure that the fund will have enough money to meet its obligations. But if a defined contribution plan is invested in assets that do not appreciate, that is the employee's problem.

As those plans spread in the 1980s and 1990s, Americans who never invested in the stock market found themselves under pressure to do so. The choices offered them usually included one or more stock funds, often the same mutual funds that they could invest in on their own. Many Americans were forced to pay attention to the stock market.

It happened that the move to defined benefit plans came at the perfect time for employees, and the worst time for companies. The stock market, after fifteen years of poor performance, took off in the summer of 1982, beginning a bull market that was only briefly interrupted by the 1987 crash. Americans who were forced to take a chance on stocks found that doing so was well rewarded.

There were other 1970s developments that proved important. On May 1, 1975—known as Mayday on Wall Street in a reference both to the date and to the cry of fliers whose planes were going down— brokerage firms were forced to stop fixing commissions. Such fixed commissions had been a fixture on the New York Stock Exchange ever since the legendary 1792 Buttonwood Tree agreement, which the Big Board recalls as its beginning, and they had come to mean that an investor selling 10,000 shares would pay a commission exactly one hundred times as great as an investor selling 100 shares, even though the extra costs to the brokerage firm were far less.

The end of fixed commissions meant that commissions for institutional investors—such as mutual funds—fell rapidly. But commissions for individual investors rose, reflecting the costs involved. Even with the rise of discount brokerage firms, a decade later individual investors were paying commissions that were far higher than they had been when rates were fixed. For an investor who wanted a diversified portfolio of stocks, the commissions involved in assembling that portfolio were likely to be far greater than the fees needed to buy a similar mutual fund.

Of course, in the mid-1970s, not many investors wanted to do that. Nor were very many people interested in the financial revolutions taking place in Chicago. But these innovations brought leverage back into the stock market to an extent and in ways unimaginable in the 1920s, before the government clamped limits on the amount of money that investors could borrow to buy stocks. It set the scene for the explosive changes in the financial markets in the 1980s and 1990s.

The twin Chicago revolutions concerned financial futures and options. One—options—dealt with a product that had been around for centuries. The other—futures—was an extension of a product that had become common for agricultural commodities but was unknown in the stock market. Both came out of the futures markets.

Financial futures began in 1972. Futures on interest rates and then on stock indexes allowed for the shifting of risk and for highly leveraged bets. An institutional investor with a lot of money to put to work could do so quickly by buying futures contracts on the Standard & Poor's 500, and then could gradually replace those contracts with the desired stocks. An institution that wanted to reduce its stock market exposure could also do so quickly.

Buying a futures contract was not the same thing as buying the underlying securities or commodities, but it carried basically the same hope of reward. A contract on the S&P 500 might expire a year after the investment was made. The buyer would put down a small amount of money, and would stand to profit if stocks went up over that period. But if the market turned down, the buyer would have to put up additional money or be sold out.

For individuals, the futures made it possible to speculate on the broad stock market with little money down. The ability to place a highly leveraged bet, which had been removed by regulators in the 1930s, was back.

It could be argued that it had never gone away, for stock options were hardly new. But they too underwent a revolution in the 1970s, when the Chicago Board of Trade began trading stock options.

Call options give the buyer the right, but not the obligation, to buy a stock at a specified price until a certain date. Put options give the buyer the right to sell the stock at a specified price until a certain date. Buyers of call options put down little money but get all the upside in a stock above the money they put down to buy the option. If a person wants to do so, he or she can gamble heavily in options. The worst that can happen to a buyer of options is that he or she will lose all they invested.

The seller of the option, by contrast, has limited profits but large potential losses. The seller pockets the premium paid for the option, but then has to honor it if need be. A seller of a call option for a stock promises to sell the stock at a particular price, say $30 a share, until a certain date. In return for making that promise when the stock is trading at $26, he or she might get a premium of fifty cents a share. If the stock fails to rise, that fifty cents is profit.

But if that stock soars, perhaps because of a takeover offer, the seller can lose many times the amount of the original premium. Similarly, the seller of a put option, who promises to buy a stock at a certain price, can lose large amounts if the stock collapses.

Before options exchanges were organized, options trading had been a highly specialized and largely obscure field. There was little liquidity in the market, and no centralized trading. Options dealers would take orders for options and seek out traders to take the other side. "The largest trade I remember was an order I had for call options on five thousand shares each on twenty-two different stocks," wrote one options merchant, Herbert Filer, in 1956, recalling an earlier era. "The order was filed without too much difficulty in about three days."

Each contract had to be presented to a particular broker who had signed to honor it, before the date it expired. It was legal to trade an option before it expired, but finding a buyer could be difficult and expensive. So there was little trading. Options were available, but they were not easy to buy or sell, and they had minimal influence on the financial system.

The Chicago Board of Trade, the largest commodity futures exchange, began trading options in 1973, in the board's smoking room. While other traders puffed away, options merchants operated in a corner of the room. Soon the volume was enough to justify its own trading room, then its own building, which became the Chicago Board Options Exchange. Other markets soon began trading stock options.

Since then, the market for derivatives has grown tremendously, and has had effects on the stock market that are difficult to measure but no doubt large. While some derivatives are traded on exchanges, many more are traded over-the-counter, with markets made by Wall Street firms and commercial banks.

As many companies' stocks soared in the 1990s, a significant product for Wall Street became the "zero-cost collar," which enabled an executive whose wealth was tied up in one stock to protect against a decline without selling the stock. Such sales might have been impossible, given the rules limiting how much stock corporate insiders can sell, or at least impolitic, given how other investors can react if corporate officials liquidate large parts of their holdings.

The term "zero-cost" was misleading. The executive paid a premium to buy a put contract, which gave him or her the right to sell the shares at a specified price below the current market price—thus assuring that losses would be limited. But that fee was covered by the fee received for selling a call option, which gave the buyer the right to buy the shares at a price above the current market price. The executive had given up part of the possible upside for protection against the downside.

As that illustrates, derivatives enable risks to be carved up and traded. They can allow traders to minimize risks, or to take only one part of the risk of a given trade, such as the risk that a Japanese stock will fall in yen but not that the value of the yen will decline against the dollar. The flip side is that derivatives can allow some traders to take on enormous risks undetected by others.

There have been a number of examples. When the bond market stumbled in 1994, a host of abuses in trading came out. It turned out that some traders had been placing large bets that interest rates would not rise—bets that insured they would profit handsomely if rates fell and that had enabled them to post excellent returns before rates began to rise.

In 1998 the near collapse of Long-Term Capital Management, a hedge fund, showed just how much leverage a fund could amass if it put its mind to it. Fears that the fund's collapse would bring down major financial institutions led Wall Street to put up the cash needed to keep it alive. The bailout was organized with the full involvement of the Federal Reserve Bank of New York, although it did not put up any money.

One irony of the Long-Term Capital Management debacle is that partners in the firm included scholars who had shared in the Nobel Prize for economics for their work in developing the theories of how options and other derivatives should be priced. They had helped to create a Wall Street revolution, and they had become the victims of their own work.

None of these innovations seemed especially important in the 1970s, when they were being made. To become so, investors had to become comfortable with them and gain a desire to use them.

The road to wider use of derivatives, and the rising faith among investors that greater risks would bring greater rewards, began in the summer of 1982—three years after the "death of equities" report—when the Dow industrials bottomed at 777 and began to rise, climbing above 1,000 in October, falling back and then conquering that level for the final time in December. A great bull market had begun.

By the summer of 1987, the Dow had more than tripled from the 1982 low and investor enthusiasm was high. At the peak, the S&P 500 stock index was trading at nineteen times that year's earnings for the index, a level not seen since the 1960s and triple the low seen in the late 1970s.

The crash that year was an epochal event, but not for the reasons that seemed apparent. At the time, the lesson of the crash seemed to be one of taking on too much risk. It was noted that the dividend yield on stocks had fallen to a record low of 2.6 percent, less than half the yield at the 1982 low.

In fact, the lesson investors should have learned related to the risks derivatives had introduced into the market. Both the boom and the fall were magnified by derivatives, specifically the use of a mis-named product called portfolio insurance. Many institutional investors had decided that they could ride the market up without risk, because they planned to get out when prices began to fall. They figured they could do that by selling stock index futures as the market weakened, thus reducing their exposure.

When prices did start to fall, the futures were sold. But the volume of that selling was so great that it forced prices down more, leading to more selling. The buyers of the stock index futures being sold tried to hedge their risks by selling stocks, which pushed those prices down. Prices fell far farther than they would have without the availability of such derivatives.

After that selling was done, stocks were free to bounce back and did so. No recession followed, in part because the Federal Reserve quickly lowered interest rates. The lesson many investors came to learn was that falls in stock prices were a great buying opportunity. The crash came to be a symbol of how good stock market investing was. Investors became more and more certain that the stock market would yield riches, and so, as the 1990s progressed, it did.

Options, the New Corporate Currency

During the 1990s, stock options became an important part of compensation for employees at many companies. As in the creation of 401(k) accounts, the accountants played a role. Accounting in force for many years allowed companies to issue options to executives without recording an expense, so long as the options allowed the recipient to buy the stock at the prevailing market price when the option was granted.

Companies could grant large amounts of options without recording an expense, and they came to do just that. They were justified as giving employees the same incentives as the shareholders, but that was only partly true. Because options holders profited from increases in the share price, but not from dividends paid while they held the options, the options gave executives an incentive to hold down the level of dividends.

In addition, it became common practice for companies to reprice options when the stock fell. After all, they argued, the old options were so far out of the money that employees had no real incentive to stay with the company, and were likely to jump to the competition. Something had to be done to keep them. The repricings all but assured that options holders would end up making money.

Options became most prevalent in technology companies and

had the great advantage of being a powerful lure for employees to move to companies that could not necessarily afford to pay large salaries in cash.

By the mid-1990s, when accounting rulemakers woke up to the fact that options were very valuable, and that the current accounting rules were ridiculous, it was too late. Corporate America ran to Congress, and the political pressure became so great that the rulemakers backed down. What is often the most valuable part of an employee's compensation package still is treated by the company as costing nothing when it tallies up its expenses and profits.

As the stock market soared in the late 1990s, it was technology companies that led the way. The computer revolution, much discussed since the 1960s, finally seemed to be having a major impact on the productivity of American industry.

It is too early to be sure whether those productivity gains were real, but there is no question that rising stock prices combined with widespread options issuance to make many people rich and, in some cases, to distort regional economies. Microsoft made so many millionaires in the Seattle area that it sharply drove up housing prices. That fact goes a long way to explaining the bad labor relations that came to haunt Boeing, which had been the area's dominant company. Its employees saw their paychecks were inadequate in a market being driven by Microsoft.

While it lasted, it was a virtuous circle for the economy. Options profits did not reduce reported corporate profits, thanks to the absurd accounting rule, but they did stimulate the economy, which raised profits for many companies. Investors felt rich because of rising stock prices, and many of them were rich when they cashed in their options. The fact that options could make a low-level employee of one company wealthier than a high-ranking executive of a company whose stock price languished helped to create an atmosphere that encouraged workers to join young companies.

Many Internet companies were the beneficiaries in the late 1990s, often to the eventual regret of all investors who did not cash out before the bubble burst. But the impact of the Internet went far beyond providing speculative stocks.

The most obvious effect is that the Internet has made it far easier for investors to get information. Corporate reports that once were difficult or expensive to obtain now can be accessed in seconds. It is not clear whether investors have made much use of that information, but it is available.

The Internet is also drastically changing the way stocks are traded. Internet brokers now offer commissions on even small trades that are lower than the old pre-1975 fixed rates, and a fraction of the levels seen after commissions were deregulated. It is now quite possible to buy stocks with very low transaction costs.

As Internet brokers expanded, they also encouraged very active trading. With virtually instantaneous action and low commission rates, traders could bounce in and out of stocks within very brief periods of time. That stimulated volume but, for most of the traders, does not seem to have improved results.

The I.P.O. Economy

The most exciting investments in the late 1990s were initial public offerings, a category that became far more popular than during previous booms. Within a few years, a new issue that doubled on the first day became commonplace.

There had been, of course, great successes among investors buying new issues. While more money has probably been lost by investors seeking the "next Microsoft" than was made by those who bought the first one, the fact remains that Microsoft was a phenomenal success and those who bought it when it was a young company did very well.

When it went public in 1986, shares sold in the offering for $21 each, and ended the first day of public trading at $28. An investor who bought 100 shares on the first day, paying the public market price of $2,800 plus commissions, would have had 14,400 shares by late 1999, with a value of $1.7 million, when the stock peaked.

Microsoft went up 33 percent that first day, a move that in those days was deemed a good one. And while Microsoft was a newly public stock, the company had been around for some time, and was well known thanks to having provided the operating system for the IBM personal computer.

At that closing price on the first day, Microsoft was trading at twenty-one times the profits it had earned in the previous twelve months. The company, whose lead underwriter was Goldman Sachs, had originally filed to go public for as little as $16 a share—a valuation of twelve times historic profits. That was viewed as a premium multiple for a software company in those days, with some other public software companies trading for nine times profits.

In 1986 Microsoft was not the new issue that captivated investor attention. That honor went to Home Shopping Network, a cable television channel that did nothing except sell things to customers who called in. Home Shopping was a pioneer in its industry, and it had been profitable for three years before it went public and created an investment frenzy.

Home Shopping shares were priced at $18 in the offering, but opened for trading at $42. Within a few months they traded for as much as $133. In the fullness of time, such inflated values proved fleeting, but that is not what seems surprising from the perspective of fifteen years later.

In those days, an offering that rose more than 100 percent on the first day was big news—and it was deemed to be an embarrassment for the underwriter. "The perception on Wall Street is that they blew it," said one money manager after the Home Shopping offering soared. There were calculations regarding how much money the company had left on the table because Merrill Lynch had priced it at what was clearly an unreasonably low price.

(Home Shopping Network is still around, owned by USA Networks, a company that was spun off from HSN in 1993 and that then acquired its former parent. In mid-2001, investors who bought HSN at the high in 1986 and stuck around for all the maneuvers had an investment worth about half what they paid.)

A decade later, in 1996, it was Yahoo that had the big new issue. The stock was priced at $13 by underwriters led by Goldman Sachs and traded as high as $43 the first day, before settling back to $33 by the close.

That 154 percent rise sparked a lot of talk, but little criticism of Goldman. By then, the focus was on the lucky investors who had gotten in, and amazement that a company formed only the year before, which had yet to report its first dollar of profits, was valued by investors at nearly $1 billion. In 1995 the company had lost more than $600,000 on revenues of $1.3 million.

Yahoo proved to be a good investment, as absurd as those numbers sounded. By the peak in early 2000, a purchase of 100 shares on that first day of trading, which would have cost $4,300 plus commissions, would have grown to 1,200 shares valued at $300,000. Yahoo's shares plunged after that, but in mid-2001 they were still worth about $21,000 for that block, or five times what the investor had paid.

Those changing attitudes toward new offerings—in which a soaring first-day price was viewed as a mark of success, not one of underwriter incompetence, and in which short-term expectations of profits, let alone actual profits, were not viewed as necessary—reached a peak in early 2000.

During a fevered six-week period, from January 31 through March 10, 2000, there were seventy-seven new offerings priced. Of those, thirty-eight, or just under half of them, at least doubled the first day of trading. A quarter of the offerings tripled the first day, but most of them gained little attention from investors. Such movements had become routine.

Far from being embarrassed, underwriters appeared to be proud of such movements. Companies focused less on the money they could have raised and more on the immediate profits for "friends and family" who were offered the sure profits of being allowed to buy at the initial offering price.

In such an attitude, corruption—or at least what in an earlier generation would have been seen as conflicts of interest—became common. It was not unusual for a company to gain the credibility needed for a new offering because an established technology company was a customer. Sometimes that company would have been given the right to buy shares—or even granted options to buy stock at prices well below the public price. In other cases, those shares would have gone to the executives at the big company that decided to buy the technology.

To the underwriters, the ability to dole out sure profits was an opportunity for marketing. The old way of getting prospective issuers to consider using a firm for underwriting was to boast of how well its bankers understood the market. The new way was to cut executives of prospective issuers in on the profits from current offerings by selling them shares that were sure to go up.

As the profits grew, so did the temptations. Institutional investors, who normally get the lion's share of stock allocations in new offerings, wanted more, for obvious reasons. For a small mutual fund, an allocation of a hot new offering could produce fantastic performance, and bring in money from investors eager to get in on such performance. That performance could determine whether a manager got a big bonus, or was fired. And that performance would be affected by just how large an allocation of hot new issues that manager could get.

By mid-2001, the Justice Department and the Securities and Exchange Commission were investigating to see whether what amounted to payoffs had been made to get such allocations. No charges had been filed, and many on Wall Street were scornful of the investigation, but the suspicion among regulators was that some money managers were given allocations in return for agreeing to kick back a part of the realized profits. The kickbacks may have been paid through inflated commissions on other trades, after the money manager made his profit by selling the shares allocated in the offering.

If that did happen, it could be deemed fraud. The prospectus for new offerings lists the compensation the underwriters are receiving. Any such kickbacks would be in addition to the disclosed fees, and some securities lawyers speculated that the underwriters might be forced to offer to rescind the trades—in effect, to buy back the shares they had distributed.

Had the hot offerings stayed hot, that would hardly be a problem for the investment banks. Anyone who would like to sell Yahoo, for example, at the original offering price would find ready buyers. But that was not what happened.

A Torrid Market Freezes

The hottest period for new issues came during that six-week stretch in early 2000. During that period, the Nasdaq composite index rose 30 percent, from 3,887.07 to 5,048.62, and many of the hottest stocks were among the youngest. Getting in on a new offering—almost any new offering—was viewed as a great opportunity for profit, and there was ample demand from investors in the aftermarket for almost any stock.

By the end of 2000, it appeared that never had so many investors paid so much for so little. Assume that an investor somehow had the pull to get an allocation of 100 shares of each of the seventy-seven deals at the offering price, and had sold each of them at the first day's close. That investor would have put up $135,440 and received $319,863, less commissions. That would have been a profit of 136 percent on money that was never invested for more than one day.

If instead that same investor held on, by the end of 2000 the value of that portfolio would have shrunk to $61,548, a fall of 55 percent from the offering prices and a drop of 81 percent from the first day closes. Of those seventy-seven issues, only two ended higher than their first-day closes, and each of them was up less than 10 percent. Neither of them was especially hot the first day, either.

During that period, there were a few companies with impressive operating histories that went public. Most notable was Palm, the leading company in the growing market for handheld organizers. It had earned $36 million in the prior twelve months. But the vast majority of companies had lost money.

All told, the seventy-seven companies had reported revenues of almost $5 billion in the twelve months before they went public, and had losses of $1.7 billion. Nearly half the companies reported losses larger than their revenues.

Imagine for a moment that all those companies had been merged together, with that history. The combined company was deemed so attractive by investors that they put $11 billion into it, at the public offerings, and on March 10, the day the Nasdaq peaked, that company had a market value of $196 billion.

To put that in perspective, IBM, another technology company but one that seemed less exciting at the time, had a market value that day of $194 billion, a bit less than our crop of new offerings. In 1999 it had revenues of $87.5 billion and earnings of $7.7 billion.

At the peak, most of the seventy-seven were deemed to be worth at least $1 billion. And that came less than four years after many eyebrows were raised at the fact that Yahoo's value had approached $1 billion.

Those valuations seemed ridiculous to some then, and they were. But by then the doubters had been totally discredited. Had not Yahoo been a phenomenal performer? Had not other stocks gone up far more than anyone who concentrated on fundamentals would have expected?

Some of the companies that went public then had fatally flawed business plans, and were destined to collapse within months. A few were successful companies that were simply overvalued. Palm Inc., the class of the new issue field during that period, would have qualified for underwriting even under those 1968 standards of Merrill Lynch. It was profitable and it was the leader of a rapidly growing industry. It also faced growing competition, but the indications were that it was not only meeting that competition but beating it. Given that the competition was coming from Microsoft—itself one of the great new issue successes, but then facing antitrust charges that boiled down to allegations that it had used its market power to become a bully—many people were rooting for Palm, a fact that only increased the allure of the stock.

Palm was then owned by 3Com, a company best known to the public for having put its name on the old Candlestick Park in San Francisco, the home of the Giants baseball and 49ers football teams. 3Com had picked Palm up when it bought US Robotics, then a leading company in an industry—computer modems—that was about to go into decline.

When it got out that 3Com was going to sell a stake in Palm to the public, and then spin off the rest to its shareholders, there was a huge surge in the value of 3Com stock as investors figured that the Palm offering would be the next big thing. Palm's own financials showed that it had earned $36 million on revenues of $753 million in the preceding twelve months.

When a stake in Palm was sold to the public at $38 per share, the buyers stormed the market. Here was a company with a history and a hot product, and investors had to have it. At the end of the first day of trading, Palm shares were selling for just over $95 per share, giving the company a market value of $53 billion. At the high price of $165 per Palm share that day, the company was valued at $93 billion, about 2,500 times its profits and 125 times its revenues.

It was an era of absurd valuations, but that one stood out because there was a ready comparison. 3Com ended the day valued at $28 billion, about $23 billion less than the value of the Palm shares it still owned.

"3Com owns 94 percent of Palm, and the non-Palm part of 3Com is worth something," Eric A. Benhamou, the chairman and chief executive of 3Com, moaned to a reporter.

Both share prices came down in the following weeks, but the gap that valued 3Com at less than its holdings in Palm persisted until 3Com spun off its Palm shares to its shareholders later in the year. Palm ended the year around $28 a share, significantly below the offering price, a decline that seemed to reflect the collapse of a speculative bubble far more than any shortfall in Palm's operations. Yet by mid-2001 the share price was below $5, as it appeared that Palm might have trouble dealing with a business slowdown.

There were, of course, companies that went public during the height of the mania that had almost nothing to recommend them save their timing. But a look at another company, Turnstone Systems, shows the myriad of hazards during a bubble, even in a company that has a successful product and is doing well.

When Turnstone went public, it had revenues of $27 million over the previous twelve months—the first year in which it had sold products—and while it had lost money in that year, it had reported profits in the final two quarters. It made equipment to allow telephone companies to offer high-speed Internet access over normal phone lines.

The offering was an immediate hit and—unlike most of the companies that went public during that period—the stock kept on rising. The business appeared to be growing rapidly, with quarterly revenues rising from $12 million in the last three months of 1999 to $23 million, $41 million and $56 million in successive quarters.

The stock, which had tripled the first day to $48.50 a share, adjusted for a subsequent split, did not peak until July, when it reached $107. At that price, the company was valued at $7 billion—a phenomenal valuation that could be justified only by the assumption of skyrocketing growth for years to come.

That growth was not to come. The company's sales were primarily to competitive local-exchange carriers, companies that had sprouted to compete with local phone companies using the phone companies' own wires, as regulators required as a condition of deregulation. Many such companies had sprung up and found it easy to get funding, and therefore had been in a position to place orders with Turnstone and its competitors. The bubble that had driven up Turnstone's stock price had also provided the money for its customers to spend.

Virtually none of those companies had found a way to make money, and when the Nasdaq bubble burst, their funding began to dry up. Turnstone entered the fourth quarter of 2000 expecting another gain in revenues, but when the final numbers were in the sales came to $29 million, barely half the previous quarter's. In the first quarter of 2001, revenues were less than $7 million.

What went wrong? Many of the company's customers were going bankrupt, canceling orders and in some cases not paying for equipment that had already been delivered. The technology was improving, leaving Turnstone with an inventory of obsolete merchandise that had to be written down. And for anyone who really wanted Turnstone's equipment, a gray market had sprung up as customers tried to sell equipment they had bought but did not need.

When all that was digested by investors, the stock fell to about $7 per share, about half the offering price and less than a tenth of the peak price. Turnstone was scrambling to find companies with money to spend—such as the incumbent local telephone companies—but it was not clear if those efforts would succeed.

There were other lessons to be learned from Turnstone. One was the increasing ability of companies to make the numbers say whatever they want them to say—at least in their news releases. In recent years, companies have emphasized "profit" numbers that are adjusted in various ways from the net earnings that they must file with the Securities and Exchange Commission. Such figures get a variety of names, including cash earnings, proforma earnings and, in Turnstone's case, adjusted net income. Companies that use a particular label may or may not be adjusting the figures in the same way as other companies using that label, or in the same way the same company adjusted the numbers in a previous period. Those numbers almost always make the results look better than the net income figures and require investors to figure out whether or not the adjustments make sense.

In Turnstone's case, the "adjusted net income" for the fourth quarter of 2000 showed a profit of $5.1 million, in contrast to the loss of $4.1 million using generally accepted accounting principles. What accounted for that $9.2 million after-tax swing? The largest part was an $11.4 million pretax write-down of inventory, reflecting the fact that the company had equipment it could not sell for what it was carrying it for on its books. There was a $2.1 million charge to increase bad debt reserves, reflecting the inability of some customers to pay their bills. There was also $1.5 million in amortization of deferred compensation—money paid in the past but not counted against earnings then. And there was $404,000 of amortization of goodwill, an accounting adjustment stemming from an acquisition.

Why take those numbers out? It could be argued that they did not really reflect what had happened in the quarter. The inventory had built up to excessive levels earlier in the year, and the bad debt reflected sales earlier in the year as well. The amortization figures were noncash charges, and companies frequently try to ignore them.

But even if one accepts the quarterly argument, it is less easy to understand why the company also released "adjusted net income" figures for the full year, showing a profit of $35.1 million, as opposed to the actual net income figure of $22.4 million. It is hard to understand how the overpriced inventory and the bad debts should not be viewed as a proper part of the full year's results.

The other lesson is that those who buy new offerings should pay attention to whether corporate insiders are selling. Most prospectuses will contain information on what promises insiders have made to delay selling their shares. Frequently, the "lock-up" period ends six months after the company goes public, but they vary. In Turnstone's case, the insiders were allowed to start selling their stock on May 15, a bit over three months after the company went public.

As a result, while public investors in Turnstone have suffered, the founders of the company have done brilliantly, even if the company never makes another dime.

The three founders, P. Kingston Duffie, Richard N. Tinsley and M. Denise Savoie, started Turnstone in 1998 with a total investment of $8,500. On May 15, the day that they were allowed to begin selling shares, all three of them did. And the selling continued until September, when the company raised more money with a new offering, at $50 per share, or less than half the peak price. The three founders tagged along on that sale, taking in $17.3 million. Those shares were sold at less than half the stock's peak price, and the willingness of insiders to sell after such a sharp fall is seldom a good sign.

All told, the three founders made a profit in 2000 of $63.9 million from selling shares, or nearly triple the amount of profits the company posted during the period. Their average sale price was more than $52 per share.

Such wild periods of new offering excess come along only rarely, but they create a bonanza for companies and their insiders when they do. And, to be fair, they can create a bonanza for outside investors as well, assuming they know enough to get out before the end.

The final exhibit in that regard is Internet Capital Group, which within a few months went from being one of the most successful initial public offerings ever to being one of the worst performing stocks.

In 1999 the stock more than doubled the first day from its initial offering price, and it did not stop there. The company owned stakes in many Internet companies, and investors soon concluded that it was worth more than the sum of its current investments, since it was investing in new operations that would also make investors wealthy.

By the end of 1999, the stock was up 2,722 percent from its initial offering price, making it arguably the best-performing new offering ever. In fact the shares had peaked just before Christmas, and they began falling even before most Internet stocks did. By the end of 2000, the shares were trading for well below the initial offering price, and the stock ended that year down 98 percent.

Challenges to Investors' Faith

By mid-2001, many stock prices were down dramatically from their highs and the new issue market was far less lively than it had been. But faith in the stock market as a long-term investment has not wavered. Nor has the belief that money is to be made by buying when the market is weak.

History would seem to support that faith. After all, even those who bought in 1929 would have done well if they had held on long enough. However, that history inevitably reflects very different times from the present. Stocks are still very expensive, as a multiple of earnings, relative to earlier periods. A return to historic valuations would imply sharp drops, particularly for the large technology companies.

If history teaches anything, it is that one generation's certainties can be deemed ridiculous by the next generation. The "young executive" who told *Business Week* in 1979 that stocks were not "where the action's at" probably was still working in 2000, when Ameritrade, an online brokerage firm, was running commercials featuring an older executive who was desperately trying to get hip by trading over the Internet. Gold, which sold for more than $800 an ounce two decades ago, languishes under $300, and even soaring oil prices in 2000 did not revive inflation fears.

Many companies that are traded now would not have been able to go public a generation ago. The existence of such lower-quality stocks could easily drag down overall returns in the future. The widespread use of derivatives has clearly allowed risk to be moved around like never before, but it is less clear where that risk has settled. There may yet be unpleasant surprises regarding equity derivatives if stock prices fall substantially. A change of investor sentiment, perhaps brought on by a sustained period of poor economic performance, could be devastating for stock owners as both profits and price-earnings ratios come down sharply.

It is, in other words, a time when investors need to be cautious, searching for changes both in the economic environment and in the sentiment that has made stocks so very profitable over the past quarter century. It is when an investment strategy is most popular that it may be most risky.

2.

Investing for the Ages: Long-Term Strategies

KURT EICHENWALD

Time was when saving for expenses like retirement was something that few people thought about. Early in the twentieth century, those who stopped working at age sixty-five had, on average, fewer than five years left in their lives. As life expectancies increased, retirees relied on the promise of fat pensions. Individual investing for retirement was far from the norm, meaning that most folks really didn't think much about their life after employment until they were well into their fifties.

No more. In the last few decades, virtually everything has changed, leaving investors with far more responsibility than ever before. People often live a quarter-century beyond the traditional age of retirement. At the same time, pensions and Social Security are playing a far less significant role in financing retirement, leaving the biggest chunk—from personal savings—all up to you. Basically, whether you want to or not, if you are planning to be anything other than poor in your golden years, you will become a money manager sometime in your life. The only question is when.

Fortunately, while the rules have changed in terms of what you have to do for yourself, the fundamentals for investing at various stages of life have remained remarkably constant. Sure, markets have zigged up and zagged down at unnerving speed in recent years, and many companies that shouldn't have qualified for a bank loan have been able to raise billions in public cash, but the basic, long-term strategies have not changed.

That is one tenet that too many investors seem to forget: The markets live and breathe with slow and powerful rhythms that, at least historically, are predictable enough to make long-term planning possible, and wise. They survive the folly of a generation's exuberance or pessimism. The business cycle does not die with the promise of new technology, or with the excitement over a new management technique. Today's boom is tomorrow's retrenchment is the next day's advance.

That certainly should inject a dose of humility—and a healthy sense of respect for the markets—into anyone who sees investing as a get-rich-quick scheme, an alternative to the casino. But, to anyone else, the historical consistency of the markets contains the secret for potential gains.

Now, with all the new challenges, how can an investor use the consistencies of the markets to survive and profit?

Here is where some of those five-dollar investing phrases come into play, terms like "risk-reward ratio," "risk tolerance" and "the time value of money." These are relatively simple concepts that perhaps just sound daunting. Risk-reward ratio is the easiest—this means that the greater the risk you take on your investment, the greater your potential gains. However, those potential gains could also be potential losses, and your ability to withstand wide fluctuations in the value of your investments is an important part of your risk tolerance. Investing for the long term allows you to bear market downdrafts, as the occasional fall in prices is offset by a return to growth.

Then there is the time value of money, meaning that investment dollars compounded over many years—in other words, with dividends and any other gains being reinvested—grow at an exponential rate. Dollars socked away early in life historically pile up far faster than much greater amounts saved later. So don't skip the first few years of investing with plans to set aside more as you age.

Chart 2A

Why to Start Now

At the end of 1960, four people of different ages invested in stocks, and reinvested their dividends. Here is what each invested dollar was worth at retirement.

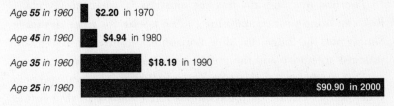

Age **55** in 1960   **$2.20** in 1970

Age **45** in 1960   **$4.94** in 1980

Age **35** in 1960   **$18.19** in 1990

Age **25** in 1960 $90.90 in 2000

Returns are assumed to match the S&P 500.   Data source: Ibbotson Associates

Sometimes investors can look out into today's marketplace and decide that things look too scary—with prices dropping or rising too quickly. For investors with longtime horizons, that doesn't matter. With markets up and down all the time, folks who invest over a forty-year period historically make tidy sums. Looking at these numbers, you'll see that investors who put their money in the markets with reinvested dividends for forty years made about 9 to 12 percent on their money each year—and that includes people who invested just before the stock market crash of 1929.

That high return can make all the difference in reaching your financial goals. Suppose you invested $1 per year in a savings account that offered 4 percent on your money, compounded annually. In thirty-five years, you would have an account worth $95.03. But shift that modest investment into something earning 10 percent annually, and your returns would more than quadruple—to $442.60. That's the magic of compounding.

The truth is, for higher returns stocks are pretty much the only game in town. The average stock gained 11.4 percent annually over the past seventy-four years, according to Ibbotson Associates, a financial consulting firm in Chicago. That compares with earnings for bonds of around 5.1 percent, and for Treasury bills of just 3.8 percent. Over that same time, inflation averaged 3.1 percent.

Very simply, saving and investing should be part of a lifetime strategy, one that incorporates every facet of your financial life, including decisions about homes and even insurance. Then, and only then, can you be assured that you will meet your financial goals at each stage of life.

The first question any investor must ask is, what are my plans? Risk can bring profits, and time can be a salve for risk's downside. Simply put, the longer the time horizon for an investor, the greater your risk tolerance and the greater your potential rewards.

This is why an investing plan that makes sense when you're in your twenties can be pure foolishness when you are in your forties. The investment goals of an unmarried twenty-something who lives in a rental apartment and is excited about having an entry-level position at a big corporation should have little relationship to those of a middle-aged middle manager with a wife, kids and mortgage. Goals change as you age, and as a result, your investing and financial strategies should change with them.

Now, of course, there is no one-size-fits-all strategy, even age group by age group. There are fifty-five-year-olds who return to college and nineteen-year-olds who are raising a family. But there are rules for investing and financial management that can help every investor prepare for their future.

To understand aged-based investment strategies, start with this test: The amount of risk you can bear in your financial life is directly proportional to the average willingness of someone your age to go bungee jumping. The reasons are basically the same. Younger people have more time, and are more able to withstand the damage if their risk-taking creates problems. In bungee jumping, they are better able to recuperate; in finance, time can heal the wounds of a bad call. Thus, if you're five years from retirement, and someone comes to you with what sounds like a particularly risky idea, it's probably best not to take the plunge.

Before putting your money at risk, remember that everyone, at every stage of life, needs a safety net, cash that's available in an emergency. If all your cash is tied up in stocks, you could be forced to sell in a downdraft—regardless of your time horizon—if you don't have the money to cover a sudden hospitalization or major home repair. The foundation of a smart investment strategy is a cushion of money that's easily available. The amount experts tend to recommend is as much as six months of salary, and no less than three months.

There are plenty of places to invest this money. A savings account at a bank is the most obvious; however, don't just stick your money in day-to-day savings without speaking with bank tellers or advisers. Most banks these days offer an assortment of savings vehicles—money market accounts, preferred money market accounts and accounts tied to certificates of deposit—which offer better returns, depending on set minimum deposits. Go for the highest return, as long as it maintains reasonable access to your money. You can also try Treasury bills (though they have a $10,000 minimum) or short-term bond funds; money in any of these investments should be safe and available in emergencies. And remember, as will be explained in chapter 5, the highest yields and lowest expenses are generally available from money market and short-term bond funds at no-load fund groups like Vanguard.

Bearing that in mind, let's take a look at financial strategies for each stage of life.

At the Starting Gate: Your Twenties

1. Ready: Get Your Finances in Order

At age twenty-nine or younger, you stand a strong chance of investing strategically to afford that house, put your kids through college, and retire comfortably with the money you need for your golden years. Some portion of this good fortune will come from sage decisions, but in truth your promising future results from thinking about your finances at an age when small steps can, with little effort, quickly transform into giant, compounded returns. All you need now is to decide to begin.

While today your future may seem like some far-off neverland, it will arrive faster than you imagine. Today, that run-down apartment may be fine; tomorrow, you and your spouse will want a house. All of the big expenses in your future—houses, cars, college, retirement, whatever—will be in easy reach only if you begin saving today. But you can only do that if you take a few steps that give you money to invest.

The first step is simple: Decide that your financial goals matter. Once you fully accept that, all other parts of successful financial planning are easy. This step will help you impose a discipline on yourself that in turn will give you the ability to save.

The second step is a little less philosophical, and more of an "eat-your-vegetables" instruction: Set up a budget. Whatever your income, whatever your living situation, you have to make choices on what to spend. Those choices can be imposed by your own planning, or by third parties—credit card companies, other creditors. Leaving the decisions to the third parties means sacrificing your potential for financial freedom.

What does limiting spending have to do with investing? The answer is: everything. In this world, it is far easier to spend a dollar or two more—perhaps on that double cappuccino on the way to the office, where the coffee is free—than it is to earn a dollar more. Every dollar of your earnings is taxed; every dollar cut out of your expenses is not. So a dollar more of salary is worth significantly less than a dollar saved by cutting out unnecessary items. And without limiting your spending, you will never be able to accumulate the initial pot of cash you need for investing. While you might think that small amount—maybe five to ten dollars a week—makes no difference, don't forget the magic you saw in the time value of money.

Start by reviewing all of your records. How much is your gross pay? What are your taxes—federal, state, local (and don't forget Social Security and Medicare)? Then figure out what you pay for housing, utilities, transportation and food. Look for items that aren't so necessary—if you're tight on money, why eat at the office cafeteria when it's cheaper to bring your lunch? Don't forget leisure, pleasure and appearance expenses—movies, dry cleaning, the gym.

Before you begin distributing your after-tax income through all of your expense lines, add two more items: money to yourself by investing through your own savings, and, if available, money to your 401(k) retirement plan or to an Individual Retirement Account (I.R.A.). Now, as you assign budget numbers to each line, remember that each dollar you take out of one item goes straight back to you, in the form of savings. Make saving easy with automatic deductions from your checking account into a savings account. Most banks, brokerages and fund companies offer such automatic withdrawal and investment programs for free.

If you can't find any savings, you may have mixed up your desires with your needs. No one *needs* an expensive car or a bottle of expensive wine. Those are just things we want. In the modern era of easy credit, the distance between desire and gratification is no more than the length of a plastic credit card.

The credit card is the bane of sound financial planning when you are in your twenties. It's easy to use, and expensive to boot. If you rack up huge balances, your savings will never materialize as you struggle each month to pay the interest. Many people in their twenties are already carrying heavy debts like student loans. But you should avoid assuming new debts—other than a home mortgage—with all your being. If you want to use the cards, that's fine—just pay them off each month. And if you need the credit in any situation other than a dire emergency, go back to your budget. You need to cut back your spending some more.

2. Set: Define Your Financial Goals

Once you're ready to start saving, you need to decide what you're saving for. What are your financial goals? The seemingly obvious answer—to make as much on your investments as possible—does not inform a smart investing strategy. Suppose you want to buy a house in three years; you won't invest your money in the same vehicles as you would if you were saving for retirement. The longer the time horizon for your financial goal, the greater the risk you can take on your investments.

Most people in their twenties have two or three financial goals. The first is to buy that house. The second is to start saving for retirement. Those who are really clever want to start putting money away for the education of their future children.

When it comes to buying a house, be realistic and remember that there are steep transaction costs associated with buying and selling real estate. It can make a lot more sense to rent a few more years until you can afford a house that you can live in for years to come. When you shift your savings into home equity, you're not spending the money. You're investing it in an asset that can appreciate. So if you want one, a home should be an important goal, to be achieved within a realistic time frame—such as five to ten years—at a realistic price.

Retirement, of course, is fairly predictable. Unless you are planning on retiring early, you can work on about a forty-year timetable. But when you calculate how much you may need to retire comfortably, remember a few things. Pensions and Social Security are going to be playing far less of a role in your retirement than they might for your parents' golden years. And these days, retirement is the beginning of a third stage of life that can last as much as twenty-five to thirty-five years. Your money will need to last a long time.

Make sure, in running these calculations, to take advantage of some of the technological advances that make saving easier: personal financial software, such as Quicken or Microsoft Money, or even online retirement calculators (to find one on the Web, just type "retirement calculator" into a search engine, and choose one you like).

Finally, saving for children's education deserves the least attention, unless you have already made the decision to start a family. For one thing, who knows if you'll even have kids? But if you're the type who is always looking for a little more reason to save, it makes sense to put a small portion aside for education, with the assumption that the earliest you will need it is in about twenty years.

3. Go: Invest Your Money

Once you have a budget, a small flow of savings each month, and financial goals, you're ready to start investing. Your time frame on saving for a home is dramatically less than for education or retirement. That means one thing: The risk profile for investing your home savings should be lower than that for your retirement savings. Again, in the markets, time can heal all wounds, but only if there's enough time.

One chunk of your cash should go into safe havens, like short-term Treasury securities, bank accounts or money market mutual funds. This is your safety net, the money that will help you survive any sudden plunge. But if you are saving to purchase a house within the next ten years, you should put a portion of that cash into stocks; the amount you save, of course, is dictated by how expensive a house you want to buy. As each year ticks by, cut back your stock exposure in your house money, shifting more of it over to the safe havens.

The largest chunk of your savings—indeed, more than half—should go into retirement, through I.R.A.s (especially Roth I.R.A.s), 401(k) plans or other retirement accounts. These types of investments have the extra kick of tax benefits, and sometimes matching payments by your employers, meaning you get far more bang for every buck you invest. Do everything you can to contribute the maximum allowable, particularly since the 401(k), if used properly, is likely to be your primary source of retirement income. For more on investing with taxes in mind, see chapter 7.

Now, sticking your money in a retirement account doesn't do it all. Since most of those plans are self-directed, you have to be sure that you invest the money properly. Surprisingly, many people don't. A recent analysis of the asset allocation decisions made by 180,000 employees at AT&T, the IBM Corporation and the New York Life Insurance Company found that a significant percentage of young workers were saving heavily in their 401(k) plans, but investing none of that money in stocks. Bad move. That study, by the Employee Benefit Research Institute, a nonprofit group, underscores how much more work has to be done in getting young people to understand that their golden time for taking on risk is now.

Investing all your money in one place or one sector increases the probability of disaster. If you want to take part in hot, new market crazes, make these investments only a small portion of your portfolio. Instead, diversify your investments by sector, by region, and by company size. With a twenty-five- to thirty-year investing time line, a plan with moderate risk would place 80 percent of your money in stocks, with half of that—40 percent of the total—plowed into a range of large company stocks, either directly or through targeted mutual funds. The other half would be divided about equally—20 percent each of the total—between small company stocks and foreign stocks, or related funds.

If you have an investing strategy that allows you to be more aggressive, shoot for 95 percent in stocks, with the largest chunk in large companies and the remainder divided between small companies and international investments. Keep nothing in bonds and just 5 percent in cash equivalents.

To make decisions about the stocks and mutual funds, see the appropriate chapters later in this book. If you're the type who doesn't want to spend time researching each individual investment you make, it's best to make stock funds the centerpiece of your portfolio. Even here, however, you need to do some research. Before committing any cash, read chapter 4 for guidelines on choosing funds and be sure to check the fund ratings with a service like Morningstar. You should also keep an eye on the fund manager—if the person who brought the fund its strong record takes a hike, move your investments until the new manager has made a mark.

One other key to investing: Don't buy anything you don't understand. Too often, investors think they have stumbled onto some holy grail of the financial markets with an investment that is billed as high return and low risk. But there is no such thing. Investment return is what you are paid for assuming risk—the higher the potential return, the higher the risk, and vice versa. Think of it this way: You wouldn't bet your money on a game of blackjack if you didn't understand the rules. So why would you invest your money in something you don't understand? Stick with what you know.

Pushing Forward: In Your Thirties

1. Assess Your Situation

If you're not married already, you might be in the coming years. You need to be prepared to dramatically realign your financial goals. Perhaps you have children, or perhaps you're planning on them in the near future. That puts time pressure on two of your biggest financial goals—saving for children's education and saving for a house. Education is the easiest. The clock starts ticking the day that pregnancy is confirmed. You have nineteen years until the first big payment. That's a long enough time frame to assume some bigger risks in your investment portfolio.

Buying a house is still not necessary—although on balance it becomes more attractive. Remember, every month you pay rent is money sent to someone else; every month you pay mortgage is a little money you're putting away for yourself. Your mortgage interest and property taxes, unlike your rent, are tax deductible.

But don't plan to buy anything huge—if you haven't been able to save much yet, you sure don't want to load yourself down with a heavy mortgage. And remember, the cost of a house doesn't end after the closing. You'll have home repairs and the like that hit your wallet almost every month. So plan ahead.

At this stage in your life, there are some additional things that you need to be doing. Some you should do at whatever age you start a family.

First, you should buy insurance, the bedrock of a secure financial plan. Suppose you have woven your safety net and grown a large investment portfolio. Then you're crippled by a falling tree. Or you die. Or your spouse dies, leaving you as the sole guardian of your children. Or your house burns down. Now, all your time horizons

Long-Term Performance:
No Contest

Over the long haul, stocks have far outperformed
bonds. The chart shows the value of $1,000
investments made at the end of 1925 in the S&P 500
stock index, long-term Treasury bonds and 30-day
Treasuries, based on total return, plotted annually.

*The upper portion of the scale is collapsed. Plotting
the whole chart on the scale used at the bottom
would make it more than three pages tall.*

Data source: Ibbotson Associates

Millions $3.0

$2,586,517
2.5

2.0

1.5

1.0

0.5

0.4

0.3

■ **Stocks** *S&P 500*
0.2
■ **Bonds** *Long-term Treasuries*
■ **Cash** *30-day Treasuries*

0.1

$48,856
$16,563
0.0

1930   1940   1950   1960   1970   1980   1990   2000

vanish, your safety net is tattered and your plans are destroyed. With no insurance, you will burn through cash like a dotcom, and everything you have worked for will be shattered. Insurance protects your family and your future and preserves your investment strategy.

The types of insurance you need run the gamut. Health, life and disability insurance may be available through your employer, but still, check out the terms. Policies that come with your job may need to be supplemented by private coverage. Most states require some level of car insurance, and you should maintain it for both the vehicle itself and for liability in any accident. Finally, if you own a home, you'll need homeowner's insurance to cover damage to the dwelling and its contents.

2. Consider Getting Help

If by the time you turn thirty, you haven't begun an aggressive savings and investment plan—or if you have, but find that you can't dedicate enough time to watching your investments—consider hiring a broker or other type of financial adviser. In these days of no-load this and discount that, online and off, this advice may sound counterintuitive. But let's face it: those do-it-yourself options are best for folks who are ready to commit the time necessary to be sure they know what they're doing. By this point, if that's not you, go to a full-service brokerage firm, or find a trustworthy financial planner. The money you spend on advice may well help you in the long run. As we point out in chapter 8, a broker at a major firm can protect you from many investment pitfalls.

In relying on a broker, there are some important don'ts. Don't become a trader based on a broker's advice; brokers rarely can make calls good enough to know when to rapidly jump in and out of a stock. If they were any good at that, the firm would put them on the trading desk, where the real hotshots sit. Don't slavishly follow whatever the broker or adviser tells you; if you don't understand an investment or transaction, look into it. And if you have a broker who tries to bully you into making a particular trade—or who does it without your approval—promptly close your account and find another firm. Remember, a broker should be your adviser, not your dictator.

How do you go about finding a knowledgeable and honest adviser? The same way you pick a stock—with research. Ask your friends and family about brokers and planners, but consider their suggestions only as leads for further research. Arrange meetings and ask them about everything—education, experience, references, their investment philosophy, their long-term strategies. Don't accept vague answers, press for specifics. Beware of anyone who appeals to your greed, with promises that you'll get rich. Call their references, and be sure to ask them how they came to invest with this person. (The last thing you need is a glowing recommendation from the broker's college roommate.)

These professionals come in all stripes; they can be be independent agents or commissioned representatives of a company. They can be licensed to sell only mutual funds, only insurance, or a broad range of investments. They call themselves by many names: financial planners, investment advisers, financial advisers, or plain old brokers.

Make sure you understand who you are dealing with, what they are able to sell and how they are paid. Some receive a commission or fee based on your individual investing decision, while other fee-only professionals are paid by the hour. If you are looking for a fee-only professional, check with the National Association of Personal Financial Advisors (www.napfa.org), an organization made up of advisers who are mostly Certified Financial Planners.

Stockbrokers can be valuable, but you should remember that they are salespeople, who often make their money when you buy or sell a stock or mutual fund. The National Association of Securities Dealers (NASD) and your state securities agency can provide extensive background and disciplinary information on any broker. Be sure to check with one of those agencies before hiring a broker.

Once you feel satisfied with your research, open an account. But if ever you feel queasy or uncertain, start again and pick a new broker

or adviser. Remember, your future is at stake. The person helping you must be someone you trust.

Rounding the Bend: In Your Forties and Fifties

1. Reassess Your Priorities

These years can be, surprisingly, among the most challenging for savers. They are among the highest earning years in your life, but also the years of your big preretirement expenses. You probably own a home already, and are enjoying all the big-ticket expenses associated with it. You have learned that furniture is not something you buy only once in life. The ridiculously far-off notion that you would have children going to college is now at hand. For these expenses— depending on the ages of your kids—you might have missed most of the window for the advantages of saving over time.

Whether or not you have begun saving for retirement, this is the time to sit down and make an honest assessment of where you stand. How much will you need when you retire? Over how many years or decades? What kind of lifestyle do you want? Remember, the world has changed; pensions and Social Security will not bail you out. If you haven't put enough money away yet for the life you want to live, you're running out of time. You are in charge of the lifestyle you will lead.

Maybe, to make up for a lack of savings, you shouldn't retire as soon as you have planned. The time value of money can work on both ends—if you either start to invest early in life or allow those investments to keep climbing a few years longer by delaying your retirement date. Whatever time you can give yourself will translate into extra money.

Maybe now you're earning a substantial salary. That's good, because it allows you to compensate some for failing to put your money away when you were younger. Over the years, you have almost certainly begun to spend more as your income went up. If you haven't made savings a part of your financial plan until now, you're going to have to cut back—way back—on discretionary spending. Plan on driving your old car around a few more years, or doing whatever you need to prune your living expenses. Whatever you do, if you haven't started saving until your forties, you need to put away at least 20 percent of your pretax income each year.

2. Get Your House in Order

For those of you who have been faithfully investing over many years, you need to do some housekeeping as well. You probably have collected an array of financial "stuff"—investments that have languished, or that no longer make the sense they may have when they were purchased—and at this point you might have little idea about your total financial picture.

It's time again to sit down and break out the pad and pencil. First of all, you need to determine what investment vehicles you have. How much do you have in defined contribution plans where you regularly put in fixed amounts, like your employer's 401(k)s? And what about retirement plans you finance yourself, like I.R.A.s? What about your personal assets, from individual investment accounts to home equity, from bank accounts to the cash value of your life insurance? And don't forget the value of personal property, like jewelry. Add all these up, and you'll see your total savings so far. Now, at this point, you should also be able to better assess your big non-retirement expenses. Do your college savings for your children meet your expected needs? Everything that's left is the amount you have saved for retirement.

Now is also the time to reassess your investments. In particular, if you will need to pay for college soon, you should consider shifting a percentage of your money out of higher-risk investments like stocks and into lower-risk investments like bonds, particularly if you are close to meeting your financial needs for that goal. Check out the performance of your various retirement investments, and clear away the junk. If you've been aggressive and attentive, with a record of success in picking stocks, then continue following your habits. But if you've been shooting a lot of blanks, consider shifting to mutual funds and turning to a professional money manager. As chapter 4 on mutual funds points out, however, you must remain involved in your investments and do some research even when you decide to let someone else do the work.

3. Adjust Your Risk

As you age, you gradually approach the time when you are going to need your money. So once you've assessed your investments and their quality, you should take another look at your allocation strategy. Your risk profile has changed some, since the time horizon has shortened. It would be a good idea, as you move from your forties into your fifties, to reallocate your assets, with more going into bonds and cash equivalents.

Stocks and stock funds should still be the largest portion of your long-term holdings. With people living longer and remaining active, anyone who abandons stocks and mutual funds as the core of their investment strategy is opting to be poor or constrained in retirement. For a plan with moderate risks, stocks should make up about 60 percent of your holdings, divided in the same categories as before— the major portion in large company stocks, with the rest divided between small companies and foreign companies. Thirty percent should be in bonds or bond funds and the last 10 percent in cash or cash equivalents.

You should review your asset allocation plans continuously throughout these years, to be sure that you adjust your risk profile as your circumstances change. As you get closer and closer to your financial goals, you may want to readjust your risk exposure.

Even if you choose to keep your risks constant, review your asset allocation every year or so. As markets fluctuate, the percentages of your portfolio in each type of security can change dramatically. If you've put 60 percent of your money in stocks, a booming market could result in that being boosted to 75 percent, without you lifting a finger. Or, in a falling market, you could find yourself with less than half your money in equities. So keep an eye on your percentages, and make sure you don't let the market make your asset allocation decisions for you.

Adjusting your risk generally means deciding to sell, a prospect that can be very daunting. A stock that's done particularly well over the years can be hard to part with, not only because of an emotional attachment but because of the potential capital gains taxes as well. That's why it's best to make any adjustments in your tax-advantaged accounts, like I.R.A.s and 401(k)s. See chapter 7 on taxes for more.

If you do have to make sales in a regular account, it's possible to minimize the tax hit if you've been good with your record keeping. If you just sell shares with no designation, the Internal Revenue Service assumes you are selling the earliest shares you purchased— which are probably the shares that cost the least. However, the law allows you to specify which shares you want to sell—in stock or in stock mutual funds. Find the ones you purchased with the highest price, then designate them as the ones to sell to minimize your taxes.

4. Watch Out for Crooks

When asked why he robbed banks, Willie Sutton famously replied, "Because that's where the money is." That simple philosophy is shared by almost every investment crook and con man. Except now you are where the money is.

You are now at your prime period for earnings, and your savings should be piling up. Crooks know that. They also know that your anxieties about retirement and other financial goals are reaching their peak. You are now their prime target.

Chapter 8 covers some of the latest traps and growing sources of risk: Internet chat rooms, borrowing on margin, the high but hidden costs of investing online, the failings of Wall Street research, the dangers of overly frequent trading and the lack of effective protection for victims of brokerage theft, bankruptcy or fraud. Given our advice to use a broker if you don't have the time or talent to manage your own money, here are some tips for protecting yourself from those who see your nest egg as their opportunity.

Securities regulators, stock exchanges and brokerage firms cannot stop a crooked broker from lying. They are not on the phone when a sales pitch is under way. But that doesn't mean investors should start stuffing the mattress. Instead, they should step up their own supervision.

"People cannot approach a brokerage believing they will treat you with only your best interest at heart," said Douglas J. Schulz, who does consulting work for arbitrations on securities cases. "In today's environment, it is more and more evident that investors need to do their own self-policing."

This is not as easy as it sounds. Victims of investment scams always feel stupid once they realize they have been taken. In fact, they are often fairly savvy, but were unprepared for the sophistication and talent of modern-day con artists. Boiler room operators and other con men have scammed millions; their pitches can be surprisingly persuasive.

How do you protect yourself? Primarily, recognize that almost all scam artists depend on creating a sense of urgency, saying such things as "This is really selling—you need to decide now" or "I don't know if I can get any more of this." But *no* deal is worth going into blindly. This pitch is intended to appeal to investors who fear missing out on a good deal. The undertone is "Nobody who understands investing would pass this up." The opposite is true. No sophisticated investor would sink money into something without research. There's always another investment, so safely pass this one up.

There are plenty of other lines that scam artists use. Here are a few of the most common:

"This stock is guaranteed to make profits." Every investment involves risk. This line is often used in selling penny stocks or other low-priced securities, with sly hints of hush-hush deals in progress that will make the stock soar. Those deals never materialize, and only one person profits: the broker.

"Don't worry about it." The primary way crooked brokers take advantage of customers is by dismissing their concerns. A good broker will listen to your concerns and make sure you are comfortable. "If you hear 'don't worry,' hang up the phone," Schulz says.

"This investment is so safe, I even put my own family into it." Investment decisions must be based on your objectives and financial condition—and yours are unlikely to be the same as the broker's family. Still curious? Ask for the family's phone number. If the broker won't tell you, you know the truth.

"This investment is really complicated. Let me take care of it." If an investment is so complicated you don't understand it, you shouldn't buy it. And a broker has no business trying to sell it to you.

"You don't need to read the prospectus." If you hear this, or you are not sent a prospectus, your broker may be hiding something. Telephone fraud works only if customers never see anything in writing.

Each of these approaches is intended to make the investor feel foolish for being cautious. No legitimate investment adviser or broker would take that approach. So anytime you feel rushed, or anytime a salesman makes you feel silly for wanting to know more, hang up the phone. There are plenty of brokers and plenty of investments out there.

There are other types of con artists, who are far more insidious— and far more dangerous—than the scamsters who phone you. Too frequently, families lose everything to someone they thought they knew. Almost every time, these are people they met through their participation in some community or social group, or even church. It may be difficult to accept, but con artists join these organizations for the very purpose of scouting out new targets. They can appear to be the most devout or committed member, a facade that they know makes them all the more persuasive. But there is a very simple way of avoiding these crooks: Do not do business with anyone you know personally. That allows you to maintain objectivity in your financial dealings, and it sidesteps the possibility that you are being taken by someone posing as a friend. Remember, it is important that you always feel able to change financial advisers. Work off references, and check up on the people you retain.

5. Starting Late

All right, let's face it. There are those of you in your late forties who are only now starting to think about how to invest for retirement. You're starting to feel a little bit desperate and uncertain, and perhaps you are looking through this book for shortcuts, tips that will put you up where you should have been.

Well, here's the bad news: There are no short cuts. There are no secrets for making up for lost time. And whatever you do, don't compound your mistake by chasing some high-risk fad that offers the prospects of a quick, big hit. At this point, you don't have much margin for error, because you don't have the time to recover from another major mistake. To a large degree, starting late on investing is like leaving late for an important meeting. Sure, you can take the risk of driving fast and recklessly, but you're as likely to have an accident as make up for lost time.

When it comes to investing, you're not much different from others your age who have been saving for decades. The key to fixing your situation is not to find the riskiest, most aggressive investments, but instead to boost the amount you invest to the highest level possible. Increase your 401(k) contributions to the maximum, sign up for automatic investing plans through a brokerage firm or mutual fund company, and sock away at least half of every raise or bonus you receive from now on.

If you are grumbling that this will cut into your lifestyle, just remember—you overspent for that lifestyle in your younger years. You probably knew it, too. This is the price you pay, but it should be enough to help you build a sizable retirement fund. But don't delay. Eventually, you run out of time to fix your mistake, and then the price is working well into what should be your retirement years.

Beginning the New Race: Your Sixties and Beyond

1. What Now?

If you've been sticking to a financial plan for the last few decades, by now you should have built up a very tidy retirement fund. The question is, what do you do with it? At this point, you have a series of very important decisions to make, and you have to pay very close attention to your circumstances to avoid making a critical mistake.

While reaching your sixties once meant that you were in the closing days of your life, that is not true anymore. Advances in medical science have lengthened the average American's life span; according to the Centers for Disease Control, the average sixty-five-year-old man has 15.9 years left, the average woman of the same age, 19.2 years. Perhaps more important, these advances have also made active retirement the norm. Not only are you likely to live longer than your parents and grandparents, but you're also likely to remain busier. Rather than looking on retirement as an ending, look on it as a new beginning, one that presents some of your most complex financial challenges.

The first big decision is when to retire. Unfortunately, your ability to retire might not match your desire. Calculate the cost of the lifestyle you want, then take a realistic look at what your savings will allow you to afford, for at least another twenty-five years. Whatever the actuarial tables say, plenty of people live into their eighties, nineties and beyond, and if you've blown through all of your money before then, your final decades could be ones of hardship.

If the numbers don't work, there are plenty of options. For one, if you can, continue working a few years longer than you had planned. At this point, you should still be in the peak earning period of your life, and another few years of saving money—rather than drawing it down—can substantially improve your retirement. Beyond that, there are plenty of incentives built into Social Security and company pension plans to delay retirement, so look into these before deciding anything. If you're not up to working full-time, check into the possibility of working part-time.

2. Stick with Stocks

While it makes sense to reduce your risks, stocks should remain the centerpiece of your portfolio. The reason is obvious—with an extended life expectancy, you are, once again, saving for the long term.

In other words, it can be just as dangerous to your financial health if you take too little risk as if you take too much. If you focus on generating a high level of current income, you'll be putting your money in fixed-income investments like certificates of deposit or bonds. But you will have little or nothing in the way of growth, meaning that you will struggle as inflation gradually raises your cost of living. Even when inflation is down at the 3 percent level, where it hovered for much of the 1990s, it would cut your purchasing power in half in about twenty-four years.

To keep ahead of inflation, retirees and those approaching retirement should keep as much as half their portfolios in stocks, and certainly should not allow their holdings to drop below 30 percent. But you don't have to buy only aggressive growth stocks. Instead, you can invest in dividend-paying blue chips, or mutual funds that hold such stocks. Such investments provide good income and some growth while historically avoiding big losses in market pullbacks. To further help your investments stay ahead of inflation, include some foreign and small-cap mutual funds or stocks. Take on as much risk as you can without making yourself uncomfortable.

3. How to Withdraw Your Money, and Limit Costs

Almost everything you do from this point on should be planned, even how you withdraw your money for retirement. There are plenty of rules to follow to avoid penalties and minimize taxes.

Rule number one is simple: Always draw from your non-retirement accounts first. Remember that the tax advantages of retirement accounts supercharge your returns. You want to keep those returns going as long as possible.

As you'll see in more detail in chapter 7, if you have a traditional I.R.A., you can start your withdrawals after age 59½, and you must start receiving the required minimum distribution by April 1 of the year after you reach 70½. When the withdrawals begin, you will finally have to pay taxes on that money, as if the withdrawals were ordinary income. By waiting as long as you can, you avoid penalties, delay taxes and allow your money to keep working for you as long as possible.

If you've saved money in a Roth I.R.A., you have greater flexibility. You can withdraw your *profits* from the account tax-free if you are over 59½, and you can withdraw your *contributions* tax-free at any time.

4. Playing with Social Security

Throughout this chapter, little has been said about Social Security, and with good reason. Regardless of what form Social Security will take, it will not allow most people to live as well as they want in retirement. However, there are ways to maximize your benefits, providing an extra back-end option for those who failed to start saving early enough.

At its adoption in the 1930s, Social Security was meant as a short-term benefit to help the elderly avoid poverty, not necessarily to live well. At the time, the government selected a retirement age of sixty-five because life expectancy was sixty-seven. In other words, the government was counting on the average retirement lasting all of two years.

That has changed. Beginning in the year 2000, the Social Security retirement ages are being gradually increased, based on your year of birth. For those born in or before 1938, the retirement age remains at sixty-five. For those born in 1939 and before 1960, the retirement age has been increased to sixty-six, and for those born in 1960 and later, sixty-seven.

Regardless of the changes, retirees can maximize their payouts. Retiring early means a reduction in benefits, by five-ninths of 1 percent for each month, or 6.6 percent a year, that benefits start before the set retirement age. On the other hand, for every year you delay retirement, your benefits increase. That gain will gradually increase to 8 percent in 2009 for each extra year you work, up until age seventy.

5. Hidden Savings: The Reverse Mortgage

Maybe you're the type who managed to save for a house, but didn't do such a good job saving for retirement. Well, in recent years, a new type of loan has been gaining popularity, called the reverse mortgage or home-equity conversion. Effectively, it is a means of tapping into the equity you've built up in your home over many years, without going to the trouble and expense of selling it.

This type of loan depends not on your income but on your age, your spouse's age, and the amount of equity you have in your house. Since the loan is based on life expectancy, the older you are the more you can borrow—through monthly checks, a lump sum or a line of credit.

Unlike a home equity loan, a reverse mortgage requires no month-to-month interest payments on what you borrow. Instead, the interest compounds and is paid off when the loan comes due—when you either sell your home or die. Then, the loan and accumulated interest are paid with the proceeds from the house. But remember a few things about the reverse mortgage. First, it virtually guarantees that you will not have a home to leave to your heirs. Second, the reverse mortgage can be very expensive, and very complicated. But for people who want to continue to live in their home—and who are faced with enormous costs such as bills for live-in health aides—the reverse mortgage offers an alternative with the flexibility that people need to continue living the lifestyle they want.

6. Prepare for the Inevitable: Estate Planning

There is one thing that can be written without fear of error: Every person reading this book, regardless of their age, regardless of their health, will die. It is an uncomfortable reality, one that everyone should eventually prepare for. These days, there is plenty of reason to expect that the estate-tax system will dramatically change. But regardless of what changes are made, a critical last element of any investor's plan is preparing for death.

The first and most obvious stage in that preparation is making sure you have an up-to-date will that clearly specifies what you want done with your assets. If you're married, you want to be sure that your assets and your life insurance will be sufficient to allow your spouse to maintain an accustomed lifestyle. Without taking the steps for estate planning, it is possible, if you are moderately wealthy, that a large portion of the money that you have saved over the years will pass on to the government, rather than to the people and organizations of your choosing.

This is not an area where amateurs should venture. As you'll see in chapter 7, you should, before setting up a trust, find a qualified professional who can tell you which types of trusts meet your need. That person—usually an estate lawyer—will then be available to make sure that the trust is properly established and executed. With that little bit of effort, you will gain much greater control over the distribution of your assets.

The Finish Line

By now you should have a strong understanding of the challenges you face in protecting your financial future. If this chapter could be summarized in a single word, it would be "planning." Far too often, people ignore the effect they can have on their future lifestyle because it seems so far off, so intangible. But that is just foolishness. Time gives you the ability to save for your future with as little pain as possible, and allows you to take advantage of the highest-risk, highest-return investments without having to worry about the impact any short-term market collapse will have on your lifestyle. As the years go by, your ability to withstand risk drops. Regardless of your age, regardless of what mistakes you may have made, start today.

3.

Stocks: How (and How Not) to Invest Directly

LESLIE EATON

It wasn't long ago—a decade, maybe—that investing was like surgery, a practice almost everybody left in the hands of professionals.

If they were wealthy and lucky, investors got real money managers as their financial guides, managers who had a philosophy they followed and who got paid based on how well their clients' portfolios fared. If the investors were unlucky—and most were—they entrusted their money to their brothers-in-law or their old science teachers or their pals from college. Most of these guys (they were almost always male) were stock brokers, who simply divided the money among the stocks their employers favored—or put it in the mutual funds that would pay them the biggest commissions.

Then came the 1990s, and the rise of do-it-yourself investing. Two developments contributed to the investing boom. The first was necessity. As discussed in chapter 1, companies used to promise their employees fixed pensions after a couple of decades of work. But in recent years, millions of us have been switched into newfangled retirement plans with names like 401(k)s and 403(b)s. The plans all vary, but most have one thing in common: They shift at least some of the responsibility for choosing how to invest for retirement onto individual employees. Suddenly, how well we all make investment decisions determines whether we'll spend our golden years dining on caviar or cat food.

Fortunately, in this case necessity was greeted by invention. The second big investing development of the 1990s was the boom in technology—the Internet in particular—that made it possible for amateurs to get the same information the pros had hoarded all those years. And so, propelled by the advent of so-called self-directed pension plans and empowered by new information technology, more average people than ever before plunged into the stock market.

They used the Internet to do their own research. They swapped tips in online chat rooms. They traded stocks using low-cost online brokerage firms. They made a bundle. And because the market kept going up, these new investors began to believe that it was easy to do better than the pros, sort of the way parents look at a Jackson Pollock painting and think, "My kid could do that."

But the new century changed everything. In 2000, the Nasdaq—full of the stocks of high-tech companies favored by amateur investors—began to drop, and drop, and drop. As it plunged, eventually taking the broader market with it, amateurs began to wonder whether those amusing brokerage ads ought to come with warnings like some auto ads do: "Professional driver on closed track." In other words, do not try this at home.

The truth, of course, is somewhere between these two views. Investing in stocks is not as easy as filling up your car with gas, nor as hopeless as building an auto engine out of toothpicks. It requires a little knowledge and a whole lot of patience.

The knowledge part has grown more important in recent years. It's no longer enough—if it ever was—simply to decide what a stock is worth, because it's absurdly cheap or has a genius C.E.O. or is introducing the greatest product since microwave popcorn. You also have to figure out what other people are likely to think the stock is worth. Because of the Internet, online trading and other high-tech developments, all kinds of things—even investment techniques you think are foolish—may well affect your investments. Hordes of people you have never seen, following a market fad, can send your stock sinking or soaring. Understanding how they think and how they invest can help you decide whether to buy, hold or run screaming in the opposite direction.

The good news is that the same developments have made it far easier to adopt and execute any investment strategy you believe in, and to understand the forces buffeting the shares you own.

- Picking stocks requires careful, patient research on both company performance and broader market trends, since other investors' responses to economic shifts will affect your investments.

The Cons and Pros of Direct Stock Investing

There are people who believe that markets are so irrational that you should just keep your savings in large bills between the sheet and the mattress pad. But as Jeremy J. Siegel has demonstrated, stocks are, indeed, excellent investments provided you have a longtime horizon. For almost two centuries, stocks have returned an annual average of 7 percent on top of inflation, far more than bonds. Of course, you have to have a very longtime horizon; there have been stretches, lasting more than a decade, when stocks haven't appreciated at all.

But if stocks are clearly the way to go, it is less clear whether it makes more sense to own individual stocks directly, or indirectly through mutual funds. In part, that depends on whether you have the time and interest to do your own careful, solid research into the markets, specific industries and individual stocks. If the answer is no, you're much better off letting a professional mutual fund manager do your stock picking (or, as described in chapter 2, finding a reputable stock broker, especially one who gets paid when your portfolio appreciates rather than through sales commissions).

Chart 3A

Smooth Returns from Stocks

Stocks rise and fall from year to year, but over long periods their returns have been remarkably consistent. Here are average annual total returns for stocks in the S&P 500 index over a typical working life — 40-year periods ending with each year.

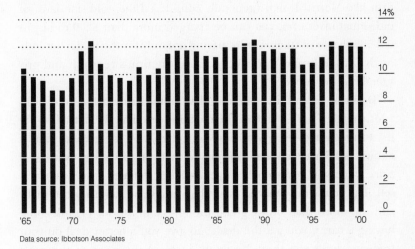

Data source: Ibbotson Associates

There's also an academic argument against trying to profit by buying individual stocks. The markets, this theory goes, are totally rational. Because stock prices perfectly reflect all available information, no one has an edge (except for the crooks who illegally trade on nonpublic information). That means it is impossible to consistently beat the market.

The adherents of this "efficient markets" theory admit that stocks have been far better investments than bank accounts or bonds (or bedding) over the long haul. But they generally argue that the only way to prosper is to put your money into a broad stock index fund. These funds try to duplicate the results of specific baskets of stocks, like the Standard & Poor's index of 500 big companies. If the fund is well managed and tracks a broad enough index, it can be a low-cost way to match the performance of the overall market—which, after all, is as well as the efficient-market types say you could hope to do over the long term. Vanguard Investments' S&P 500 index fund springs to mind (it's well managed and cheap, meaning no up-front fees and low annual costs).

By contrast, investing in individual stocks can be expensive—especially if you trade a lot. If you trade through a broker at a full-service firm like Merrill Lynch (generally considered the gold standard for individual investors), you can be charged more than $200 to buy or sell 500 shares of stock. You're paying not only for the trade, but indirectly for the broker's advice, access to the firm's research and presumably other services.

Don't be fooled into thinking that online brokers are necessarily a lot cheaper. Sure, some of them charge less than $20 a trade—but if you are not careful, you'll pay in other ways, by getting what is known as poor execution. This means that you pay a slightly inflated price when you buy a stock, or get a slightly deflated price when you sell. The actual amounts on each share are small, but they can really add up, more than outweighing the low commission. (Think about buying a car; if you get the dealer to give you a better deal on your trade-in, don't you think he might increase the price of the car a little to make up the loss?) Big stocks that lots of people trade, especially on the New York Stock Exchange, are less prone to these hidden markups than less liquid shares on Nasdaq and over-the-counter. For more on the risks of trading online, see chapter 8.

One final advantage of funds: Every investment adviser out there recommends diversification—spreading your risks across different stocks, different industries, different markets. That's a lot easier to achieve in a mutual fund, which typically invests in many different stocks, than in an individual portfolio.

So why bother with individual stocks? Some people shouldn't. If you'd rather defrost a frozen pizza than make one (or even order a pie from Domino's), stock investing probably isn't for you.

But you may not have a choice. Many companies today pay their employees with stock options or offer shares at a discount. These deals are usually too good to pass up, but a little knowledge about investing and the stock market helps calm the mind. (For example, the stock of newspaper publishers sometimes plunges because of increases in the price of paper, rarely because of faulty journalism.)

Some people inherit shares, get them as gifts or find moldy old certificates in their attics. You may feel compelled to invest in the company started by the smartest girl in your high school or the genius in the garage down the block. And you may very well have special knowledge you think you can turn to your advantage. Doctors, for example, are often drawn to investing in medical companies, while teachers have a great grip on what craze is about to sweep teenagers and which companies will empty their pockets. Propellerheads know all about the hottest high-tech equipment, while constant travelers may know what products really will be sold to every soul in China.

Then, too, a lot of people find investing interesting, plain and simple. Investing in stocks isn't gambling, of course, but it can offer the combination of intellectual challenge and sweaty-palmed excitement that comes only when you have real money riding on a true game of skill.

There are some practical advantages to buying stocks directly. If you feel tortured by the tax man, you may prefer to buy shares rather than mutual funds because of the way funds handle capital gains. At least once a year, funds must distribute to their investors all their profits from selling stocks. Lucky you: those capital gains are taxable. Worse yet, it sometimes happens that a fund sells some winners, generating capital gains, but holds on to a bunch of losers that drag the value of the portfolio down. You end up having to pay taxes on an investment that has actually lost money. And buying a fund just before it distributes gains, typically near the end of the year, may leave you paying the taxes on gains others enjoyed. With individual stocks, you choose when to recognize gains or losses.

Another big advantage of individual stocks is that you can bet against them, as well as for them. To profit when a stock sinks, you simply sell short, in Wall Street's lingo. Actually, there's nothing simple about it. You have to borrow shares from a brokerage house and sell them. If you've guessed right and the stock's price falls, you replace the borrowed shares—a step known as "covering"—by buying shares at the new, lower price. Your profit is the difference between the price at which you sold the borrowed shares and the price at which you bought the replacements (minus the rather substantial costs involved).

If the stock price goes up, however, you can lose your entire investment, or more. This happens a lot because, even if you successfully identify a stock to sell short, you can't profit until loads of other investors share your opinion and send the stock price down. Plenty of bankrupt short-sellers were right that a stock would plunge, just wrong about when.

- Trading individual stocks can be expensive and an obstacle to diversification.
- Employees should take advantage of discounted shares or options given by employers, despite the time it takes to manage direct holdings of stocks.
- Owning individual shares can give flexibility to get out of a sector of the market, to bet against a stock and to pay taxes on your own schedule.

Be Your Own Buffett: How to Find Your Investing Style

Many traditional stock-picking methods work—some of the time. A few of them have been successful over the long haul. But none of them work all of the time (or investors would be richer than they are).

Take, for example, Warren Buffett, an investor so successful that he has been called the Sage of Omaha, where he works. Over the past thirty-five years, the value of Berkshire Hathaway, his investment company, has risen by an average of 24 percent a year, twice the gain of a portfolio based on the Standard & Poor's index of 500 big companies. But in at least four of those years, Buffett's portfolio lagged the S&P 500. In 1999, for example, Buffett shunned tech stocks. He didn't understand them, he said, and he wouldn't invest in something he didn't understand.

His holdings gained less than 1 percent that year—far below the 21 percent gain for the S&P 500. All of a sudden, the sage was being described as a technophobic fogey who had lost his touch. Yet in 2000 his portfolio gained in value (by 6.5 percent), while the S&P lost more than 9 percent.

It's not just Buffett. Investors who take completely different approaches to picking stocks have the same uneven results, if you look at them year to year. Richard Freeman, who manages the Smith Barney Aggressive Growth Fund, has one of the very best records of the past decade, with an average gain of almost 20 percent a year, according to Morningstar, the fund-tracking outfit. But his fund actually lost money in 1994, and barely eked out a gain in 1996, despite a strong stock market.

So there's no investing magic that will help you make money year in, year out. (Try a bank CD instead—but good luck staying ahead of inflation.) Most successful investors simply pick an approach that they are comfortable with and believe in, and stick with it, trusting that gains in good years will outweigh losses in bad years. But there's no denying that it can be a trial to stay with your approach when other people are making more money.

Is it possible to change your investing style to match the market's whims? Moving in and out of specific stocks or industries, or even the entire market, in response to short-term changes in the investment climate is called market timing, and it is exquisitely difficult to do consistently. True, amateur investors with just a few stocks are lighter on their feet than pros with big portfolios, and so can add a stock in a hot sector that they might not normally favor, for example. And figuring out what investing style has been working lately is easy; just read the interviews with the top-performing mutual managers in *Barron's,* the *Wall Street Journal* or online.

It is hard to know exactly what kind of stocks will be in favor in the future, however. About all you can do is note what's doing well right now, and hope that continues. That's not an intellectual framework for investing—it's chasing the past and crossing your fingers. Investors who do that tend to end up with a motley and expensive collection of last year's hottest stocks, which often turn out to be this year's losers.

- Evaluating a stock-picking approach requires looking at its record over a decade or more.
- Pick an approach that makes sense to you, and that you think you can comfortably stick with given your investing goals.

Stock-Picking Techniques: Birds in the Hand and in the Bush

You can divide stock-picking techniques into a few categories. There's the big-picture method, which on Wall Street is known as "top down" analysis. Say you think energy prices are going up. You buy the stocks of companies that will benefit (like oil producers) and sell those that will suffer (truckers and airlines). Some investors simply buy all the stocks in an industry group—a basket of stocks—while others search for the individual companies that will benefit the most from a trend. At the end of 1999, as investors worried that Y2K glitches would lead to worldwide chaos, one of the big winners was the stock of Hormel (worrywarts stockpiled cans of Spam).

Then there are the approaches that Wall Street calls "fundamental," because they involve analyzing a company's performance. Basically, you look at a company and decide if you'd like to be its owner. Then you figure out if the company's stock price is right.

Two versions of fundamental investing have rewarded their followers over the long run. Most famous, perhaps, is the value method, which was developed by Benjamin Graham. Investors who use this system are bargain hunters. They look for stocks that are underappreciated by the rest of the market, and so are priced lower than they should be given their prospects, assets like factories and cash, or the strength of less tangible properties like patents or brands. If the value investor is right and the market ultimately agrees, then the stock will rise.

One of the most famous and successful of these investors, Warren Buffett, describes this approach as "a bird in the hand is worth two in the bush." In a recent annual report for his company, he writes that before springing for the bush (a company he does not already own), his method requires him to answer three questions: "How certain are you that there are indeed birds in the bush? When will they emerge and how many will there be?" Also how much money could you make if you did not take the risk of buying whatever is in the bush (and put the money in, say, Treasury bonds, instead)? Answering these questions helps him decide whether it makes sense to give up the birds (the bucks) that he already has and buy the bush.

Some value investors focus on old-fashioned companies that do things like make cars or produce chemicals. Such industries are cyclical—closely tied to the ups and downs of the economy. Their stock prices tend to sag, along with their profits, during an economic downturn. The bottom of that downturn is when value investors want to buy them, in the hope that their stocks will rebound as the economy recovers. These cyclical companies also tend to have lots of fixed assets like manufacturing plants and patents—the kind of intrinsic economic worth that can be underrecognized in a depressed stock price.

The opposite approach is called growth investing. In this case, investors seek companies that will enjoy such rapid earnings growth that their stocks are worth buying at almost any price. There may not be many birds in these bushes right now, these investors allow, but they expect flocks to emerge. Often these are companies with hot new products, or prospects for rapid expansion into new places.

During the late 1990s, many growth investors tended to focus on high-tech stocks. The Internet boom, the thinking went, was so big and so significant that a company that managed to stake out a prime piece of it faced virtually unlimited prospects—no matter if it had

Chart 3B

Growth Stocks and Value Stocks

Growth stocks, chosen mainly for their potential to grow rapidly in size and profitability, often have been better performers when the market as a whole is strong. At other times, often when the market is tepid or cold, investors were better off with value stocks, chosen for their low price relative to assets and future earnings.

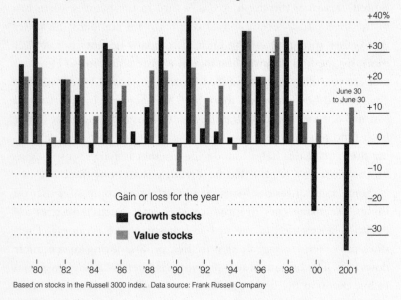

Based on stocks in the Russell 3000 index. Data source: Frank Russell Company

nothing in the way of profits, or even sales, right now. Such strato-spheric expectations for growth at Internet companies like Amazon and Yahoo led growth investors to pay equally stratospheric prices for their stocks (to their eventual regret).

Both of these investing approaches, growth and value, can be applied to companies of all sizes, in many industries. There may be (almost) no older an industry than retailing, yet Wal-Mart was, for many years, the premier growth stock. That wasn't because the con-cept of a big discount store was new, exactly, but because of the way the company carried out the concept (to the detriment of competi-tors like Kmart).

By contrast, WorldCom, the telecommunications upstart that

gobbled its way to titanhood in voice and data communications, was a darling of growth investors. Now, its stock has fallen on such tough times that value investors are casting covetous glances its way. And both kinds of investors might be able to find (different) reasons to buy Microsoft.

How can you choose which fundamental approach to take? There's no easy answer. Only you can decide what makes sense for you, intellectually and emotionally. People who love to shop the sales might be drawn to value investing; those who are looking for the next great product or high-tech gizmo may be happier with a growth approach.

If you have no strong feelings either way, you might try to combine elements of the two, as in "growth at a price," the best strategy if you are saying to yourself, "I want growing companies but I'm not willing to pay the moon for them." Or you might consider which approach would diversify your portfolio. If your 401(k) investments are in value-oriented funds, you might want to try the growth approach on your own, or vice versa.

Another school of investing is known as technical analysis. This method ignores the company underlying the stock. Technical analysts don't care about what a company makes, or how much it earns; only the movements in its stock price matter.

Some technical analysts say their craft relies on historical patterns; over the past few years, they might say, whenever a stock does x, the next week it does y. Many academics have a hard time with this kind of thinking. A stock, they point out, has no memory of what its price was last week. Other technical analysts, who are perhaps more sophisticated, argue that what moves stocks is mass psychology, psychology that can be divined by looking at stock prices and trading volumes.

The simplest kind of technical analysis is known as price momentum. Its adherents look for stocks that have been going up, figuring that the trend will continue no matter what is happening to the companies on a fundamental level. This is also known as the greater fool theory, because its users don't care how much they pay for a stock, figuring that some other idiot will take it off their hands for more.

At the extreme, technical analysis can become a sort of stock market tea-leaf reading, with charts of stocks' past performances serving as the teapot dregs. Usually these techniques are incomprehensible to anyone who is not a devotee. Self-styled gurus will sometimes sell their "sure-fire system to double your money every four months!!!" Usually they have their own money invested in gold jewelry, leased Bentleys and criminal defense lawyers.

Some trading techniques are not strictly technical but not really fundamental, either. For example, some investors pay a lot of attention to the recommendations of Wall Street analysts. And, indeed, their reports can move stock prices—almost always up, since Wall Street analysts are really salesmen, and they almost never tell investors to sell shares.

Analysts' reports are, in theory, based in fundamentals, and yet they often have more to do with what the analyst's employer wishes would happen. If the brokerage firm wants investors to buy a certain stock, why, the analyst who covers that firm might issue a buy recommendation, whatever he or she really thinks.

Why would a brokerage firm want to stir up investor interest in a particular stock? It might have a lot of that stock on hand, and want to unload it or see its own holdings rise in value. Or the company might be an important client of the brokerage firm's investment-banking arm. (Investment banks help companies with corporate transactions, like issuing stock or making acquisitions.) For example, many Internet-stock analysts have come under harsh criticism for talking up the stocks of companies that just happened to have been taken public by those analysts' very own firms. (For more information on identifying these conflicts of interest, see chapter 8.)

While analysts' broad recommendations have lost much of their credibility, their estimates of companies' future earnings may still be worth noting, if only to explain short-term swings in stock prices. Investors who buy a share of stock are buying a partial ownership interest in those future earnings. As a result, stock prices are acutely sensitive to such estimates, and to the degree that a company's actual results meet, beat or miss them. Many financial Web sites compile analysts' estimates.

Occasionally, these estimates may provide opportunities for investors who have really done their homework on a company. For large, well-known companies that are followed by many analysts, earnings estimates tend to be clustered fairly tightly together, around a figure known as the consensus estimate. Every once in a while, though, the analysts can't seem to agree; some will expect a company to earn much more, while others will expect it to earn much less. That's a fairly rare anomaly with major stocks—and one worth looking out for. If analysts can't make up their minds about a stock, chances are investors can't, either. As a result, the stock price probably won't be as high as it should be if the optimists are right, or as low as it should be if the pessimists are right. An investor who has done enough research to be convinced that one side or the other is right has a chance to make some money, or avoid some losses.

Computers, and particularly the Internet, have made it easier to choose stocks that fit your style, by methods once available only to professionals. Sites like Yahoo display charts, graphs, financial ratios and all sorts of arcana at the click of a mouse. At sites like Morningstar (www.morningstar.com) and Quicken (www.quicken.com) you can create "screens" to select all the stocks that fit certain criteria, like fast-growing small medical companies. Smart Money (www.smartmoney.com) has a feature that creates three-dimensional maps of the stock market that show at a glance what sectors and companies are soaring or swooning.

- Fundamental analysis—looking at a company as if you were going to buy the whole thing and become its owner—has a good long-term track record, and has outlasted all the fads.
- The two broad kinds of fundamental analysis are value investing, or looking for companies with strong existing

businesses and relatively cheap stock prices, and growth investing, or looking for companies that will grow so fast that their stocks are cheap at almost any price, no matter how high.

• Take Wall Street analysts' recommendations with a shaker of salt, but you may want to be aware of their consensus earnings estimates.

• Ultimately, in stock investing, you have to be right about a company's financial prospects and have a lot of other investors come to agree with you (and bid the stock price up).

The Start: Finding a Promising Company

Very experienced (usually professional) investors often have a long checklist, like rising earnings, low debt, great management and a cheap stock price that they use to decide which companies to invest in. There are also novices who pick a stock because they heard it talked up on television or got a "hot tip" from a pal.

But many amateur investors start by buying a stock because they like the company's product or service. And they are not the only ones; Peter Lynch, the legendary former manager of the Fidelity Magellan Fund, often picked stocks based on his wife's experiences (she liked L'eggs pantyhose and Easy Spirit pumps).

It would be more accurate to say that, for Lynch, knowing the companies' products was just the starting point for a complex financial analysis. To understand why, think about what happened to investors in Heartstream, which produced a portable defibrillator that even people with minimal medical experience could use to jump-start the heart. It was the holy grail of defibrillators, one investor (and doctor) said—"simple, inexpensive, small, and idiot-proof."

Since they had a better mousetrap, Heartstream investors and its executives thought the public would beat a path to their corporate offices. Wrong. The medical-equipment distributors who buy defibrillators were reluctant to rely on a small company with only one product and no track record. Eventually, Heartstream was bought by a bigger company, and investors who came in close to its peak share price lost a lot of money.

Going to the Real Source

Once you've settled on a company to investigate, where do you go from there? It was not so long ago that much of the information you needed was available only to professional traders and money managers. The only time regular investors would hear about price-earnings ratios or free cash flow was when their brokers were trying to snow them. And even the brokers didn't know about EBITDA (earnings before interest, taxes, depreciation and amortization; it's a cash-flow measure popular among acronym-crazed money managers).

Today, on financial Web sites like Yahoo Finance, you can find a company's stock price history, news and financial summaries. You can also go to the company's own Web site, or punch its name into an Internet search engine.

But the smartest thing you can do is to check out the filings the company submits to the Securities and Exchange Commission. Everything you want to know (and lots more) is disclosed there. Best of all, lying to the government brings serious penalties, so the filings are much more reliable than, say, a company's press releases or Web site. The commission's own site (www.sec.gov) allows you to search the electronic data gathering and retrieval (Edgar) archives for publicly traded companies. Type in a company's name, and see what pops up.

If the answer is nothing, and you've tried every spelling you can think of, watch out. Companies that do not file with the commission are usually so small and risky that their stocks have no place in an amateur investor's portfolio. But if you hit paydirt at the S.E.C., you will be faced with a long list of filings, many identified only by cryptic letters and numbers. It looks daunting, but it's not. In fact, Diana

Henriques, an investigative reporter for the *New York Times* who often teaches number-phobic journalists about S.E.C. filings, tells her students that they need only "five easy pieces" from the S.E.C. that will answer almost all their questions about a company. These are the Registration Statement, the 10-K and 10-Qs, the Proxy Statement, the Form 13s and the 8-Ks.

- A great product may be a good start, but it is not enough.
- To investigate a company, begin with its S.E.C. filings. They're free, detailed and reasonably reliable.

The 10-K: Almost Everything You Ever Need to Know

First, go to the 10-K, the company's real annual report. This does not have the cheery letter from the company's chief that you'll find in the glossy annual report you get in the mail, nor does it have the lovely photos of smiling workers. But it has information, lots and lots of it.

For starters, it will give you the company's address and phone number, the number of shares it has outstanding, and any former names it has used. That can be extremely revealing. A company that was once known as, let's say, Humungo Gold Mines, then Astroid Technology and now TJLC Restaurants has either changed its line of work a worrying number of times, or gone public by merging with a shell corporation, always a red flag for scam stocks. For more on how to spot signs of stock fraud, see chapter 8.

In the 10-K, a company describes its business or businesses, gives you its history, tells you how many employees it has, who its competitors are, who regulates it, whether its business is seasonal, and how much it spends on research and development. It covers any major lawsuits that have been filed against the company (though only those management thinks could have a "material" impact; a personal injury suit filed by someone who fell in a pothole in the company parking lot probably doesn't qualify).

In the case of TJLC Restaurants, we would discover (if this company really existed, rather than being a composite) that it has two lines of business: it owns and operates three restaurants called Tastes Just Like Chicken!, which specialize in french-fried frogs' legs, and it raises frogs for sale to other restaurants and to shoppers, via the frozen-food aisles of grocery stores. It has 233 employees, has regulatory dealings with the Environmental Protection Agency and the Food and Drug Administration, and competes with many larger restaurant chains, including Alligator Al's and Rattlesnake Pete's.

A 10-K also includes reams of financial data, including three to five years' worth of figures on how much money the company brought in (its revenues); how much money it made or lost, both overall and per share; the value of its assets; and the amount of its debt. There are more detailed figures for the last two or three years, including how much it cost to produce its products, how well each segment of the business did, how much it spent on general corporate expenses like sales and administration (called the SG&A by Wall Street) and its tax payments. Sales, costs and earnings show up on the income statement; assets, receivables (money that the company is owed) and money that it owes show up on the balance sheet.

Even amateurs can look at these financial figures and get some idea of a company's prospects. What's the biggest figure under revenues? What's the company's biggest expense? Has it changed over the years? Are revenues growing? Are costs? Do revenues seem to be growing more slowly than costs? (Not a good sign.) Are sales in one line of business growing, while those from another part of the business are shrinking? Is the company adding debt, or paying it off?

For our hypothetical company, TJLC, we would see that its sales grew last year, but its earnings shrank. Furthermore, its best years are behind it; sales peaked in 1996. (Was there a fad for frogs' legs that year?) And the company lost money in 1997, though it blames an accounting change. On the other hand, the company owes less money: its debt has been shrinking and shareholder's equity, or its assets minus all its debts, has been rising.

But don't take my word for it. In every 10-K, management has to describe, in plain English, what happened last year and how it was different from what happened in the previous year. Sometimes these discussions are less than illuminating ("sales fell 10 percent compared to last year because consumers bought fewer of our products"). Yet often they are very interesting indeed. You should get a description of the company's strategy, its explanation for why sales or costs are rising and some interesting tidbits of information ("we sold the corporate headquarters to the president of the company for $11.96, but he's letting us keep our desks there").

At TJLC, management reports that while sales of frozen frogs' legs have been rising a bit, by 6 percent, sales of legs at its restaurants have been declining, and one restaurant is likely to close. Meanwhile, management has hired an interior designer to spiff up the frog-themed décor and add lily-pad-shaped tables. To cut expenses, TJLC sold its small corporate airplane, known as the puddle jumper.

The financial statements in the 10-K are audited, which means that an accountant has checked them over. Read them, including the footnotes. (You may not understand every word, but there are nuggets there you won't find elsewhere.) Check the name of the accountant. Have you heard of the firm, or does it sound like one guy working out of his basement in Bayonne, New Jersey? Is the opinion "unqualified"? That doesn't mean the accountants don't know what they're doing; it means they haven't taken exception to anything in the statements.

Watch out for what is known as a "going concern" statement in the auditor's letter or notes, where the auditor raises doubts about whether the company can remain in business without, say, raising a lot of money or suddenly getting a bunch of new customers. This is a very bad sign indeed. Read the "Certain Transactions" (or similarly titled) section carefully; it describes relationships among people involved with the company that may raise questions in your mind (like the fact that TJLC's new interior decorator is married to its chairman).

Cash-flow statements, which are also part of the 10-K, show you the sources and uses of a company's cash, or where a company has been getting money, and where it has been spending it. Is the company making money from operations, or just from its investments? Or is all of the cash coming in from so-called financing activities? (Translation: We're borrowing, or selling stock, as fast as we can to stay afloat.)

The phrase "cash flow" is often used another way, to describe the overall amount of money a company gets from and can use for its core businesses. A common measure is the previously mentioned EBITDA (again, that's earnings before interest payments, tax payments and depreciation and amortization—accounting charges that take into account the fact that most assets, such as equipment or a new building, become less valuable over time). You can calculate it yourself; it should be rising.

Who is running this company, anyway? The executives and directors are all listed in the 10-K, along with their ages and what other positions they've held for the last five years. A strong board of directors will include a lot of people who do not work for the company, do not get substantial business from it, are not related to its chief executive and seem likely to know something about its industry (not, say, the minister of the president's church and the professor emeritus of Finnish at the local university).

The 10-K will probably tell you how much money the executives made in salary, bonuses and stock options. You may also find out how much of the company's stock is owned by management and the directors; it should be a big chunk, but not so much that management is likely to consider the company "theirs," to do with as they like.

For all this information about management and the board, the

10-K may simply refer you to the proxy, which is the ultimate and best source for it; we'll discuss the proxy more below.

Finally, the 10-K may also include exhibits. These are worth scanning. You may find the president's employment contract, or the deal the company forced the former treasurer to sign when he was fired. Most likely it'll just be copies of real estate leases and bank-loan agreements, but you may find some valuable information about the company's management and future.

- Be sure to check the 10-K, a company's real annual report. Look for the Legal Proceedings section, the Certain Transactions section and any going concern warning from auditors about a company's financial prospects.

Beyond the 10-K: The Other Things You Want to Know

What if the company you are interested in is new, or is only now selling shares to the public? In that case, you want the registration statement, which will usually include a prospectus. This, also filed with the S.E.C., will tell you everything there is to know about the company, including its history, its financial track record and what it plans to do with the money it is raising. Look for the underwriter— the Wall Street firm that is selling the shares. Have you heard of it? If not, check it out by visiting the Web site of the National Association of Securities Dealers regulatory arm (www.nasdr.com). A well-known underwriter does not guarantee that the company is a good one, but an obscure underwriter should give you second thoughts.

Who will make money from the stock sale? Sometimes when a company sells shares to the public for the first time, or even later, most of the shares come out of the hands of insiders, early investors and the founder's friends and relations. These folks make a profit, but the company itself doesn't benefit. That's a worry if the company really needs cash to finance its business; even if it has plenty of money on hand, you might want to ask yourself why the insiders are selling if this company's prospects are so good.

That also goes for more established companies that are selling shares, for the fifth or fiftieth time. If you see a registration statement (on the S.E.C. list, it will likely begin with the letter "S"), read it. It may be dull and straightforward—the details, say, of the employee stock-purchase plan—but it could tell you that the company's early investors are bailing out. You may want to follow them.

If, as is the case with our hypothetical TJLC, the company has not sold shares since 1993, you will not find a registration statement on the S.E.C.'s Edgar site.

Unfortunately, 10-Ks and registration statements go out of date quickly. For the most recent information, you want to get the current 10-Q, a sort of mini 10-K covering three months. The financial data in 10-Qs are not audited, but useful nevertheless. Reading the Qs lets you see how well the company is executing the strategy it outlined in the K.

It can also give you early warning of problems. In the case of TJLC, the financial statements in the 10-Q show some large and mysterious changes. The amount of current assets has soared, which seems like it should be good, except that the increases have occurred in the areas of inventories and receivables, which is money owed by customers. Meanwhile, both the balance sheet and the income statement show a charge for "doubtful accounts," or money owed to the company that it is unlikely to collect. In fact, the company lost money in the quarter.

A careful reading of footnotes and management's comments would reveal that the company's largest distributor of frogs' legs, Frenchy's Products, filed for bankruptcy protection owing TJLC a lot of money. Thus the charge, the receivables and the piles of frozen frogs' legs building up in the company's freezers. The company is looking for a new distributor, has finally closed that money-losing restaurant and is keeping its fingers crossed.

If you were a shareholder already, you might be pretty disgruntled. And, in fact, a large shareholder is pressuring TJLC to merge with another company or sell itself to the highest bidder. How do you know this? Because the shareholder, Amphibian Fund, has spelled it out in a filing called a 13-D.

These filings must be submitted to the S.E.C. by any shareholder who owns 5 percent or more of a company's stock. They will tell you who is buying the stock, what they paid for it and, vaguely, where the money came from. In amendments to this filing, the investors must also tell you about any changes in their holdings. Finally, these big shareholders must say if this is a passive investment, or if they intend to try to force a change at the company, as Amphibian does. Since it owns just 12 percent of the stock, and management controls 43 percent, the fund's chances of forcing a sale aren't great. But if another company does try to buy TJLC, it, too, will probably have to file a 13-D at some point.

It's worth checking out 13-Ds to see who else has invested in the company you're investigating. Sometimes you'll find the name of a famous investor, like Mario Gabelli, who manages mutual funds and pension accounts. You may take comfort in the fact that a seasoned pro is your fellow investor.

On the other hand, you may find that the only other big investors are index funds, which are not buying your company because of its intrinsic value but because they have to invest in every stock of a certain size, say, or in a certain index. Such investors often file a 13-G, which is just an abbreviated version of a 13-D filed by financial firms that are passive investors.

How will you know if anything important is happening at TJLC in between its 10-Qs—something like a merger? Well, the company will probably issue a press release, but that by itself doesn't always mean much. Some companies issue a press release a week, whether they have anything important to say or not. (TJLC's last one announced that it was adding Caribbean-style jerk frogs' legs to its menu, which already features Cajun blackened legs and Texas jalapeño legs.)

If something really earth-shaking is happening at a company, it will file an 8-K, "a report of a significant event." If the C.E.O. quits, if the company loses a big court battle, if regulators come down on the company like a ton of bricks, there should be an 8-K.

Our hypothetical TJLC would have filed one, reporting that it is in discussions with an outfit called Mollusk Mania, which wants to buy the company. The directors are considering the offer; there can be no assurances that a sale will go through. Mollusk Mania is a purveyor of specialty foods; it runs the popular Escargot-To-Go chain.

- If there is a recent registration statement from a past or pending stock offering, make sure to read it.
- See the 10-Qs for up-to-date details above and beyond what may be in a company's press release about its quarterly earnings.
- 13-Ds, and their relatives, 13-Gs, tell you who is making a big investment in a company, and if they intend to be passive investors or will try to force change (or buy the company outright).
- Also check the 8-Ks, where companies must report significant events.

Mergers and What They Mean to Your Investment

Mergers, and potential mergers, can drastically affect the value of your stock. Returning to the fate of our investment in the hypothetical TJLC, we get news that Mollusk Mania has agreed to buy TJLC, but not for cash. If the shareholders approve the deal, holders of TJLC would get one share of Mollusk Mania for every four shares of TJLC that they own. At the time the deal is announced, Mollusk's stock is trading at $36, TJLC's at $8, so TJLC's shareholders seem to be getting a pretty good deal ($36 instead of the $32 market price of four shares). Or are they? To really answer that question, you need to look at the proxy statement.

The proxy is supposed to tell shareholders everything they need to know to vote at the company's annual meeting (or at a special meeting called to consider something important like a merger). It's not quite the League of Women Voters Guide; corporations will spin the information as best they can to get shareholders to vote the way management wants. On the other hand, the S.E.C. mandates a lot of disclosure, so there's a limit to how much propaganda the company's executives and directors can get away with. In most companies, each share is worth one vote. (Some companies, including the New York Times Company, have two classes of stock, and one, controlled by the company's founding family, has far more votes per share than the regular class of stock.)

Often, what shareholders get to vote about is not very exciting. They might get to ratify management's choice of an accounting firm; they might get to elect a handful of directors. But proxies are always interesting, because they tell you even more than the 10-K about the company's management and directors, how much they are paid, how much stock they own and any special deals they have struck.

In the case of our hypothetical TJLC, we find that one of the outside directors works for the bank to which TJLC owes a lot of money; another works for a construction company that built its three restaurants. And that the money-losing restaurant was sold to the chairman's son for what seems like very little money.

Most important, the chairman of the company controls 41 percent of its stock. This means that if only a relatively small number of shareholders vote with him, the merger will go through (it also makes it highly unlikely that anyone will mount a hostile takeover bid for the company, because they'd have to get so many votes to prevail over the chairman). We discover his son and two nephews, none of whom appear to have graduated from college, work for the company, which pays for special insurance for the family, as well as for their cars and their security details and their use of a vacation house in Louisiana. It also covered their personal use of that company plane before it was sold. Nice work if you can get it.

Another interesting fact is that if TJLC's executives lose their jobs because the company is bought or merged, each of them gets a payment equal to three times his or her average salary for the last three years. No wonder Mollusk Mania has agreed to keep most of them on in executive positions.

Given everything that you have learned from reading all of TJLC's S.E.C. filings, you can be pretty sure now that the merger will go through. After all, the company's executives control much of its stock, and they look like they'll make out awfully well in the merger. Now you have to decide whether to keep Mollusk's shares or sell them. Time to check out a new 10-K, registration statement, 10-Q, and other S.E.C. filings.

Since we're talking about mergers, should you become an amateur arb? To arbitrage means trying to profit from two different prices for the same thing. Usually this means buying something one place and selling it in another (buy rice where it's cheap, say, and sell where it's expensive). But in the 1980s, arbitrage started to refer to betting on takeovers and mergers. Those who practiced it were and are known as arbs.

If a company you already own is bought—or is buying someone else—you are involved in a merger, and must try to evaluate the new company just as you did the one you already own. But sometimes there's a frenzy of takeover speculation, and investors start chasing companies that they think are candidates for mergers. They also start betting on the outcome of hostile takeover offers.

This can be a profitable strategy. But it is practiced by pros who can devote their whole attention to it, and who are therefore almost certain to beat out amateurs trying to speculate in their spare time. And that's even if the pros do not have inside info, as some of the most successful did in the 1980s, before they spent time in federal detention centers.

Digging Deeper

A final word on fundamental research: There are plenty of other sources to turn to if you want to keep digging into a company. Read the specialized publications that cover the company's industry (*Sand & Gravel Today* may be more interesting than it sounds). If you are really dedicated (or planning to make a living off investments), call its competitors, its customers, the corporate recruiters and temporary employment agencies that it deals with. Check the company out with federal, state and government officials. (Polluters, scam artists and other reprobates often have a history of run-ins with regulators.) You can even track down former employees, and read every lawsuit the company has been involved with. Investigative reporters do all of these things.

If you'd like to own a business, at some point you have to stop evaluating the company itself, and move on to the second step of investing—figuring out how much to pay for the company (or at least your stake in it, as represented by shares of stock).

- Even when there's nothing much on the ballot for the annual meeting, proxies are always worth reading to learn everything from how much money the president makes to which director skipped most of the board meetings.
- When there's a takeover or merger in the works, the proxy contains details the press release doesn't.
- Short-term trading strategies, such as speculating on mergers, should probably be left to professional money managers.

The Price Is Right—Or Is It?

How can you decide if a company's shares are cheap, expensive or just the right price? Looking at the price alone won't tell you. A company with a very high stock price, but very few shares outstanding, may be worth less than a company with a low stock price and a lot of shares outstanding. When you multiply the stock price by the number of shares outstanding, you get the value the stock market puts on a company, called the market capitalization—but, as an investment, you still can't compare it with other companies, or with the market as a whole.

This is where ratios, or multiples, come in. The best known is the price-earnings (P/E) ratio, in which you divide a company's share price by its earnings per share over the last twelve months. This tells you how much other investors are willing to pay for a year's earnings. Lower multiples suggest investors are less confident about future earnings, while higher multiples suggest investors are optimistic. The P/E ratio for any company that has earnings is easy to find. On Sundays, the *New York Times*, for example, prints them for every stock that trades on the New York Stock Exchange, the American exchange and Nasdaq. Far more information is available on the Internet, on sites like Yahoo Finance.

Using the P/E ratio, you can easily compare a stock with others in its industry, as well as to the market as a whole; the P/E ratio of the S&P 500 index is widely available from financial publications and Web sites. Because a company's ratio is so easy to calculate, you can use it to see whether its stock is trading for more than usual, or for less (which might signal a bargain). You can also tell whether investors are becoming more or less optimistic about a company's prospects.

How does this work? Take IBM, International Business Machines. In the spring of 2001, the company's stock was trading for about $117.50 and had a P/E ratio of about 26. Was that a lot, or a little? Well, in the past five years, IBM's P/E had been as high as 37, and as low as 13! So the stock was trading sort of in the middle of its P/E range, not a steal but not overpriced, either. If you were eager to own it, that might not have been a bad time to buy.

But remember, the overall stock market is far less euphoric now than it was in, say, 1999, so you'd expect IBM's ratio to be well under its high. After all, the P/E of the stocks in the S&P 500 index had been as high as 50 in the same five-year period, and as low as 14. The index's P/E was recently about 29, also in the middle of its range—and slightly higher than IBM's ratio.

How does IBM compare with other companies that also make computers? Well, a few mouse clicks would tell you that Dell, which sells a lot of PCs to companies and individuals, has a P/E of about 31, higher than IBM's but a lot lower than Dell's peak of 106 (when investors apparently thought that every person in the United States would order a new computer every three months). And as you checked into IBM's competitors, you would find that its P/E is among the lowest of the computer hardware companies, not counting those that are losing money.

Why? Well, you can also figure out that IBM's sales are growing more slowly than some of its smaller competitors'. On the other hand, it has continued to post earnings during tough quarters when others were losing money. There may be some benefit to being a behemoth that sells a lot of different kinds of computers to many different customers, and has become the leading provider of computer services as well.

Some investors like to compare a company's P/E ratio to its earnings growth rate over the last twelve months (this is sometimes called the PEG ratio). If the P/E is lower than the earnings growth rate (the PEG is less than 1), it might be a good value; if the P/E is much higher, the stock price may be poised to tumble.

Growth stock investors are even more likely to calculate the PEG using a future, or forward, P/E and a projected rate of earnings growth. How do you figure out future earnings? Well, companies will sometimes announce how much money they expect to make in a year. And Wall Street analysts forecast earnings (usually with a lot of guidance from the company). Rather than rely on any one analyst's forecasts, savvy investors usually look at the consensus forecast, which is available on many financial Web sites.

The problem is that Wall Street analysts are not very reliable forecasters. In fact, they're congenitally optimistic. Recently, they have come under fire for being slow to cut their estimates and in general more interested in pleasing the companies they cover than in guiding investors (see chapter 8 for a fuller discussion). So take any projected PEG ratios with a pound of salt.

Value investors prefer to look at the price-to-book, or P/B, ratio. Book value is basically the net worth of a company, or what you could get if you liquidated it. You figure book value by looking at the company's balance sheet and subtracting all the liabilities (bonds, and money owed to Uncle Sam, customers, banks, partners and the like) from all the assets (property, equipment, cash in the bank, etc).

In the case of IBM, the book value of the company divided by the number of shares outstanding was about $12.20, while the stock price was almost ten times that amount. So IBM's price-to-book was about 9, a fairly high number. That's in part because IBM has a lot of assets that don't show up on its balance sheet: patents, the value of its brand name, business relationships, the loyalty of all the scientists who work there. So some investors have dismissed P/B as too old-fashioned a measure of value in this high-tech age. But paying attention to the P/B would have protected a lot of investors when the Internet revolution turned out to be an investing illusion, based on companies with virtually no book value. It can also be useful for evaluating businesses, like oil companies, whose value is based largely on their tangible property.

Another ratio that is sometimes called old-fashioned is the dividend yield, which is basically a comparison of a company's stock price with its annual dividends. As discussed in chapter 1, back in Ben Graham's day dividend yield was considered a primary measure of stock value, because dividend payments, not rising share prices, were the chief source of stock market wealth.

In the last half of the twentieth century, companies began keeping the cash they generated and investing it in their operations (rather than paying it out to their owners). Companies like Ford still pay dividends; companies like Yahoo don't. Conservative investors should remember that dividend payments will buttress your portfolio, giving you some income even when share prices are falling or flat.

There are plenty of other ratios. Aggressive investors, who may be interested in companies without any earnings, may look at price-to-sales and price-to-cash-flow. All of them are easy to calculate (or look up on a financial Web site) and all can be helpful when you're trying to figure out how a company compares with its competitors or the overall stock market.

One other ratio to be aware of is the volatility measure known as beta. This tells you if a stock is more or less volatile than the overall market. A stock with a beta of 1.0 tends to move in line with the S&P 500; a stock with a beta of 2.0 would rise (or fall) twice as much as the index. Going back to our examples, IBM has a beta of about 1.3, Yahoo has a volatile beta of about 3.7, while Ford's stolid beta is about 0.9.

A caveat: You can't compare apples with blueberries; small, volatile Nasdaq stocks, for example, don't correlate well with the S&P 500, so the beta ratio for them is almost meaningless.

- Valuation ratios allow you to compare a company with its competitors and the overall market, and can give you an idea of whether a stock is relatively expensive or cheap.
- Growth investors look at the price-earnings ratio; value investors generally prefer the price-to-book ratio. Aggressive investors might check out price-to-sales (after all, they may be interested in companies without any earnings); conservative investors will look at dividend yield.
- Also look at beta, a measure of a stock's volatility, compared with an index, usually the S&P 500.
- Assess a stock's price by reviewing a company's P/E, PEG, PB, and beta ratios as well as dividend yields. In most cases, your investing strategy will determine what you glean from these numbers.

4.

Mutual Funds:
Leaving It to the Pros

DANNY HAKIM

Mutual funds? At the turn of the millennium, those two words didn't exactly light up a cocktail party. The bull market agenda went like this: Dump the broker. Dump the mutual funds. Buy dotcoms. Retire. Move to Boca.

Okay, scratch that. The bear market made many investors realize that picking your own stocks can be entertaining, so long as the market is perpetually going up. But that doesn't always happen, which brings us back to mutual funds. The idea behind mutual funds is that picking a portfolio of securities assembled by a professional manager, whether it be a collection of stocks or bonds or both, is a whole lot easier than puzzling over which securities to buy on your own.

In practice, however, picking mutual funds is not a whole lot easier than picking stocks or bonds. There are more than eight thousand different mutual funds with objectives as diverse as investing in Japanese technology to buying Ohio municipal bonds. How do you pick one that is right for you? And where can you go to find the information you need?

We'll explain how funds work, and how to go on the Web and use tools that can help you. We'll also go over some of the traps you can fall into, like the dangers of buying fund shares near the end of the year. And we'll look at some of Wall Street's newest financial gadgets that are meant to compete with mutual funds.

First, however, we'll see how the mutual fund industry got started, and how it took the Great Depression to make funds popular.

How Funds Started, How Funds Work

Sherman Adams had an idea and $50,000. This was back in 1924. Adams was a broker in Boston, which was the center of the nation's investment industry and remains home to investment giants like Fidelity and Putnam.

Like many other Boston businessmen, Adams and his two partners, Ashton L. Carr and Charles Learoyd, wanted to start an investment fund. This was hardly new. Investment funds called trusts had been around for decades. Robert Fleming, a Scotsman, made a fortune after the Civil War by buying up a portfolio of depressed American railroad bonds and creating a trust for European investors. In 1868, an early British fund, the Foreign and Colonial Government Trust, started investing in debt from fifteen different governments, including Egypt, Turkey and Peru.

By Adams's day, the American public was on the cusp of going gaga for stock trusts, which became a popular shortcut for investors who wanted a passel of hot stocks. In 1929 there were hundreds of trusts, with $7 billion in assets, an enormous sum in those days.

Adams's fund, Massachusetts Investors Trust, was different by design. The conventional trust of the day was an investment company that offered the public a fixed number of shares, much as a normal company does. Thus, these investment trusts themselves traded like stocks. Their price was set by supply and demand, often higher than the value of the underlying stocks. Today, such trusts are more commonly known as closed-end funds.

In a market environment like that in the Roaring Twenties, closed-end funds heaped speculation on top of speculation. First, there were wild fluctuations in the stocks the funds held. Then, there were wild fluctuations in the funds themselves, on the belief that they were must-have portfolios of hot stocks.

Adams's idea was to create something more grounded. His Massachusetts Investors Trust was the first mutual fund and, unlike conventional trusts, continuously issued new shares to meet new demand and liquidated shares when investors decided to cash out. The price of the fund was determined only by the value of the stocks that the Massachusetts Investors Trust held.

With his two partners, Learoyd and Carr, Adams put up $50,000 to start the Massachusetts Investors Trust. They invested in forty-five companies, including some that are still around today: General Electric, General Motors and Eastman Kodak. While closed-end funds grew ever more speculative, this trust was intended to spread risk across a diversified portfolio of blue chip investments. By the end of the decade, it had $14 million in about 130 different stocks.

Of course, play-it-safe was one of the less effective sales pitches of the 1920s. The new trust was not a hit, nor was a mutual fund started by the State Street Corporation that same year, 1924. By 1929 there were nineteen mutual funds with less than $200 million among them—compared with the $7 billion in the closed-end trusts.

But Adams, who came up with the open-ended concept, was either brilliant or lucky. In the stock market crash of 1929, closed-end funds imploded, and many went under. Not that the Massachussetts trust fared too well itself, because anything that touched the stock market turned from gold to lead. From its peak on September 3, 1929, to its low on July 9, 1932, the fund fell 83.4 percent.

In the meantime something remarkable happened. As the public fled from stocks and trusts, the Massachusetts trust's shareholders more than tripled from 5,000 in 1929 to 16,225 in 1932. While many trusts were going bankrupt, the Massachusetts trust, because of its open-ended structure, remained solvent. It even still paid a dividend of eighty-nine cents a share in 1932, down by about half from 1929. By 1934 the fund had 21,000 shareholders. With Franklin Delano Roosevelt in office and the nation focused on austerity and recovery, the concept of safety suddenly didn't look so bad. The fund, now called the MFS Massachusetts Investors fund, still exists today. Its assets have grown to $14.1 billion.

Keep in mind that the industry's founding principle was to give investors a simple way to build a conservative, diversified portfolio. Though most fund companies preach diversification, many simultaneously push the latest hot sector fund on the public. The industry's largest funds, the Vanguard 500 Index Trust and Fidelity Magellan, both hew to the industry's traditional broad-based approach, though by very different means. More on that later.

First, let's look at how mutual funds work. There are four kinds: stock funds, bond funds, balanced funds that invest in stocks and bonds, and money market funds, which invest in short-term securities and can be thought of as a near equivalent of cash, though they are not immune to problems. Each has its own net asset value, or N.A.V., the value of the fund's assets divided by the number of shares. But because funds distribute capital gains from stocks they have sold, at least annually, and subtract distributions from the N.A.V., don't regard a fund's N.A.V. like a stock price in calculating your returns.

Mutual funds, as investment companies, are much more like normal companies than you might expect. An investor is a shareholder and has the right to vote on various matters that might come before the fund. Proxy statements are sent out to inform shareholders of such issues. Each fund is also required to have a board of directors who are supposed to ensure that the fund is properly managed. The directors are responsible for representing the shareholders' interests, and some of them are required to be independent, meaning they are not employees of the fund manager. In fact, the actual independence of directors is a matter of much debate, and review by the Securities and Exchange Commission, since it is rare to hear of an independent fund director seriously challenging a fund firm.

Much basic information about a fund can be found in its prospectus, the document an investor must receive. Read it before you buy the fund. The prospectus includes information about fees, past performance, minimum investment, the effect of taxes and investment style. Annual and semiannual reports are sent out to shareholders or can be consulted by the public at the S.E.C.'s Web site (www.sec.gov). All of these documents should be studied, but only as a starting point.

In this chapter, we will be dealing mostly with stock funds, though we will discuss how all four categories of funds can be used to build a diversified portfolio. For advice on choosing bond funds, see chapter 5. Before you worry about choosing an individual stock fund from among the more than four thousand available, you should narrow your choices down to a category. Here are some of your basic choices:

1. *Diversified funds or sector funds?* Stick mostly with diversified funds, which invest across a broad range of industries and make good core holdings in a portfolio. Sector funds, which focus on particular areas of the market like technology or financial services, are more speculative than diversified funds, especially in recent years as the market has grown more volatile.

In the bull market of the late 1990s, flashy fund categories cropped up in every imaginable strain. Internet funds proliferated by the dozen and attracted billions of dollars. When mutual fund companies saw how successful Internet funds could be, many embarked on a strategy of marketing fission. Find a popular sector. Subdivide it into every possible atomic permutation.

What we'll call the Mutual Fund Industry Leading Indicator theory explains what happens next. By the time a glossy new niche sector of funds is actually assembled and passes muster with securities regulators, the very sector they plan to exploit is often primed for collapse.

New Internet funds were arriving almost weekly by the beginning of 2000. At the end of the year, many had fallen 50, 60, 70 and even 80 percent. Several closed and returned what cash was left to their investors. Other funds changed their names and strategy. Merrill Lynch and Strong Capital liquidated their struggling Internet offerings by merging their assets with other funds.

Harold Evensky, a financial planner based in Coral Gables, Florida, believes that a 10 percent allocation to sector funds is the maximum for any investor, and only that much if you have money to fool around with. "My opinion is that people in sector funds are playing, not investing," added Evensky. "Trying to pick sectors, long term, is a losing game."

The lesson here: Sector funds should be bought in moderation.

2. *Actively managed vs. index funds.* Index funds are probably the best first fund purchase because they offer a no-frills, cheap way to buy diversification, and because it's easy to understand what you are buying. Such funds use computer models and various strategies to follow market indexes. The largest fund in the nation, the Vanguard 500 Index Trust, tracks the Standard & Poor's 500 stock index, as do about sixty other mutual funds.

Index funds are the ultimate in if-you-can't-beat-'em-join-'em. In his seminal 1973 best-seller, *A Random Walk Down Wall Street,* Princeton professor Burton G. Malkiel argued that no active stock-picking strategy could topple the law of averages over long stretches of time, so it made more sense for investors to buy index funds than worry about beating the market.

Index funds are also cheaper than actively managed funds, or at least they should be. It saves money when you don't have to pay to fly that fund manager and all those analysts to four-star hotels around the world. S&P 500 index funds can make for good core holdings in a portfolio or good first purchases for beginning investors. Another group of popular index funds track the Wilshire 5000 index, a broad market index that also includes small and medium-size companies. A Wilshire 5000 fund can also make for a good first investment, as can the Schwab 1000 index fund for investors who have Charles Schwab as their broker.

"For any individual out there, having an index fund in the beginning part of their investing life is a smart investment," said Charles Schwab himself. "That's the way to get started."

Some index funds are better as second or third investments, because they track indices that are narrower. The Russell 2000, for instance, is an index of small company stocks, while the Nasdaq 100 focuses on large but volatile technology companies.

Studies, often cited by the media, show that the great majority of active funds don't perform as well as their index benchmarks over time, although some do. We don't mean to dismiss actively managed funds, which are the majority of the mutual fund business. Just keep in mind that, when picking out an actively managed fund, what makes it more appealing to you than an index fund. One advantage is that actively managed funds come in a wider variety of styles and types.

3. *Growth investing vs. value investing.* Play it safe and buy both. As discussed in chapter 2, the terms "growth" and "value" refer to stock-picking styles, in this case the picking style of fund managers. Though there are many different approaches, they roughly break down into two categories, value and growth, which represent different ways of looking at the investing world.

Value investors are bargain hunters. They look for stocks that they believe the market has priced below what they are worth. They can be good companies in slumping market sectors. They can be companies that are overshadowed by more prominent rivals. They can be companies that have had a publicized misstep but in which an investor remains faithful. Warren Buffett made his name by buying bargains, like McDonald's and Coke, and holding on to them until they recovered, or by buying junk bonds when the market was not and waiting for them to revive, which they did.

Growth investors buy stocks that they believe have the potential for rapid earnings growth, with less concern for their price or their price-to-earnings ratio, or if they even have a P/E ratio. Some growth investors jump on companies whose stocks are moving rapidly upward, hoping to catch the ride. Aggressive growth managers say it often doesn't pay to worry too much about prices, especially given the lure of promising technology companies. During the bull market for technology in the late 1990s, growth fund investors triumphed and value investors looked, frankly, quaint.

By 2001, however, growth investors had either conveniently forgotten what they had said or were miraculously reborn, talking about earnings, earnings, earnings. To value investors, the lesson was clear enough: Earnings never really go out of style. But longtime investors in growth funds like the Janus Twenty had their own argument. Even after a precipitous decline in 2000, they had been left with a considerable gain.

The reality is that growth funds and value funds tend to thrive at different times, which makes it sensible to balance investments in both. How can you tell which is which? Look up a potential fund on the *New York Times* Web site (www.nytimes.com) or Morningstar (www.morningstar.com) to find whether it's a value fund, a growth fund or a blend of the two.

4. *Small, medium or large cap.* Same as above; buy the right amount of each, depending on your strategy. There are funds that focus on small, emerging companies, funds that invest in burly blue chips like IBM or Citigroup and funds that invest in medium-size companies. Others invest in all sizes.

Funds that do not specify a range often pluck stocks of any size. These can be called multi-cap, all-cap or "go anywhere" funds. A point to keep in mind: Generally avoid small-cap funds that have grown over $1 billion. Large mutual funds have trouble making meaningful investments in small companies. If managers of big funds put too much money into a small stock its price can soar, or the price can collapse if managers change their minds and try to sell.

5. *Income vs. growth.* Income funds aim to provide shareholders with a substantial dividend, which can be important for retirees. As

a result, these funds tend to invest more in companies that provide high payouts and less in hot, emerging growth companies. Growth funds, by contrast, focus on rewarding investors from growth in stock prices, rather than providing a stream of income. In practice, the high dividend payers favored by income funds also tend to be value stocks. It's no surprise that the sort of low- or no-dividend stocks favored by growth funds tend to be growth stocks.

Other varieties of funds include:

Enhanced index funds, which use borrowed money, or leverage, to try to outperform stock indexes by various percentages. Such a strategy makes them combustible, and most individual investors should avoid them.

Hedge funds, exclusive private funds that are not available to the general public. There are, however, a small number of mutual funds that hedge by using various strategies like short selling, or borrowing stock in the hope of buying shares at a lower price to pay back the loan. Or they practice such arbitrage strategies as taking advantage of discrepancies between the prices of a company's stock and its convertible bonds, or bonds that can be converted into stock. These funds often have the term "long/short" or "market neutral" in their titles. Some of them are quite interesting, but as a group they vary widely in their effectiveness, are more expensive than the average fund and should be approached with caution. Unless you are willing to do a good deal of homework, avoid them.

Wealthier investors might be tempted by hedge funds, but keep in mind that they are largely unregulated and, as such, risky. The classic hedge fund seeks to minimize a fund's losses, and risks, by selling some stocks short. In reality, hedge funds have come to include almost any private funds, with styles ranging from global currency trading to arbitrage to technology investing to making enormous bets on macroeconomic trends.

Smaller investors can gain entry into hedge funds through funds of funds, or funds that invest in several hedge funds. There are hundreds, if not thousands, of these funds of funds, and most major investment banks have several. The minimums have come down as low as $25,000. But they, too, should be approached with caution.

Momentum funds, a hot variety of growth funds that jump on fast-moving stocks and try to jump off before they sputter. They tend to be speculative and should be avoided by risk-averse investors. Expect increased volatility and the potential for high tax bills. They usually are labeled as growth funds, but a good sign of a momentum strategy is a fund that trades so rapidly that its annual turnover ratio is well in excess of 100 percent.

Focus funds, like the Janus Twenty or the Marsico Focus Fund, distinguished by investing in just twenty to forty stocks, fewer than most other funds. They can have higher returns, but they can also be more volatile. You should have a compelling reason for buying one, like a belief that the manager knows what he or she is doing.

Quant, or *Quantitative,* funds, which use complex computer models to guide buy and sell decisions. Quant funds are more than a fad, and they seem to hit and miss just like conventionally managed funds. Many of these funds work the term "quant" or "quantitative" into their titles, like the Fidelity Technoquant Growth Fund. But many that do not label themselves quant funds use some of the same techniques.

Keep in mind that a single mutual fund can touch on many of these approaches. Often, a fund's style can be gleaned from its title. Take the Vanguard Small-Cap Value Index Fund. The fund a) focuses on small companies; b) buys stocks that are considered to be good values; and c) follows an index. Vanguard also has a fund that tracks a small company growth index. Just remember to determine your strategy to diversify properly and then figure out how your funds fit into that strategy.

Size matters. Really big funds have a harder time performing as well as smaller funds. A fund like Magellan, at more than $80 billion, cannot move in and out of stocks without affecting their prices as easily as, say, the $1.1 billion Thornburg Value Fund. Remember that small company funds lose their edge when they grow to the neighborhood of $1 billion. But size does not matter for index funds, because they seldom trade.

- Picking hot-sector funds can defeat the purpose of investing in mutual funds. Choose a broad index fund, then add a balanced group of choices from main fund categories.
- Diversify by size and style. Balance an index fund with one that invests in small companies, a growth fund with a value fund.

Funds, Fees and Investment Value

The chief executive of Ohio National Financial Services, a mutual insurance holding company based in Cincinnati, began his company's 1999 annual report with this sentence: "You look to your financial institutions for products that meet your needs and deliver excellent value."

True enough. But what is excellent value? If you could fill up for $20 at one gas station or $200 at another, would $200 be an excellent value?

Among the seven equity mutual funds that it offers through its ONE Fund subsidiary, Ohio National has an S&P 500 index fund that is more than ten times as expensive as some of its competitors', even though all such index funds are essentially commodities, tracking the same benchmark. If the S&P 500 averaged a 12 percent return over the next twenty years, an investor with $10,000 would gain nearly $84,000 from Vanguard's fund but just over $59,000 from Ohio National's, at current fees. That's a $25,000 difference.

Keep a close watch on costs and make sure you are getting services you want and need in return. Fees should not drive your investment decision by themselves, but they should play a major role in your choice of funds, fund groups and brokerage firms.

Every fund charges expense fees, to compensate the management

Chart 4A

The Effects of Expenses

Though differences in expense ratios between funds may sound small, they can accumulate over time into significant differences in performance.

Here is what a $10,000 investment in 1990 would have yielded in five hypothetical funds that differ only in their expense ratios; all five perform as well as the average stock fund before expenses.

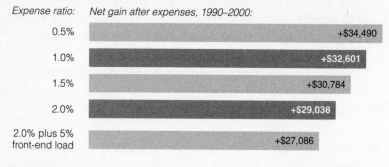

Expense ratio:	Net gain after expenses, 1990–2000:
0.5%	+$34,490
1.0%	+$32,601
1.5%	+$30,784
2.0%	+$29,038
2.0% plus 5% front-end load	+$27,086

Data source: Morningstar Inc.

firm and pay operating costs. Though expenses are levied daily, they are expressed as annual expense ratios. The average domestic stock fund has a 1.49 percent expense ratio, according to Lipper Inc., the fund tracking firm. That means 1.49 percent of the average domestic stock fund's assets are deducted during the year to pay various fees and expenses such as the 12b-1 fee, which covers marketing and distribution. Most performance figures in newspapers and on Web sites already account for the expense ratios.

Before you buy a fund, check its expense ratio and compare it to its competitors' in the same category. Index funds are less expensive than actively managed funds, a savings that helps account for index funds' strong performance.

For actively managed funds, an expense ratio of 2 percent or more is high. But keep in mind that small or new funds have higher fees because they have lower asset bases over which to spread their expenses. Sector funds and foreign stock funds are more expensive because of their specialized disciplines. Despite the disadvantages of large funds, the more responsible firms lower the fees as the funds, and the economies of scale, grow.

How you buy a mutual fund can determine your costs. Do-it-yourselfers usually choose the options with the lowest costs, investing either through those fund companies that deal directly with investors, like Vanguard or Fidelity, or through a mutual fund supermarket.

The most popular supermarkets offer investors choices between thousands of different funds. Two of the biggest are run by Charles Schwab and Fidelity. In Fidelity's supermarket, one can choose from thousands of funds managed by its competitors. Fidelity presents these choices because its own brokerage and fund supermarket operations are lucrative enough to be worth the compromise. Fund supermarkets generally offer some funds with extra transaction costs, typically $18 to $75 a trade. But they also offer some without any added costs, like the ones included in Schwab's OneSource plan, because they charge the funds themselves for distribution.

Several fund firms and brokers have fees for small accounts that can erode your gains. Even Vanguard, the king of low-cost investing, has a $25 annual fee for accounts under $10,000. Other firms charge investors for switching funds, even if you are switching within their fund family.

An even more common charge is a redemption fee for selling a fund within a certain period, usually ranging from sixty days to two years. Some redemption fees have the legitimate purpose of discouraging short-term trading by fund investors, which drives up fund expenses and can force fund managers to sell stocks quickly to meet redemptions. Any realized gains are taxable—and often it is the responsible long-term shareholder left holding the tax bill.

One of the heaviest fees a fund investor might face are loads, or sales charges levied by most funds sold through brokers and financial advisers, and some sold directly by fund groups. Why pay a load at all? If you want to get professional advice and service, as many investors do and should, consider it a way of paying the costs. If you are a do-it-yourself mutual fund investor, stick with no-load funds.

How do load funds work? Get ready for a tour of the mutual fund industry's alphabet soup. Most load funds offer several classes of shares, according to when the loads are collected. Investors therefore have to figure out, before they buy, how long they are likely to hold their shares.

A load fund's A-shares impose their charges up front. They carry a traditional front-end load, as much as 5.75 percent, which is lopped off the initial investment. An example: If your fund has a 5 percent front-end load, and you invest $10,000, you pay a $500 fee and start with $9,500.

B-shares impose their fees on the back end, when you sell, unless you hold them for many years. They have higher 12b-1 fees, typically a full percent annually, compared with a quarter of a percent for A-shares. What they call contingent deferred sales charges start at about 5 percent but decrease over time to reward long-term investors, typically falling as low as 1 or 2 percent after five or six years. Generally, B-shares convert to A-shares after six to eight years, by which time the higher 12b-1 fees have fully compensated the broker.

C-shares also charge higher 12b-1 fees of, typically, a full percentage point. But C-shares almost never convert to A-shares and usually charge redemption fees for only the first year or two.

Confused yet?

Some brokers like it that way, because it makes it easy to wring more money out of their clients, especially those who object to paying expenses up front. Here's what you should do:

If you plan to hold the fund for fewer than three or four years, C-shares will cost you the least. Longer than that, but less than about seven years, B-shares make the most sense. Longer still, buy the A-shares. Also, wealthy fund investors should stick with A-shares because, unlike other share classes, they charge you less depending on how much you invest.

"For long-term investors, the cheapest way to go is generally to buy A-shares and pay the sales charge up front," said Burton J. Greenwald, a fund industry consultant. "For wealthier investors, A-shares are almost always the better way to go if the load decreases to 3 percent or less."

Brokers often recommend the funds and fund share classes that bring in the most money for their firm. So, even if you invest through a broker, it pays to do your own homework. But remember, if you're going to take the do-it-yourself route, do not buy load funds. For every load fund there are plenty of no-load alternatives rated as good or often, considering the lower expenses, better.

- Compare fees. Differences in sales loads can add up to tens of thousands of dollars over time.
- Do not buy load funds if you are a do-it-yourself investor using a discount brokerage. For long-term investors who want the advice of brokers, paying loads up front through A-shares is generally the way to go.

The Tax Bill

Taxes are another important cost. The S.E.C. now requires funds to disclose their after-tax performance in their reports. If you are investing through a retirement account, don't worry about after-tax returns. If you are investing through a regular account, however, pre-tax performance is really less relevant than after-tax performance.

Mutual funds generate tax expenses for their investors by paying interest and dividends, which are taxed as normal income, and capital gains. Capital gains, which funds pay out at least once a year, are simply the profits from any sales from the fund's portfolio, whether bonds or stocks. But capital gains are usually a much higher portion of a stock fund's total returns. Funds often pay out both long-term gains, from securities held more than twelve months, and short-term gains. The maximum federal tax rate for long-term gains is 20 percent, while short-term gains are taxed as ordinary income at rates as high as 39.6 percent.

To keep your taxes down, check a fund's turnover ratio, which measures how much it trades. Many growth fund managers who trade aggressively, with turnovers of 100 percent or more a year, rack up huge tax bills.

During the bull market, investors paid little attention to tax efficiency. They took notice in 2000, however, when many stock funds ended up punishing them twice—with falling prices and record tax bills.

"It was an eye-opener," said John J. Brennan, chief executive of the Vanguard Group, "a seminal year in the decade, where investors could lose substantial money and get a capital gains distribution."

Many investors suffered a double burden because many funds sold stocks at prices lower than their early 2000 peaks, but still much higher than when the funds purchased these stocks in the years before. In fact, 2000 was the worst for mutual fund tax bills, according to Wiesenberger, a fund tracking firm. The average stock fund had a taxable capital gains distribution equivalent to 9.2 percent of its value, up from 6.4 percent in 1999. So the biggest losers in 2000 bought hot funds early in the year, only to see them plummet while still generating huge tax bills from prior gains.

Other funds keep their taxes to a minimum. Several companies offer *tax-managed* funds, which use accounting and trading strategies to minimize taxes. The tax-managed funds are worth considering, though they have varying degrees of success. By design, most do not aim to shoot out the lights. Some, like Vanguard's, are index funds that use extra strategies to minimize taxes. Others, like those offered by Eaton Vance Asset Management, are actively managed. Both types use similar approaches: restricting their trading, using accounting and hedging tactics and selling losing stocks to offset gains.

But a fund does not have to be labeled tax-managed to be tax efficient. Most index funds, because they trade infrequently, are quite tax efficient. Managers who buy and hold, with turnovers of 25 percent or less, tend to be tax efficient as well.

You can also reduce your tax bill by not buying funds before they plan to make their capital gains distributions, usually at the end of the year, but in some cases, earlier. One way to avoid this trap is to make most of your fund purchases at the beginning of the year. Call your fund company, or check its Web site, to find the distribution dates.

Be especially wary of funds that have had big run-ups but have not paid out their capital gains. Some funds post this information on their Web sites, and virtually all will tell you if you call (as you should near the end of the year). You will get the distribution, and tax bills, for gains that were racked up when you were not an investor. You can often avoid this hit if you sell your fund before the final weeks of the year.

For more on tax strategies, see chapter 7.

- Funds are required to disclose after-tax returns. A turnover ratio of 100 percent or more is often an indication of high taxes to come.
- Watch tax traps. Avoid buying funds near the end of the *fiscal* year (sometimes September rather than December) without making sure the fund has already paid its capital gains taxes.

Finding a Strategy

Let's start by seeing where you can find information about funds. The fund companies themselves are not your best sources.

Instead, look to services like Morningstar, Lipper and Standard & Poor's, which all track mutual fund returns. By far the best Web site for fund information is www.morningstar.com, where investors can find detailed fact sheets for most mutual funds. Some useful features include a fund's returns for the current year, fifty-two weeks, three years, five years and ten years. Looking at past returns can be a trap, of course, because they often fail to predict future performance. But a fund's long-term returns, together with other factors found on the Morningstar Web site, like risk measures, tax efficiency and fees, are still the most valuable indicators.

When you do look at performance, check a fund's ranking, by percentile, in its peer group and its performance against its benchmark index. Morningstar classifies each fund by style and size. Magellan is a large-cap blend fund, meaning that the manager, Robert Stansky, uses a blend of growth and value styles. Stansky's predecessor at Magellan, Peter Lynch, made this style famous—he called it growth at a reasonable price.

Morningstar ranked Magellan in the sixteenth percentile compared with other large-cap blend funds over the last decade, and it slightly outperformed the S&P 500. More recently, however, Stansky has struggled. In the year that ended at the beginning of March 2001, he was in the sixty-eighth percentile, or well below average in Magellan's peer group.

Don't always look for the funds with the biggest past returns, even over the longer term. What you want for most of your funds is a steady hand. Look at a fund's standard deviation, a volatility measure that shows how widely a fund's return varies from its mean performance. Check on a Web site like Morningstar to see if your fund's standard deviation is higher than the S&P 500's.

Standard deviation indicates how much a fund fluctuates from its average monthly return, generally calculated over three years. If a hot fund gains an average of 2 percent per month but has a standard deviation of 10 percent, the fund's monthly returns have been between an 8 percent loss (or 2 minus 10) and a 12 percent gain (2 plus 10) two-thirds of the time. Add and subtract double the standard deviation and you can find a fund's range of returns 95 percent of the time: for this fund, between an 18 percent loss and a 22 percent gain. The higher the standard deviation, the more volatile a fund will be. A high standard deviation isn't a bad thing for some of your investments, but understand what you're getting into and whether a manager's returns have justified the added risk.

Another way to monitor risk is by using the Sharpe ratio, a measure developed by William Sharpe, a Nobel Prize winner, to compare risk and rewards. Technically, it's a ratio between how much a fund outperforms the Treasury bills and its relative risk. Morningstar has these figures, too. The higher, the better.

Other useful tidbits on Morningstar include how long the fund's manager has been there. If a manager is new, check the fund's prospectus for qualifications. Morningstar also lists a fund's top twenty-five holdings, what brokers offer it, other risk measures, and fee and tax-efficiency information.

Worthwhile Web sites include www.SmartMoneyUniversity.com, a good place to find basic answers to basic questions. SmartMoney (www.SmartMoney.com) itself offers nifty Internet tools like asset allocators and fund selectors, and provides performance data. TheStreet.com (www.TheStreet.com) offers personal finance and mutual fund news.

Extensive data on thousands of mutual funds are also available at the *New York Times* Web site (www.nytimes.com), where investors can easily look up performance, fee, risk and portfolio data.

Among sites with narrower aims, www.Freeedgar.com and www.10kwizard.com offer access to filings that mutual funds make to the S.E.C. Freeedgar has a handy glossary that explains what each type of regulatory filing means. Fundalarm (www.Fundalarm.com) and Brill (www.brill.com) are two mutual fund sites that have message boards where investors compare notes, but they are best left alone unless you're a fund junkie.

Newspapers like the *New York Times* and the *Wall Street Journal* list daily price changes in a fund's net asset value and longer-term performance statistics. But because there are so many funds, most newspapers omit small or new funds. More detailed information on funds' returns is available on Web sites, including www.nytimes.com. The *Times* also publishes a mutual fund quarterly report on Sunday a few days after the end of each quarter, with news and analysis of the mutual fund industry.

How much current information can you gather directly from your mutual fund company? Not much. If you want to know what stocks your fund actually holds, good luck. The S.E.C. requires fund companies to provide a full accounting of their holdings only twice a year. Most do just that and no more, though some issue lists of top holdings and sector weightings a bit more often. So much can change over six months that such disclosures give investors only a rough estimate of a manager's approach, not a clear fix on its position.

The big fund companies like it that way. "Our disclosure policy is meant to protect our proprietary research," said a Fidelity spokeswoman. "In order to secure the best possible prices, our managers make purchases over weeks and months."

Such policies understandably vex many investors who prefer the instant information flow the Internet can provide. But Fidelity's stance has some merit. Because Fidelity manages nearly $1 trillion, investors who sensed that it had shifted strategies would try to buy or sell before Fidelity could fully adjust its own portfolio. Disclosure has become a trend on the fringes of the industry, but the few new funds that release their holdings data daily have not attracted much money.

Once you have found your way to the best information sources, how do you know what categories to pick? Academia has provided some help. The 1952 paper by Harry Markowitz, "Portfolio Selection," laid the groundwork for modern portfolio theory, a strategy that aims to create a portfolio that balances risk and return. Markowitz, a professor at the City University of New York, won the Nobel Prize in 1990, which he shared with two other academics, William Sharpe and Merton Miller. Markowitz's theories underpin the Internet tools that today allow investors to plug in various factors—age, salary, savings, marital status—and have an optimum allocation strategy spit back out with a few clicks.

Many fund companies, like T. Rowe Price, offer their investors customizable asset allocation tools. A newer crop of companies, some of them charging for access to their sites, has arisen to help investors deal with these issues in depth, including Financial Engines, whose founders include William Sharpe.

We deal in this chapter with the stock part of the fund equation, though these asset allocation tools often guide investors to put some of their money in bonds. As discussed in chapter 2, you should also shift more into bonds and bond funds as you age.

A broadly diversified fund or funds should be at the core of your portfolio, be it an index fund or an actively managed fund or both. One does not need more than a handful of other stock funds. Having too many multiplies paperwork and makes it difficult to track your asset allocation. Pick a large company growth fund, or a multi-cap growth fund. Pick a large-cap value fund. Add a small-cap fund and an international fund as you build your portfolio. And, if you're within striking distance of retirement age, start shifting into growth and income funds, as well as bonds and bond funds, for their healthy current payouts and lower risks.

Roy Diliberto, a Philadelphia area financial planner, emphasizes that investors should avoid the common trap of piling into last year's best funds, which can become this year's losers. If you truly diversify, not everything you invest in will be coming off a hot streak.

"That means you're going to invest in something that didn't make money last year," says Diliberto. But what didn't make money last year is often what will make money the next year, because of the market's cyclical nature. So it can pay to stick with losing positions in market sectors that have become unfashionable and undervalued. "That, of course, is easier said than done, which is why people like me exist," Diliberto adds.

Picking a Fund

Now, let's look at one way to pick a fund. Start with some hypotheticals: a) You're a do-it-yourself investor. b) You're just starting out and you have already put $10,000 into an S&P 500 index fund. c) You're ready for your second foray into building a diversified portfolio.

Since an S&P 500 fund represents a blend of the growth and value styles, but is restricted to large companies, a good second purchase is a small company fund. There are several hundred small-cap funds to choose from. Which one do you buy?

Here's one approach, using free tools available on the Web. First, consider this: Vanguard offers a fund that tracks the Russell 2000 index of small companies. The fund is no-load, with a 0.25 percent expense ratio—quite cheap. This fund itself could make a good second purchase. But let's see if we can find an actively managed fund that has done better, considering performance, volatility and fees.

One place you can easily do this on the Web, for free, is SmartMoney (www.SmartMoney.com). First, look up the Vanguard fund, by its ticker symbol, NAESX, which you can find on the site. Write down its three- and five-year returns, its standard deviation and its expense ratio. Then, call up the site's Fund Finder. To justify paying for an actively managed fund, let's find one that has beaten the index over the past three and five years. On the Finder's performance tab, type in the Vanguard fund's three- and five-year returns, to screen out funds that didn't keep up with the index.

Second, on the Volatility tab, enter a standard deviation between zero and the current standard deviation of the Vanguard fund, to screen out funds that are more volatile than the index. Why not try to find funds that combine good performance and low risk?

Third, under the Profile tab, for Sector, choose Small Blend. We already have a large blend fund, the S&P 500 index, so let's choose a small company fund that also blends investing styles. Under the same tab, pick a fund with a Morningstar rating of at least four stars, out of five, and a manager who has been with the fund since at least 1998. If the manager is new, the performance record doesn't mean much.

Last, under the Expenses tab, put in zero for sales charge and for the contingent deferred sales charge, or back-end load. Since we are going the do-it-yourself route, there is no need to pay a load. For expense ratio, let's keep it below 1.4 percent, roughly the industry's average.

So what do we get? All of these criteria might yield too many funds, so you can further adjust by increasing the performance or lowering the volatility, or entering other factors to suit yourself. For a small-cap fund, it is also a good idea to screen out funds with more than, say, $2 billion in assets.

When we ran a screen, some of the alternatives we found included the Ariel Fund, which gained 15.4 percent annually over five years, as of June 2002, compared to a 6.2 percent annual return for the Vanguard Small-Cap Index Fund. The Ariel Fund even managed to post the better performance with less volatility, judging from its standard deviation. Things to keep in mind: going forward, the fund will have to continue to perform well to earn its 1.19 percent expense ratio. Also, its asset size of more than $1 billion is not ideal for a small company fund.

Even with such powerful tools, picking funds on your own, without the help of a broker or other adviser, involves some risks, especially if you are a novice investor. Past performance does not guarantee future returns. That is why we emphasize looking for funds that have done well, but also minimized risk, which is more predictable than raw performance. Avoid funds that have had torrid past performances, because those funds often seem to peter out.

- The Internet offers a wealth of information and tools when choosing a new fund, including comparing how different funds balance risk and return. Look for consistency.
- Don't buy last year's best performers, because they often sputter the next year. And don't try to time the market by dumping a fund if it has one off year.

What Else Is Out There?

Every year some new financial product comes along that aims to unseat the mutual fund, but fails. Still, there have been a few products worth considering. Some are low-cost alternatives to mutual funds, some combine features of funds and direct stock picking, and others are designed only for wealthy investors.

Closed-end funds still do exist, though they have been far outstripped by open-ended mutual funds. Today, there is about $158 billion in closed-end funds. Closed-end funds should be considered only by investors who are willing to do extra homework and take some extra risk.

Remember, a closed-end fund, though subject to the same regulations as a conventional mutual fund, is fundamentally different. An open-ended mutual fund trades at its net asset value, which is determined by the price of the securities the fund holds. Closed-end funds trade like stocks, have a fixed number of shares, with initial public offerings and commission charges for buying and selling. As a result, the fund can be priced at a discount or a premium to the underlying securities—and usually is. Essentially, buying a closed-end fund means doing some additional homework. Not only are there the fund's expenses, management, performance and portfolio to consider, there is the additional factor of how other investors will view the fund. If they don't buy it, it will not do well. Most individual investors should avoid them unless they are willing to do the extra work and have a compelling reason, like finding a worthwhile fund trading at an unusually high discount.

Exchange-traded funds, or E.T.F.s, are worth considering case by case as an inexpensive way to buy into indexes like the Standard & Poor's 500 and the Nasdaq 100. But since E.T.F.s are still an evolving product, it probably makes more sense for beginning investors to stick with mutual funds.

Exchange-traded funds have been around since 1993, when the American Stock Exchange created Standard & Poor's Depositary Receipts, known as Spiders. The Spiders, which track the S&P 500 stock index, are an alternative to conventional S&P 500 index funds. Like closed-end funds and stocks, E.T.F.s trade throughout the day. Unlike closed-end funds, they have features that prevent their price from drifting too far from the net asset value.

In the United States, E.T.F.s are strictly index funds, though a few companies plan to offer actively managed E.T.F.s. Regulatory approval of such a product, however, will not be simple.

Some E.T.F.s are structured like mutual funds, with boards of directors and other administration, and some are not. To date, the most popular E.T.F. by far has been the Nasdaq 100 Shares, often referred to by their ticker symbol, QQQ, which track the largest Nasdaq issues, including Microsoft, Intel and Cisco. The QQQs were started in 1999 and had grown to more than $20 billion in assets by the end of 2000. They are popular because there are relatively few conventional mutual funds that track the Nasdaq 100, and because the ease of trading QQQs makes them a simple way to speculate on the technology sector.

The Spider is the second most popular E.T.F. and, at 0.12 percent, has an expense ratio even lower than the Vanguard 500's, at 0.18 percent. Barclays S&P 500 iShare has a 0.0945 percent expense ratio, even cheaper. Studies show that E.T.F.s can be more tax efficient, too. In the past several years, the Spider appears to have been even more tax efficient than the Vanguard 500.

Among the drawbacks, since E.T.Fs trade like stocks, is that you have to pay a commission every time you buy or sell. The lower your commission and the longer your investment, the greater the advantages of E.T.F.s and their lower expenses, compared with standard index funds.

Clearly, E.T.F.s are a force mutual fund companies cannot ignore. In 2000 Vanguard, having long argued the advantages of its conventional index funds over E.T.F.s, revealed a plan for Vipers, Vanguard Index Participation Equity Receipts, or E.T.F. shares for some of its conventional index funds.

There is one other sort of E.T.F. worth knowing about: Merrill Lynch's *HOLDRs*, or *Holding Company Depositary Receipts*. These are fixed baskets of stocks, grouped by sector, that are sold in bulk and available through any broker, not just Merrill Lynch, on the American Stock Exchange. They can turn in their HOLDRs for the underlying stocks at any time. Do not buy HOLDRs at their initial offering, however, because they carry an extra fee that does not become part of their value. In general, HOLDRs are best for hands-on investors since, unlike other sector funds, they are not actively managed.

Folios further blur the line between funds and stocks. They are best suited for stock pickers, not for those who prefer the convenience of mutual funds. The first folio was created in 2000 by an Internet start-up called Foliofn, which offered investors a way to buy preselected baskets of stocks at a low price, essentially a volume discount on stock purchases. Unlike HOLDRs, folios are not discrete securities. By 2002, Fidelity and E*Trade were offering their own versions of folios as alternatives to owning mutual funds or individual stocks in brokerage accounts.

The entry into the market of those two big players signals that customized baskets of stocks have some appeal despite opposition from the mutual fund industry. But for smaller companies like Foliofn, weathering tough economic and market conditions will be a challenge. Foliofn charges a monthly fee of $29.95 to let investors choose from hundreds of baskets of stocks or build their own. Investors can fill each of these baskets with as many shares as they want of up to fifty stocks and make changes to the baskets at no extra charge over their monthly fee. HOLDRs charge no monthly fees, but don't allow investors such flexibility.

The advantages of folios include the potential for far greater tax efficiency than with a mutual fund. Folios let you make timely sales of losing stock positions, without extra commissions, to offset winning ones. "Harvesting losses," as this practice is known, is a good way to minimize tax bills. Additionally, you can customize your portfolio as you see fit. If there are stocks that you object to for moral reasons, you can exclude them from your portfolio. Or one could purchase one of Foliofn's "socially conscious" portfolios.

Of course, this flexibility negates many of the advantages of owning mutual funds. For one, nobody helps you manage the basket once you've bought it, at least not as they are designed so far. As such, a folio is not so much a replacement for a mutual fund as it is a different way to trade stocks. So far, folios have not been subject to the same stringent rules as mutual funds, which means they do not have boards of directors, publicly disclosed expense ratios or disclosure requirements. The Investment Company Institute, the fund industry's lobbying organization, has asked the S.E.C. to subject folios and any similar products to the same regulations that govern mutual funds. Shortly afterward, the S.E.C. ruled that folios would not be subject to mutual fund regulations.

"Generally, we applaud new products coming to market because they can increase competition, which can have the effect of lowering fees for investors," said Cynthia M. Fornelli, deputy director of the commission, in early 2001. "On the other hand, we have an obligation to analyze these products to make sure whether they're something we regulate."

Depending on what your broker offers, and the size of your account, *managed accounts*, or privately managed stock accounts, can be worthwhile alternatives to mutual funds. With thresholds for entry having become much lower, they are one of the hottest areas in asset management today. Private portfolio managers have lowered their minimums to as little as $50,000 in some cases, but typically look for at least $100,000 from investors who are worth at least $500,000. One reason these accounts are more widely available is that technology now allows a single investment professional to manage, in some cases, tens of thousands of individual accounts.

These managed accounts are sometimes called "wraps," because the various fees are combined. One type is the mutual fund wrap, where a consultant advises clients on how best to spread their investments across a slate of funds. Such wraps are generally not worth the trouble because they heap fees on top of fees.

More compelling are privately managed securities accounts, also known as consultant wraps. Consultant wraps are enough of a draw for the fund industry's richest clients that many fund companies are joining the business. They offer the services of their top investment managers through managed-account programs run by third parties like the leading investment banks.

The annual fees for such accounts average 2.25 percent, more than for most mutual funds, though it varies widely depending on your broker and account size. Most consultant wraps work like this: Clients visit an investment adviser, whether a big broker like Salomon Smith Barney or a small independent. With the guidance of a broker or other investment professional, clients then pick among scores of investment managers from different firms. Usually clients spread their money among several accounts and asset classes and then leave much of the monitoring and managing to the brokers.

At most big brokerage firms, minimums don't come much lower than $100,000. New Internet-based financial companies, like WrapManager.com and PrivateAccounts.com, are offering lower minimums and lower fees for private accounts, though usually without the additional advice of a broker.

Unlike mutual funds, all of the privately managed programs give clients direct investments in stocks. Participants and their advisers can therefore tailor the holdings to their preferences.

Managed accounts can also have tax advantages. Mutual funds can leave newer investors with tax bills from gains that previous investors enjoyed. A hot-performing fund that suffers withdrawals, for instance, will have to sell stocks to meet redemptions, leaving the remaining investors with a larger tax burden. In managed accounts, investors pay taxes only on their own gains. Wrap clients can also take defensive measures, like selling losing positions in one account to offset gains in others, thus reducing tax bills.

• Some alternatives to standard mutual funds are worth considering for their low costs and flexibility, but any fledgling product should be tried in moderation and requires extra diligence and attention.

5.

Bonds and Bond Funds:
Why They Belong in Your Portfolio

ROBERT D. HERSHEY JR.

To most people, the very word is soporific. What could be duller, after all, than holding someone's I.O.U. when you could have a piece of the action and enjoy, say, the 20 percent plus annual returns that investors in stocks have so often enjoyed, most recently in the five straight years of equities mania ending in the late 1990s?

Sure, Tom Wolfe dubbed bond traders masters of the universe in *Bonfire of the Vanities*, and F. Scott Fitzgerald made Nick Carraway a bond salesman in his tale of the glamorous 1920s, *The Great Gatsby*. More recently, the bond market was the playground for John Meriwether's band of Nobel-laureate speculators who made king-size fortunes before the 1997 fall of their Long-Term Capital Management made headlines in nearly touching off a world financial crisis.

Traditionally, though, bonds have been regarded as a boring, arcane investment suitable only for the aged, the already rich, the unimaginative or the hopelessly conservative. Until the 1950s, in fact, bond yields were lower than those on stocks on the grounds that stocks needed to compensate investors for assuming greater risk.

Well, you can indeed look at bonds as the province of the ultra-conservative belt-and-suspenders crowd if you like—and it's true that bond buyers are unlikely to cut much of a figure at parties, where technology stocks and real estate long dominated the chatter—but there's a useful, arguably essential, place for them in every portfolio. That's right: Even twenty-somethings weaned on the Internet, with decades of working life ahead, should probably own some bonds. The question is whether they should be something as safe as a two-year note from the United States Treasury, a subinvestment-grade debenture (which provides limited liquidity) or debt issued by a steel company whose prospects for long-term survival are chancy enough to have pushed the yield well up into double digits, or something in between.

Bonds belong in most portfolios despite the fact that their returns—interest plus any capital gains—have traditionally lagged behind stocks over the long term and may well continue to do so. The margin, however, is not as great as is widely believed. Through modern financial history, stocks have returned roughly 10 percent compared with 7 percent for bonds—and bonds have outperformed stocks for periods of as long as twenty years. And bonds far outstrip stocks for producing current income.

There's also the fact that people have different degrees of risk tolerance, though you don't really know what yours is until you have actual rather than theoretical money invested and something goes wrong. And of course people's circumstances differ, and inevitably change. Workers budget for their children's college, lose jobs, get divorced and approach retirement. As you age, the longer term becomes progressively shorter.

The array of bond choices, combined with different forms of direct or mutual fund ownership, is immense. Government bonds are the natural choice for investors for whom safety and liquidity, the ability to easily buy and sell, are paramount. Municipals are best suited for those in the upper tax brackets who keep investments for decades. Corporate bonds are for the more venturesome, seeking maximum returns. You can pay a bit extra for instant diversification by investing in any of these categories through a bond fund, which is highly advisable for corporate bonds and probably essential for

Chart 5A

Countervailing Trends

In general, bond prices have risen in years when stocks fared poorly. The chart compares an index of intermediate-maturity Treasuries with the S&P 500 index for each year since 1950 when the S&P 500 index declined. Figures are in percentage points.

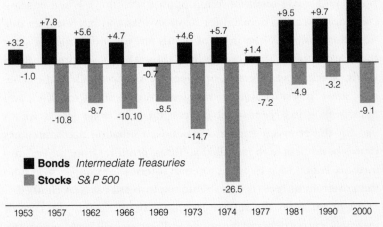

Bonds *Intermediate Treasuries*
Stocks *S&P 500*

| 1953 | 1957 | 1962 | 1966 | 1969 | 1973 | 1974 | 1977 | 1981 | 1990 | 2000 |

Data source: MFS Investment Management

lower-quality, or junk, bonds. But, as we'll see, there are pitfalls with funds, too.

Whether bonds account for 10 percent of a portfolio or 90 percent, they almost certainly ought to be represented. A traditional rule of thumb suggests a percentage of bonds and cash equal to one's age, though many advisers these days recommend a higher share in stocks (see chapter 2 for more on how to match your investments to your stage in life).

Don't let anyone talk you out of a bond stake by implying that your investment savvy is best gauged by how thoroughly you shun the fixed-income, or bond, market. Experienced and knowledgeable people know better, some of them having learned from harsh treatment at the hands of the stock market in 2000 and 2001. And more investors may gravitate toward bonds as financial havens at a time of extreme economic and political uncertainty.

How Bonds Help Your Portfolio

Bonds do two fundamental things. They provide steady income, sometimes with tax advantages, and they act as portfolio ballast. Bonds and stocks often move in opposite directions. When business conditions weaken, demand for loans shrinks and interest rates subside; this pushes up the price of bonds already in the market since they carry interest rates higher than those that newly prevail. Bond yields, which move inversely, or opposite, to prices, fall. As the economy slows, investors also become less worried about inflation, and more willing to accept lower interest rates. In other words, what's bad for the economy is good for bonds, a situation that sometimes causes bond people to be called vultures, profiting from others' misfortune. Watch what happens to bond prices, for example, next time the government reports that the unemployment rate has climbed.

In boom times the reverse is typical. Bonds decline because of fears that excess demand for goods and services will lead to inflation, which shrinks the buying power of the fixed returns of interest and principal that bonds deliver. Stocks, on the other hand, tend to thrive when the economy is strong or expected to become strong, and to sag in recessions.

Because inflation also diminishes the value of any gains or dividends from stocks, they sometimes move in tandem with bonds. For much of the three decades until the late 1990s, both types of investments were so sensitive to inflation that they tended to move in the same direction. As inflation stayed in remission and the economy slowed, however, the two markets substantially decoupled, with stocks losing and bonds gaining.

Even when stocks and bonds do go the same way, bonds tend to be less volatile. So the presence of bonds in a portfolio provides you with the psychological staying power to stick with other investments, such as stocks of solid companies that have temporarily fallen out of favor. Odd as it sounds, a portfolio composed of 80 percent of two-year Treasury bonds and 20 percent stocks is actually more stable in terms of buying power than holding cash. That's the ballast.

The shifts in stock and bond performance therefore point up the wisdom of larding any portfolio with various types of investments, including such fixed-income stalwarts as money market funds or certificates of deposit. As the Safeco Corporation, a mutual fund company, advised its clients: "It's always time for bonds because it's always time to be diversified."

In the absence of default risks that affect junk bonds in particular, bonds tend to move as one big, albeit disparate, group, responding mostly to changes in interest rates. This is in contrast to stocks, which tend to move much more by industry or individual company.

Although it seems that everybody and his stepnephew has an opinion about the direction of interest rates, timing the bond market is no easier than predicting the direction of stocks or even the economy. How many people, for example, predicted the end of potentially inflationary federal budget deficits, much less the arrival of similar-sized surpluses, at the beginning of the Clinton administration? As well as the resulting rally in bonds? What's more, there have been some extended periods, such as in the early 1980s and the mid-1990s, when bonds were more volatile than stocks.

No matter which way the markets move, however, it's a sure bet that bonds will keep churning out interest far above the dividend yield on the typical common stock. In the latter part of 2001, the Standard & Poor's index of 500 stocks yielded about 1.25 percent. Companies justified such historically meager payouts on the grounds that most investors had come to be interested mainly in growth— you're better off it we keep the profits and reinvest, tax-free, in the business, they said.

Companies also argued that buying back shares, which tends to support the stock price, was an acceptable substitute for cash payouts. In fact, these purchases generally just offset shares newly issued to executives and employees under option plans. There seems little likelihood that this trend will be reversed.

Chart 5B

For Income, Bonds Outstrip Stocks

Since 1959, 10-year Treasury bonds have consistently yielded more income than widely held stocks like those in the S&P 500. Through the 1990s, as dividends fell out of fashion in corporate boardrooms, the yield on stocks dwindled far below historic averages.

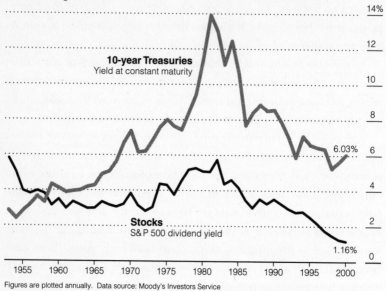

10-year Treasuries
Yield at constant maturity

6.03%

Stocks
S&P 500 dividend yield

1.16%

Figures are plotted annually. Data source: Moody's Investors Service

Bond interest, on the other hand, is a matter of contract, not management whim.

This is not to say that bonds are risk free. Any allocation of money has its dangers, including putting it under the mattress—where, except in rare cases such as in Japan over the past decade, it would almost certainly lose value to inflation if it is not stolen, burned or chewed by the dog.

One risk is that the issuer of the bond, the borrower, will fall on hard times and not be able to keep paying you interest or return your principal when the bond comes due, often in twenty or thirty years. Some bonds are still sold for very long maturities, such as ninety-nine-year bonds marketed by Disney and Coca-Cola in the 1990s. A handful, called perpetuals, have no maturity dates at all.

Credit, or default, risk can be judged, though never for certain, by ratings assigned by Moody's Investors Service, the Standard & Poor's Corporation and some lesser-known services. They rate a company's individual debt issues, which often have various repayment terms and guarantees, not the company itself. Ratings range from triple-A down to D, for bonds in default.

To spread and minimize credit risk, and get the benefits of professional selection, consider bond funds. In case a few borrowers default, the impact on a bond fund can be so slight as to probably escape many shareholders' notice.

The second major risk, perhaps less appreciated by the casual investor, is that interest rates could rise, which would mean the price of your bonds, whether individually or in a fund, would fall. That price is a direct reflection of the market's estimate of future inflation, which is subject to big swings.

The longer the bond has until maturity, the more its price responds to, say, a one-point move in interest rates. For example, if rates climbed from 6 percent to 7 percent, the price of a thirty-year bond, the longest common maturity, would fall 12.5 percent. A five-year bond would decline only 4.2 percent.

If a company is financially solid, and you are able to hold its bonds until they come due, a rate rise makes little difference other than lost opportunity to capture the higher rate. But if you need the money before maturity, a rate rise would cause you to suffer a loss— perhaps sizable.

There is a related type of market risk, one recognized by few nonprofessional investors and widely ignored. But so-called reinvestment risk can loom very large when the holding period runs into decades. This is the possibility that when your bond comes due, even if in the near future, you will face unattractively low interest rates when you seek to reinvest the proceeds. The risk also affects your reinvestment of your interest payments.

A quoted yield to maturity assumes that interest can be reinvested at the original rate. The risk that you won't be able to do so, of course, rises when rates are declining.

One way to deal with this is to buy zero-coupon bonds, with individual investors best advised to stick mainly to Treasury issues to minimize risk. While other bonds typically pay interest every six months, zero-coupon bonds are so called because they pay no current interest. You buy them at a discount from face value and your return is the difference between the purchase price and face value at maturity.

The stated interest rate is the compounded annual return that makes up this difference. This phantom interest is added to the bond's value in calculating its price if it is sold before maturity.

So long as you hold the bonds to maturity it doesn't matter what happens to interest rates in the interim. You've locked in your entire return. But keep in mind that, because all your interest payments are in effect reinvested at a fixed rate, zeros are more volatile than ordinary bonds and losses (or gains) could be steep if you have to bail out before they come due.

Investors saving for a fixed goal, such as college, are the best candidates for zeros, which, so long as the borrower remains solvent, assures you of having a certain number of dollars at maturity. There is a bit of a bookkeeping hassle, however. With some exceptions, you must pay taxes on the phantom interest you accrue but don't see in the form of the bonds' increased value as they progress toward maturity.

A popular strategy for minimizing market risk is to "ladder" your portfolio, buying an array of bonds with staggered maturities so that they come due in scheduled succession, say every six, twelve or twenty-four months. If rates have risen, you can use the proceeds to latch on to these greater available returns. Laddering minimizes both interest-rate risk and volatility.

Another way to control risk is to employ the "barbell" strategy in which you concentrate your bond holdings at both extremes of the maturity spectrum, avoiding the middle. The short-term part, maturities from months to a few years, provides flexibility; the long-term part provides high yields.

Since there is such a wide variety of bond funds, you can employ them on behalf of almost any strategy.

- Bonds belong in every portfolio. Even though their total returns lag behind those of stocks, they smooth out your investment performance and provide higher current income.

Where to Keep Your Bonds

In the old days, you bought a bond and stuck it in a safe-deposit box. From time to time you would retrieve it, go to a booth where scissors were provided and clip off an interest coupon. Then you'd go to the teller and deposit or cash it.

But coupon-clipping is a thing of the past. So-called bearer bonds—payable to whomever had them in their possession—have given way, for tax enforcement and administrative ease, to bonds registered in the owner's or a broker's name, with interest arriving automatically by mail or credited to an account. In fact, the bonds may exist as little more than an electronic impulse.

Still, as in real estate, location matters—a lot.

Even including the minority of investors who insist on having their bonds in physical possession, the chief decision beyond what proportion of your portfolio should be in bonds is what type of accounts to put them in. And in this, professional wisdom seems to be shifting.

The increasing ubiquity of 401(k) accounts and their retirement-oriented kin means that there are now tens of millions of Americans with sizable amounts of money in both tax-advantaged and fully taxable accounts.

Financial planners have tended to recommend that bonds—corporates and Treasuries—be placed in tax-deferred accounts. With relatively high income from interest, bonds seemed to need more shielding from taxes than did stocks. Most of the returns from stocks come from capital gains, which do not trigger a tax bill until the stocks are sold—or, if the stocks are willed to a survivor, perhaps never.

This "defer bonds first" strategy may be misguided, according to a study in 2000 by three professors at M.I.T. and Stanford. The old strategy ignores the ready availability of tax-exempt bonds, for investors' taxable accounts, and the fact that most investors buy stocks through mutual funds, which tend to trade heavily and rack up annual tax bills unless they are in tax-deferred accounts. So it may well pay to defer stocks first by placing them, and your stock mutual funds, in your 401(k) and I.R.A., and concentrate your bond investments, perhaps municipals, in taxable accounts.

Looking Abroad: Why It's Safer to Stay Home

Sooner or later, you will find yourself wondering whether to diversify your bond portfolio with some foreign issues. Generally, the answer is no. For one thing, there is very limited choice. Government, or sovereign, bonds tend to be either the high-quality, low-interest debt of industrialized countries—and why go abroad for that?—or speculative high-yield bonds of the emerging world where monitoring is difficult and risk of default great.

The corporate market is underdeveloped almost everywhere outside the United States and there is nothing to compare with American tax-exempts. Another negative is the currency risk, whether you buy individual foreign bonds or a foreign bond fund. You might hedge the currency risk by buying a mutual fund that does so, but with trouble and expense.

There are occasions when foreign bond values seem compelling. (Chapter 6 discusses such opportunities in detail.) But, especially for investors with limited time and money, why bother searching for foreign bonds when there is such a juicy selection of bonds at home?

To Go Short or Long: The Yield Curve and Other Bond Market Twists

One of the most common terms you hear in the bond market is the "yield curve," an important concept that is much less intimidating than it sounds. It is nothing more challenging than a graph of how bond yields vary with maturities. It is called a curve because of its normal, graceful upward sweep from lower to higher levels as maturities get longer.

This curve portrays the basic economics of the situation: Investors demand increasingly hefty rates of interest for lending money for many years instead of just a few months, to protect themselves against erosion from inflation and the risk of default. Inflation can damage purchasing power much more in the long run than in the short run. A long-term 5 percent bond can prove a very poor investment should inflation accelerate to, say, the double-digit rates experienced in the late 1970s and early 1980s.

The yield curve is not always normal, sloping gently upward. To watch it is to glean some of the most valuable economic and financial information to be found anywhere. Readily available from newspapers or various Web sites, it can be put to profitable use by all kinds of investors, especially bond buyers.

Sometimes, for example, the curve flattens or even inverts to slope downward, with short-term rates higher than long-term rates. Traditionally, this condition has proven one of the better predictors of impending recession, generally the best time to buy bonds. The longer the maturity, the bigger the likely gain.

Higher short-term rates typically result when the Federal Reserve is tightening monetary policy to slow down an economy that is growing so fast as to risk revived inflation. The Fed tightens by raising the overnight lending rate—what banks pay one another to borrow

Chart 5C

Yield Curves Tell of Things to Come

Ordinarily, yields are higher on bonds with longer maturities, because the uncertainties and risks are greater the further into the future one must look. But when the Fed raises short-term rates to counter inflation, investors may accept lower long-term rates expecting that the economy and inflation will slow. If the resulting curve inverts, that is considered a harbinger of recession. These curves are for Treasury securities.

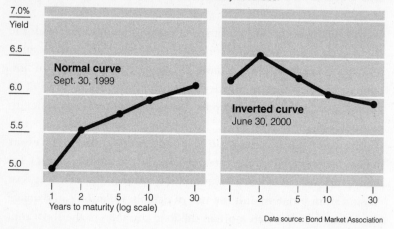

Data source: Bond Market Association

for very short periods and a benchmark for other short-term rates. By raising rates the Fed not only makes it more expensive for businesses and consumers throughout the economy to borrow, but also signals its intentions about likely future moves. As short rates rise, investors may be reassured that the Fed will not let inflation get out of control, so long-term rates tend to ease. The futures market for Fed funds, traded on the Chicago Board of Trade, tells you what sophisticated opinion thinks lies ahead.

Spotting a "flattened" curve, you should probably buy short-term bonds to take advantage of temporarily high yields while preparing to stretch your time horizon to accumulate longer-term issues that you believe, with some confidence, will hold their value as the economy slows.

If, however, long rates are far higher than short rates, this suggests rapid economic expansion ahead that might arouse fears of inflation, the great enemy of bonds. But be alert to distortions such as took shape in the late 1990s, when the government suddenly began to run budget surpluses after decades of deficits, reducing its need to borrow money in the bond market. Since long-term debt is usually the most expensive, the Treasury cut back on issuing thirty-year bonds, which it did not customarily market before the 1970s because the law did not allow it to pay more than 4.25 percent for long-term loans. The drastic shrinkage of supply artificially depressed thirty-year yields and led to the displacement in the late 1990s of the thirty-year maturity, often referred to as the "long" bond, by the ten-year Treasury bond as a market bellwether. So if you ask someone, "How's the market?" the answer, for bonds, is now likely to be the ten-year Treasury rate.

The ten-year bond was already widely used as a benchmark for home mortgages, since it roughly corresponds with how long families live in a particular home. Refinancing opportunities reduce the amount of time the average mortgage is in place to about five years.

If you might sell your bonds before maturity, you need to be able to gauge their volatility and likely value. Ask a bond specialist about what is called their duration, a complicated measure of how quickly the bond pays interest to investors. Duration is shorter than maturity for all but zero-coupon bonds, because these pay all their interest at maturity.

By the way, you'll sometimes see or hear the term "debentures" when market discussions get technical. Debentures are simply bonds backed solely by the borrower's promise to pay, while other bonds are backed by specified physical assets. It's a distinction that is often ignored, with most folks just calling everything bonds.

And don't be put off by references to notes and bills. These relate to their length, notes typically being issued for two to ten years and bills for up to one year.

Money Market Funds

Younger investors tend to take these for granted—and you can't blame them for thinking such an elegant product must have been around forever—but, as discussed in chapter 1, the creation in the 1970s of money market mutual funds was a huge stride in the democratization of credit. It brought a vast expansion of opportunities for Americans as both borrowers and lenders.

No longer were the basic instruments of the short-term market for credit, including short-term certificates of deposit, commercial paper and bankers' acceptances, the exclusive realm of large institutions and professional traders. (C.D.s are receipts for bank deposits; commercial paper is a short-term corporate I.O.U.; and acceptances are bank guarantees assuring payment for goods in foreign trade.)

Money funds, containing these securities, give the ordinary income-seeking investor the chance to get premium returns that had been out of reach for all but those with $100,000 or more to commit. Almost immediately, these safe, highly liquid instruments proved wildly popular. They now have grown to $2 trillion, or about 30 percent of all mutual fund assets.

Because the underlying securities are of such short maturity, their value is stable enough for the money funds, in all but a handful of cases, to maintain a constant share price of $1. Banks have versions that generally pay somewhat lower rates but carry federal deposit insurance. Further refinements include money funds that invest only in tax-exempt issues.

As discussed in chapter 2, to maintain liquidity some of your assets should almost certainly be stashed in a money market fund. In addition to its other qualities, it typically allows you to write checks against your balance. Some carry a minimum check size, often $500, and some limit free checks, often to three a month, but such restrictions are diminishing.

The funds are stocked almost exclusively with debt coming due in a year or less. They must, by rule of the Securities and Exchange

Commission, consist of at least 85 percent of the highest-quality paper. It's a good idea to peruse your money fund's holdings to make sure it's not holding questionable commercial paper, like the C.D.s of a bank with a swelling portfolio of problem loans. A few funds avoid commercial paper as too risky, but they also sacrifice yield.

Overall, the safety record of money funds has been superb. On rare occasions a fund has been forced to "break the buck," failing to maintain the usual $1 price, but the fund's sponsors have stepped in to make investors whole.

Two words of caution: Beware of buying municipal money funds—and to a lesser extent taxable ones—close to the end of the year because of a seasonal quirk that balloons yields temporarily, only for them to retreat in January. You may well get a lower return than you expect. (By contrast, yields on funds composed of longer-term municipals tend to shrink toward's year end and rebound in January.) And watch out for muni money funds that beef up yields by including a lot of so-called private activity bonds, used to finance projects like pollution-control equipment for the local utility, that don't qualify for exemption from the alternative minimum tax (more about this later). If a fund bills itself as "tax exempt" it must confine such taxable holdings to 20 percent or less. A "municipal" fund is not so limited.

- Longer-term bonds usually have higher yields, but also higher volatility. The yield curve gives you the market rates at the full range of maturities, as well as some insights into the likely direction of the economy.

United States Treasuries, Ginnie Maes, and Other Government Bonds

For sheer safety, the paramount consideration for most bond buyers, there is nothing like securities backed by the promise of the United States government. Nothing in the world.

Despite trillions of dollars of accumulated debt, unfunded commitments to pay more trillions to future Social Security beneficiaries and a population that year after year buys hundreds of billions of dollars more goods from abroad than it is able to sell, the Treasury's promise to pay is unquestioned. And never more so than at the beginning of the twenty-first century, when the United States has emerged as the world's only superpower.

To be sure, sovereign countries can literally create money to pay off their debts. But this does not work for long without a productive economy and a sound political system, as Russia's default demonstrated in 1997. Foreigners have such faith in the United States, however, that they hold 40 percent of its debt.

It is in this arena—virtually free of risk to interest or principal—that investors are safest buying individual bonds. Not only are these utterly secure, but there are also a huge choice of rates and maturities and a ready, round-the-clock market. The Treasury, in fact, is by far the world's biggest issuer of debt, with trading in it dwarfing the value of turnover on the New York Stock Exchange and the Nasdaq market combined.

The only hazard is that, due to the threat of inflation, interest rates in general will rise, leaving you with a loss on any bonds you must sell before they mature. And the longer the maturity, the greater this risk. As we'll discuss later, some Treasury bonds are even protected against inflation.

Treasuries can be bought with the greatest ease, with a few clicks on your home computer, at little or no cost, under the Department's Treasury Direct program (see the Internet section on page 148 for details). And since late 1999, you can even use your MasterCard to buy inflation-proof savings bonds online.

Your bank or stock broker can buy bonds for you for relatively modest fees. But they generally aren't enthusiastic about this business, which they regard essentially as an accommodation for customers.

You can, of course, invest in Treasuries through mutual funds. But unless you're unusually phobic about tracking investments, you may well decide that the fees are not worth the hefty slice they lop off from returns. One percent a year, for example, may well amount to one-fifth of your yield. And you have no control over what's bought and sold and the tax consequences of these decisions.

Yet another attraction of Treasuries—and a further inducement to handle them yourself—is that, except for bills, the shortest-term debt, they can be bought in $1,000 units compared with the $5,000 typical for other bonds. Bills, which are sold at a discount and redeemed at face value, have a $10,000 minimum. Finally, Treasury securities are exempt from state and local taxes—under the Constitution, the Feds and lesser governments can't tax one another—making them especially attractive for people in heavily taxed regions.

Just because the most conservative of investors, like widows, retirees and charitable organizations, favor Treasury securities, however, doesn't mean that their returns are always modest, or constant. The 14.25 percent bonds the Treasury marketed in 1982, when inflation had just begun to retreat from three years in the double digits, proved a fabulous investment as interest rates tumbled under Paul A. Volcker's and Alan Greenspan's regimes at the Federal Reserve.

It is also possible, however, to lose a bundle on Treasuries. Some professional investors use them to make huge, highly leveraged bets on trends in interest rates. Meriwether of Long-Term Capital Management bet that Treasuries would decline relative to various other types of bonds, a strategy that failed because of extraordinary world market conditions.

While there is considerable talk about eliminating the national debt over the next decade or so, this seems unlikely. The Federal Reserve, in fact, would find this something of a threat, since it sets the nation's monetary course by buying or selling Treasury securities to expand or diminish the money supply.

If there should be a scarcity of, say, ten-year or other popular maturities, making yields unattractive, you can buy similar "off the run" bonds, like a twenty-year bond with nine and a half years left to run, at compellingly higher rates. Quotes for the whole array of government bonds appear in many daily newspapers and Web sites. Keep in mind that these issues are quoted a bit oddly, in 32nds of a dollar and with decimal points separating whole numbers and fractions. So 102.28 means $102^{28}\!/_{32}$, or $1,028.75 for a $1,000 bond.

Investors who want the safety of government paper can still obtain significantly higher yields—typically one-half to three-quarters of a point—by shopping what is called the agency market, where the government backs the bonds with implicit, rather than explicit, promises to pay or by agreeing to make its credit available in an emergency.

Most agency issues amount to investments in huge pools of home mortgages. Among the myriad of such issues are the Federal National Mortgage Association (Fannie Mae), the Government National Mortgage Association (Ginnie Mae), the Federal Home Loan Mortgage Corporation (Freddie Mac) and the Federal Home Loan Bank System. These, too, can be purchased through mutual funds, but investors should balance the convenience against the continuing added expense.

Remember that, in return for the higher yields, such mortgage-backed securities, and funds, have limited potential for gains. While most treasuries can keep rising as interest rates fall, mortgage-backed bonds are subject to being paid off early as homeowners refinance.

Savings Bonds

Often derided as low-interest investments for patriotic suckers, United States savings bonds are actually a reasonable financial proposition, depending on your investing goals. The returns, now tied to market interest rates, usually beat savings accounts and match certificates of deposit or money market funds. Unlike most other bonds, savings bonds don't suffer if interest rates rise. What's more, they provide tax advantages. Interest is generally tax-deferred until maturity, and the proceeds of the bonds can be applied tax-free to finance school and college tuition, provided certain conditions are met.

Yet the fact that savings bonds are so easy to buy, such as through payroll deduction and by credit card on a Treasury Web site, contributes to a widespread belief that they are simple to understand. There are now several different varieties—series EE and H and series I, which is protected against inflation—and frequently changing rules and rates. And banks, a principal outlet, have so little incentive to teach their staffs about how savings bonds work that customers can get expensive misinformation.

Buyers often wind up keeping matured bonds after they stop earning interest—some $5 billion or so are currently in this category—or cashing them in when holding on for a few more days would avoid the loss of six months' interest. Most savings bonds accrue interest every six months. In fact, banks often calculate the wrong payoff amount. So if you go the savings bond route, read up on them.

Since interest accrues from the first of the next month, it's usually wise to buy savings bonds toward the end of a month, so you will receive interest right away. Cash them in at the beginning of a new six-month period, right after the interest has been credited to you. You could lose up to $300 in interest on a $10,000 bond by cashing it in a few days too early, before a six-month period is up.

Inflation-Proof Bonds

Since early 1997 the Treasury has offered another type of its bonds that is guaranteed both to pay a fixed rate of interest and to protect against inflation, a highly appealing combination. These Treasury inflation-protected securities, or TIPS, pay a set amount of interest throughout their lives while the principal is adjusted for inflation, as gauged by the Consumer Price Index.

For example, you might get a 3 percent interest rate with another 4 percent added to your principal for inflation, making this bond competitive with a conventional 7 percent bond—but with a guarantee, not just a hope, that you will preserve your purchasing power.

The bonds are best for conservative investors and those saving for specific goals who want to be assured that faster inflation won't put their goals out of reach.

British and Canadian investors are among those who have been able to buy inflation-proof, or indexed, bonds for many years. But in the United States, they are more of a critical than a popular success, probably because inflation has been low since they were introduced.

Despite their seemingly low rates—and low current inflation—they are worth considering because they are guaranteed not only to pay you interest and return your principal but also to preserve your purchasing power. In other words, they eliminate both credit risk and market risk, the two bond bugaboos. "It's a remedy that comes as close to resembling an investment with nothing to lose but a lot to gain as anything I've seen in the investment world and it's sure to put an authentic smiley face on your portfolio for years to come," raved William H. Gross, founder and chief investment officer of Pacific Investment Management Company, which offers the Pimco mutual funds, and arguably the most successful bond investor ever. "I'm extremely bullish on it." While Gross runs the biggest inflation-adjusted bond fund, the Real Return Fund, investors can easily purchase these bonds on their own.

You might want to move quickly, however, since these TIPS face an uncertain future; an advisory group to the Treasury has called them "an expensive adjunct" to the government's borrowing program.

Some savvy investors put them in 401(k) and other tax-deferred accounts because, if inflation soars, those holding them in taxable accounts could wind up with tax bills greater than the annual interest. This is because the amounts added to the bond's value to compensate for inflation, phantom income that you don't receive until you sell the bonds or they mature, are still taxable each year. The government's inflation-protected version of savings bonds, the ones that can be bought with a credit card, require a minimum investment of just $50.

- Treasury bonds are safest, but for minimal added risk, the government's mortgage-backed bonds pay significantly higher rates.
- Savings bonds, which offer some tax advantages, offer much more competitive rates than they once did.
- Inflation-protected bonds, guaranteed to keep you ahead of inflation, may be one of the smartest bond investments you can make.

Corporate Bonds: From Blue Chip to Junk

Just when you thought that colorful corporate financing came to an end with mining bonds payable in gold dust, Wimbledon bonds that pay interest in the form of tennis tickets or bonds backed by the future music royalties of David Bowie, along comes U.C. Sampdoria, an Italian soccer team. It marketed $3.3 million of euro-denominated 2.5 percent bonds with the proviso that if the club played itself back into the top division the interest rate would jump to 7 percent—and to 14 percent if Sampdoria finished among that division's top four. Unfortunately, the team fell short, missing out on the higher television and gate revenue that would have supported the higher payout.

The usual corporate bond is far less entertaining. Bought individually, it seems designed to be unfriendly to ordinary investors. Unlike treasuries and municipals, they have no tax advantages. Nonetheless, bought through mutual funds, their high yields can make them a fine addition to a portfolio.

Only 5 percent of corporate bonds are held directly by individuals. Among the drawbacks is the risk that a company will buy them back if they rise in value. Or the issuer's fortunes could dim, dragging the bonds with them. The minimum denomination is usually $5,000, compared with $1,000 for Treasury bonds, and many trade so seldom that you will probably find they fetch less than you expect.

Even understanding their prices, once issued, is complicated. They are typically quoted in terms of how much more they yield than do Treasury bonds of comparable maturities.

No wonder that individual corporate bonds are most likely to be salted away by pension funds, life insurance companies, college endowments and other institutions, and never seen again for decades.

But buying bonds through mutual funds can minimize the drawbacks. Corporate bonds do tend to pay high rates of interest, making them appealing for tax-deferred accounts like 401(k)s. Diversification lessens the risk that any one company's mishaps, or default, will seriously dent your portfolio. Funds, unlike most individual bonds, are highly liquid, or easy to buy and sell. They are a great mechanism for automatically reinvesting interest payments, which are typically not big enough to purchase another individual bond.

There are bond funds of all types, varying by length of average maturity, by credit quality and how aggressively the managers trade. Some funds are closed-end, meaning they issue a fixed number of shares, which sometimes are available at prices less than the value of the underlying bonds.

Keep in mind that some bond funds carry high fees relative to their returns. "There is a large difference between a bond fund and a bond," said Michael Shamosh of Gabriele, Hueglin & Cashman, a Wall Street investment house, likening it to a choice between processed food and the raw ingredients. "You pay for the processing—it makes things easier—but you can't control what goes into it."

Paying three-quarters of a point in annual expenses to get a 5 percent yield means that your money has to work fifty-four days just to pay the managers, Shamosh said. Many bond funds also carry sales charges, or loads, of several percent. Some of the best bond funds, like Vanguard's Total Bond Market Index Fund and its GNMA Fund, carry minimal expenses of only about a quarter of 1 percent, with no loads.

Keep in mind that the yields advertised by bond funds are history, not necessarily what you'll get. Some bond managers jack up advertised current yields—to the detriment of total return including any losses or gains—by paying premium prices for bonds with high coupons, or high interest payments. These bonds are often the most likely to be paid off early, at lower prices. So instead of shopping for the highest yield, look at a fund's record and ratings over several years and compare it with other funds.

Be especially alert also to evidence that portfolio managers are panicking. In their intensely competitive field, they may be tempted to gamble, reaching for higher returns by taking on greater risks if they find themselves slipping behind their benchmark or their peers.

Above all, do not make the common mistake of chasing last year's hot performer. Studies have repeatedly shown that winning performance for any given period is mainly a matter of what kinds of securities are in fashion and not the result of managerial genius.

Since fund managers trade rather than hold bonds to maturity as direct investors might, the result can be a tax bill for gains, apart from the interest payments. The Securities and Exchange Commission has recently required funds to start disclosing their after-tax returns. More funds are already trying to keep their taxes low.

One particularly useful type of bond fund specializes in junk: high-yielding corporate (and some municipal) bonds whose credit-worthiness is in doubt, either from the time the bonds were sold or because of a subsequent downgrade. Junk bonds, typically providing double-digit yields, can be quite appropriate even for conservative investors so long as they are bought at the right time, and only through bond funds, to spread the risk of default.

Popularized in the early 1980s—remember Michael Milken?—then crashing in the early 1990s, high-yield bonds have been stigmatized. But there is nothing immoral about them. Fledgling companies as well as established ones in out-of-favor industries, or those who use the proceeds for hostile takeovers—all have a legitimate place in the capital markets. Venturesome investors should feel free to make risky commitments in search of outsized returns.

Junk bonds, rated below BBB by Standard & Poor's, typically yield about 7 percentage points more than Treasuries of comparable maturities, though this spread can vary a great deal. The performance of junk bonds, unlike other bonds, depends more on whether the economy will be strong enough to allow issuers to meet their debt obligations, and on how well an individual issuer is doing, than on the general level of interest rates.

Recessions, of course, jeopardize the survival of money-losing or marginally profitable companies, putting both your interest income and principal at risk. But junk bonds, like other securities, trade on expectations, not necessarily current conditions. So you may want to consider junk funds when the economic outlook still appears gloomy, but glimmers of improvement are starting to become visible. Prices typically start to rally well before economic recovery is assured, while the default rate is still climbing. Junk bonds generated 40 percent returns, for example, in 1991 even though the economy remained in recession until that spring. All this is opposite the normal practice of buying high-quality bonds when the economy appears likely to sink and push rates down.

Pay close attention to the rate spread between Treasuries and junk. The wider the spread, the more appealing junk can be—but remember that these spreads represent the collective judgment of the market about default risks, which you might not want to buck without good reason. Look at such other indicators as the ratio of rating upgrades to downgrades, the higher the better.

The Standard & Poor's Web site (www.standardandpoors.com) has a wealth of data and analysis. To find the ratio of upgrades to downgrades, for example, click on Forum in the Quicklink bar at the top. Then, under Ratings Commentary, click on Corporate Finance. Then scroll down and click on the most recent quarterly Global Credit Market trends report.

Since few investors have the means to buy enough junk for proper diversification, you should almost certainly stick to funds. Professionals can afford the necessary, difficult research, and have better access to what tend to be illiquid markets.

Paradoxically, a well-chosen portfolio including junk can actually be safer than one composed solely of high-grade bonds, since junk is less affected by changes in interest rates.

Convertibles and Preferreds

Convertible bonds are bond-stock hybrids, securities that combine a fixed stream of income with a stake in the issuing company allowing you to exchange them for common stock at a specified, higher price. If the company thrives, you wind up as a part-owner; if not, so long as it is able to meet its obligations, you keep collecting interest.

While this might seem the perfect all-purpose investment, the risks, complications and limited marketability aren't usually worth the skimpy interest rates and frequently long odds against profitable conversion. And, of course, if the company fails to thrive the interest payment is probably also at risk. Many telecommunications and bio-technology convertibles that flooded the market in the late 1990s have already fallen sharply in price despite maturities as short as two or three years.

Preferred stocks might be worth a look by some investors, espe-cially retirees. They trade like bonds in that they respond much more to interest rates than to degrees of corporate success. Indeed, inves-tors in preferreds generally regard them as bond substitutes. There are also convertible preferreds, which can be converted into com-mon stock, but these share many of the drawbacks and complications of convertible bonds. Since preferreds rank behind even the lowest-rated bond in giving investors their money back should the company fail, it is important to shun any but those of very high quality. But their yields are generous; they are available in small amounts—$25 shares are typical—and many are quite liquid, with stock exchange listings and prices you can easily monitor.

- Investors seeking higher interest rates than most other bonds offer should consider corporate bond funds. But corporates are fully taxable, and riskier than government bonds.

Municipal Bonds

Whether it's borrowings for a subway system in Washington, D.C., a new high school in suburban Atlanta or the facilities needed to attract the 2012 Olympic Games, the municipal bond market is where individual investors are most likely to buy fixed-income invest-ments directly. Americans of relatively modest means routinely join with the rich and superrich in holding some $535 billion of tax-exempt state, city and project bonds, four times as much as the stash of Treasuries held by individuals. They hold 35 percent of outstand-ing municipals, also commonly called tax-exempts, compared with 4 percent of Treasury debt.

Although there are some municipals of poor quality and many that don't actively trade, their widespread appeal is not surprising. Returns are relatively high for tax-paying investors—as opposed to, say, pension funds—and the quality of the overwhelming majority is high. In short, municipal bonds represent the best remaining tax shelter left to many American investors now that the government has abolished or limited so many tax deductions. Except for any paro-chial appeal to people who will benefit from the facilities to be financed, like a Red Sox fan lending money for a new baseball sta-dium in Boston, the paramount features of municipal bonds are their safety and high relative yields.

A tax-free 5 percent return, for example, means that a top-bracket investor with a marginal federal tax rate of 39.1 percent would have to earn 8.21 percent from a corporate or Treasury bond to do as well. Even middle-income taxpayers can find municipals compelling values. The formula for comparison is

$$\frac{\text{tax-free yield}}{100 \text{ percent} - \text{marginal tax rate}} = \text{taxable equivalent yield}$$

Declining tax rates set to take effect in coming years will only mod-estly reduce municipals' appeal.

Municipals are safe enough so that investors can confidently buy high-grade issues without surrendering some of their returns to buy them through mutual funds. But because mutual fund shares are easier to sell, those who don't want to hold their bonds to maturity might find the fees worthwhile. Some of the funds with the lowest expenses and no sales charges, or loads, are among the top performers.

Defaults occur on occasion, usually when a toll road or other revenue producer fails to generate enough business. But municipals generally have a stellar record of making good on payments of interest and principal, second only to that of Treasuries. This is especially true for so-called general obligation bonds, or G.O.s, which are backed by a theoretically unlimited power to levy property or income taxes. Only 1.7 percent of total outstanding municipal debt ever missed a payment during the Depression years of 1929 through 1937. Payments in arrears and not ultimately made good amounted to less than one-half of 1 percent.

One New York City bond marketed in 1870 to finance planking over a street in what is now the Bronx has been paying a tax-free $17.50 every six months for 131 years and seems a good bet to keep doing so until it comes due on March 1, 2135.

The tax-exempt feature, which dates in practical terms from the reintroduction of the federal income tax in 1913, renders interest nontaxable not only by Washington but also by other levels of government (but see the warnings below about the alternative minimum tax).

States generally exempt their bonds, and those from in-state issuers, from their own taxes. Bonds from certain other places, including the District of Columbia and Puerto Rico, provide widespread general exemption from state levies. Investors in such highly taxed places as New York City, Philadelphia, Pittsburgh, Cleveland and Akron can enjoy a tax-free trifecta—interest on their local bonds is exempt from federal, state and local income taxes. In some places, like Maryland, counties levy income taxes but exempt interest on their own bonds.

Keep in mind, though, that the exemption applies only to interest. If you sell municipal bonds or funds that have risen in value, the profit is taxable, as on any other security. But you can also deduct losses.

One pitfall of buying municipals is that most are callable, the borrowers being public bodies typically run by elected officials accountable to citizens watching how their tax money is spent. The officials, like homeowners, want to be able to refinance if interest rates drop.

So when sizing up yields, look at whether they are calculated to the date they may be called, often at a premium, or to the date they mature. Legally, bonds must be priced to whichever yield is lower, but there is still room for variations in accounting practice. And it's futile to compare bonds whose yields are calculated using different methods. Ask your broker for information, since very little, except for the prices of some actively traded revenue bonds, is available in the news media.

As in any market, whether a bond is what the trade calls rich (high-priced) or cheap will be determined only by subsequent performance. But for municipal bonds in general, purchasers have historically been well rewarded when triple-A-rated issues pay 80 percent or more of the yield on Treasury securities of similar maturity. Not only does the tax exemption give municipals the yield advantage, but buyers can figure on an eventual rise in price as the relationship between the two types of bonds returns to a more normal 70 percent or so.

Still, it's not always easy to decide what is good value among individual bonds since it is unlikely you can learn the terms of recent trades. While the market is becoming more transparent, you may find that bonds changed hands at a certain price, but not how many, or exactly when, or whether either of the parties was a nonprofessional.

Be alert also to the fact that municipals are less desirable after retirement. For one thing, your tax bracket is likely to be lower, reducing the advantage of tax-free income. And even if you're not in a lower bracket, you may find that municipals and Social Security benefits don't mix very well. Tax-exempt income counts as much as other earned or investment income when calculating how heavily your Social Security benefits may be taxed. And although huge numbers of municipals carry triple-A ratings, this is the result of insurance, not sterling finances. In the 1990s, the practice by borrowers of improving their rating—and thereby paying less interest—by obtaining insurance or some other guarantee grew to the point where more than half of new municipal bonds are credit-enhanced in some way.

Some professionals caution investors to check whether a top rating comes about through insurance or the issuer's own solidity. The insurance premiums reduce yields only modestly, but the insurers may be less able to pay off municipal bonds in hard times than would states and cities on their own.

Despite the generally high standing of municipal bonds, there are high-yield issues, typically lacking ratings, liquidity or both, that pose serious risks to investors straining for maximum yield. Shareholders of three high-yield funds of the Heartland Group of Milwaukee found the funds frozen indefinitely and placed under court supervision in early 2001 after the firm was forced to write down their value by as much as 70 percent. There is no established way to price municipals that lack a ready market.

Investors wealthy enough to be subject to the alternative minimum tax do not lose their tax break for interest from municipal bonds, but can be taxed more heavily on their capital gains from selling municipals, or any other bonds, for more than they paid. For more on how the alternative minimum tax affects your investments, see chapter 7.

Some municipal bonds are not tax-free at all. These are so-called private purpose issues, such as for convention centers, stadiums and large industrial development projects, where the issuers are using the borrowing power of local government.

The Bond Market in Cyberspace (At Last)

For the individual investor, buying and selling bonds has traditionally been mysterious and costly. What with middlemen and high spreads between bid prices received by the sellers and ask prices paid by buyers, trades may be at prices painfully different from what was expected, particularly when the amounts invested are in four or even five figures rather than $100,000 and up.

Since the mid-1990s, however, an electronic revolution has been dragging the bond market from the dark ages of fragmentation and opaque pricing and hurtling it toward a fiercely competitive but still ill-defined future.

"There's a thick veil of secrecy in the bond market," said Marilyn Cohen, a Los Angeles financial planner specializing in bonds. "It's one of the last dinosaurs to fall."

Although cities and towns now often auction their bonds online, in many cases drawing bids from new and distant underwriters, the bulk of the bond market's evolving drama is centered on the trading markets. These are a sprawling, electronically connected network of dealers, brokers and investors quite unlike such centralized markets as the New York Stock Exchange. This network is where the debt of the federal government, corporate America and states, cities, hospital authorities and turnpikes changes hands and where dealers, in the role of King Canute, for so long held back the electronic tide.

The dollar volume of this market is a dozen times that of the Big Board's stocks. Many bonds are also listed on the New York Stock Exchange, but most of the trading there comes from the rule requiring small orders of fewer than ten bonds to be routed to the exchange.

The bond market revolution has so far attracted far less attention than the more advanced electronic revolution in stocks, where ubiquitous and instantaneous prices contributed to the end-of-the-century speculative frenzy. But the changes in bond trading are nevertheless deep and pervasive. Spreads have begun to narrow, shrinking profits for dealers and brokers worried about survival in a world where investors are increasingly empowered.

Instead of changing hands through a patchwork of private channels on terms hidden from view, a growing share of the market is to some degree transparent, with visible inventories, prices and in some cases trades.

Institutional investors are the main initial beneficiaries, but consumers stand to gain directly in buying and selling bonds and indirectly through their stakes in mutual funds and pension funds. They will also benefit as taxpayers, as governments are able to market their bonds more efficiently. Increasingly, individual retail customers will emerge from their long enfeeblement by the bond market fraternity that costs them, according to one estimate, $20 billion a year in transaction charges and unfair prices. The proportion of retail bond trading conducted on the several electronic systems will leap to 24 percent in 2005 from less than 1 percent in 2000, according to TowerGroup, a consultant. Merrill Lynch and other full-service brokerage houses will spur this increase in response to customer demands that include the chance to peruse the firm's inventory.

This is not to say, however, that the retail share of the bond market is likely to supplant investment through mutual funds and other institutions. Individual investors directly hold only about 6 percent of all outstanding bonds, according to TowerGroup and the Bond Market Association. Institutions own the other 94 percent, in a market that totals $15 trillion.

Experts say they don't expect a big jump in how many smaller investors buy individual bonds just because they become more accessible over the Internet. But those who do buy bonds will be much more likely to buy them directly online.

Then they will drive better bargains. Since the bond market has no central exchange market where anything more than the smallest orders can be matched, your broker generally must buy them wholesale from other professionals and carry an inventory. The cost of

Chart 5D

Online Bond Trading

Though only a tiny fraction of bond purchases were made online in 2000, analysts expect the proportion to grow rapidly.

Online purchases as a percentage of all bond transactions

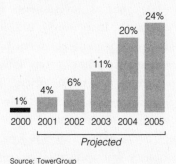

Source: TowerGroup

holding these bonds for weeks or even months is reflected in spreads, the less active issues carrying the highest margins. The Internet allows brokers and dealers to form alliances that in effect combine their inventories, each of them displaying their wares to more people while reducing the number of issues each keeps on hand.

One of the most useful Internet resources is the Web site run by the Bond Market Association, a trade group whose origins are in the tax-exempt market. Since late 1998, investors logging on to www.investinginbonds.com have been able to check prices, yields and other information on more than one thousand tax-exempt bonds actively traded the preceding day. Corporate bonds are now also included on this site, which offers a basic education about bonds as well.

Another useful source, geared to those who want to research or explore without making a commitment, is www.lebenthal.com, sponsored by the Lebenthal & Co. brokerage. This site, though oriented toward tax-exempt bonds, provides prices and other data about all kinds of bonds, as well as certificates of deposit.

For those ready to deal, some highly evolved systems allow you to buy and sell with the click of a mouse, with no involvement by a broker or trader. These include www.csfbdirect.com, for Credit Suisse First Boston, and www.schwab.com, for Charles Schwab, which offer current, or real-time, prices and the firm's bond inventory levels, adjusted after each transaction. You can also buy new United States Treasuries by going to www.publicdebt.treas.gov/td/tdstore front.htm.

"Live and executable prices displayed on the screen represent the future of retail bond investing on the Web," Andy Nybo, a Tower-Group consultant, predicted. If so, the days of seat-of-the-pants bond quotations and rip-off executions are numbered.

- Take advantage of the information newly available on the Web that is making it easier for investors to shop for bonds and trade them at fair prices.
- Corporate bonds offer high interest rates, but buy them through funds to minimize risk.
- Municipal bonds represent the best remaining tax shelter for many investors.

6.

International Investments:
The New Landscape

JONATHAN FUERBRINGER

David Bowers arrived from London early in 2000 as Merrill Lynch's new chief global investment strategist and set about to shake up the firm's view of the world. Yet only after he spent the summer and fall crunching numbers and examining the interplay between foreign stock markets and Wall Street did he suspect how great a change he would usher in. He and his colleagues concluded that investing abroad is nowhere near as good an idea as conventional wisdom dictates.

Money-management mavens have long said that, by owning foreign stocks, American investors can hedge against a downturn here. Sprinkle your portfolio, they said, with stocks from Britain, Germany, France, Japan and even some emerging markets like Brazil. Then, presumably, as one market or stock goes down, another will go up.

Bowers and other strategists are challenging that approach. The assumption that foreign markets will often rally when Wall Street falls has not panned out in the past few years. And, they say, there are better ways to reduce risk—namely, by choosing industry sectors or other financial markets, like bonds, that are less in sync with the United States stock market.

That revelation led Merrill Lynch to take a bold step. It advised its wealthy private clients to limit the foreign stocks in their portfolios to 0 to 10 percent, down from the 35 percent recommended by the former chief investment strategist, Charles I. Clough Jr.

But reducing the recommended exposure abroad does not mean abandoning foreign investment altogether. Why? Other analysts who have cut back their allocations abroad have not gone as far as Merrill because foreign investing can offer more than just diversification and the risk reduction that used to come with it. With the globalization of the world economy, there are many more foreign companies that are international players and offer the opportunity for great returns. More and more, some of the better companies in various sectors are not the American ones.

In fact, there are ways to invest abroad that avoid the traditional country-picking approach under fire by Merrill Lynch and others. The most promising alternative is investing by sectors—like technology, pharmaceuticals, telecommunications, even autos—and picking the best stocks you can find, an approach that will include foreign companies.

A shift from investing abroad as a way to reduce risk to concentrating on sectors and the world's best companies in those sectors would change the investment landscape. The once popular country funds that made it easy to diversify abroad are becoming a lot less attractive, hurting their returns. But money managers, including those at mutual funds, who apply the sector approach, and global sector funds based on new indexes, are attracting new investors.

Americans have always fallen short of meeting conventional money-management guidelines, which said they should put about 25 percent to 40 percent of their equity portfolios into stocks outside the United States, or 15 percent to 30 percent of their entire portfolios (including bonds). InterSec Research Corporation estimates that individuals had 5 percent of their money invested in stocks and bonds abroad at the end of 2000. Many of Merrill Lynch's own clients, Bowers has said, do not own enough foreign stocks to reach its new, lower guidelines.

It was even harder to interest Americans in foreign stocks in the last six years of the 1990s, when they rose just 37 percent as American equities climbed 190 percent. "The U.S. is doing so well. Why should I invest overseas?" was the refrain from many investors, said Stacey Ho, co–fund manager of the Wells Fargo International Equity Fund.

Americans have long kept most of their money at home. There was not a significant spurt in the flow of American money abroad until 1989, when net purchases, subtracting sales, jumped to $22.1 billion, up from an annual average of $3.4 billion since 1960. By 1996, Americans made $149.8 billion in net purchases of foreign stocks. But that dropped to $97.7 billion in 2001.

Net inflows into international equity funds, which invest mostly outside of the United States, also tailed off. From a peak in the early 1990s of $33.8 billion, they fell to $2 billion in 1998 before recovering to $13.1 billion in 2000, according to AMG Data Services. But net inflows plunged by $9.8 billion in 2001.

Besides the distraction of the technology and Internet stock booms at the end of the previous millennium, the foreign financial crises of 1997 and 1998 also discouraged American investors from looking abroad. The first began in Asia, the second in Russia. Both resulted in very difficult years for emerging foreign markets, killing much of the taste for investing there.

The introduction in 1999 of a single currency for eleven European countries (now twelve) added to American reluctance to buy foreign stocks when the euro turned out to be a weakling. In its first year it fell 13.8 percent in value, taking a big bite out of that year's gains for American investors. The 2001 terrorist attacks also blunted the appetite of some investors for foreign stocks.

So it is no surprise that some famous investors will tell you not to invest outside the United States. Listen to John C. Bogle, the legendary founder of the Vanguard Group and the creator of index mutual funds. "When you go abroad, you are taking on more risk to reduce your risk," he said. "I would just prefer to reduce my risk in the United States."

There is political risk: A country may have a revolution, an election may go the wrong way, a leader may be assassinated, he says.

There is financial risk: The banking system may be weaker than that in the United States. There is legal risk: A country may have bankruptcy laws, or other laws, that are unfavorable to investors or other laws that are harmful to shareholders.

There are plenty of strong voices, however, recommending that Americans buy foreign stocks. And investors should listen, especially because most of them own few or no foreign stocks at all.

The New Rationale for Investing Abroad

David Antonelli, director of international equity research at MFS Investment Management, a mutual fund company in Boston, notes that Americans are using products made by Nokia, Ericsson, Sony, Toyota, BMW, Glaxo Wellcome and Nestlé all the time. "If these are the choices you have made day to day as the best products, why would you not want to invest in some of them?" he asks.

Other reasons for looking beyond our borders include the possibility for higher returns by finding values not available at home, and the chance to diversify, which can still provide investors some risk reduction, if not as much as previously thought. And while the correlations between Wall Street and foreign stock markets are now quite close, they could reverse, making diversification more valuable again.

But the clincher is that almost half of the world's market capitalization—stock prices times shares outstanding—is outside the United States, based on indexes compiled by Morgan Stanley Capital International. So if you choose to be an isolationist you are missing a lot of opportunities. "Limiting the population of choices you have to one country," Antonelli said, "is really selling yourself short."

Still, you have to be clear on why you are investing abroad. Are you doing it for return, for risk reduction or for a combination of both?

In any of those cases, there will be times when foreign stocks are more attractive and you might decide to tilt your commitment abroad to more than your usual percentage. Europe could be beginning an economic rally while the United States is slowing down, giving European stocks a better outlook. Or if the dollar is in a deci-sive downward trend, foreign exposure can help because your gains from abroad increase when they are translated back home.

But remember that widely accepted currency forecasts, like stock market forecasts, often do not come true. Most of those who bet on the new euro when it debuted in 1999 said it would be strong, forcing the dollar lower and making European stocks even more attractive to American investors. That turned out to be one of the worst fore-casts ever.

The best advice is to consider foreign stocks as a part of your portfolio while remembering that Bowers of Merrill Lynch advises, "You have to actively manage your international exposure." This doesn't mean trade all the time. It means pay attention. Wall Street is often swept by fads, and it is best not to get caught up in one. But if the world is changing, investment approaches have to change, too.

Looking at why Merrill Lynch has changed its approach to for-eign markets and how other strategists are adjusting can help inves-tors decide when and how to diversify abroad. For years, money managers and analysts have argued that the key reason for investing abroad is to lessen risk through diversification. Diversification can provide a collection of investments, spread across many markets, that have a tendency to move in opposite directions. This nega-tive correlation lessens the overall risk to an investor's portfolio, because when one market or stock is going down another would be going up.

In just the last few years, the data show that much of the foreign benefit has been lost because world markets follow the United States more closely than ever. They also tend to follow the United States even more closely when Wall Street is declining—just the time when American investors want the protection of diversification the most.

For those interested in statistics, the numbers make the case. On a scale from zero, for no correlation, to one, for perfect correlation, Merrill Lynch found that its measure of the correlation between the United States and the rest of the world's developed markets, including

Chart 6A

A Smaller World

From the late 1970s through the mid-1990s, stocks in the United States and abroad followed their own rhythms. Diversifying with some foreign stocks therefore tended to smooth out a portfolio's performance. More recently, American and foreign stocks have tended to move so closely in step that buying foreign stocks has hardly reduced risk.

In the chart, a figure of 1.0 means that American and foreign stocks always moved the same way; zero means they were no more likely to move together than in opposite ways.

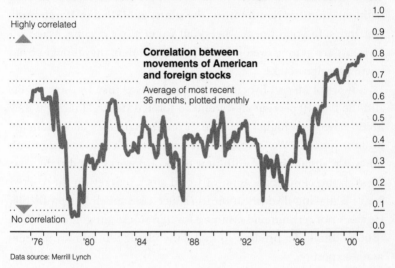

Data source: Merrill Lynch

currency movements, rose from 0.145 in 1993 (the lowest since 1979) to 0.786 at the end of May 2002. (Merrill compared foreign stock market performance to that in the United States using rolling monthly returns over three years, with each new month beginning a new three-year period.)

With this global narrowing of divergences, the usually close correlations between the United States and Europe have become closer still and so have the historically wider correlations with Japan and emerging markets. Ibbotson Associates, using a slightly more conservative approach of measuring rolling monthly returns over five-year periods, found similar patterns.

Although these numbers alone undermine the argument for

overseas diversification by country, a recent study adds fuel to the flame. Conducted by Kirt C. Butler of Michigan State University and Domingo Castelo Joaquin of Illinois State University, it shows that when the United States stock market goes into a tailspin, the rest of the world is even more likely to follow.

"An internationally diversified portfolio becomes riskier in bear markets because of higher volatility and greater correlation among national equity market returns," the study, published in March 2000, concludes. In other words, when Wall Street is in a decline, American investors are getting even less risk protection than they thought from buying foreign stocks.

Bowers of Merrill Lynch was taken aback, at first, by these results and the 0 to 10 percent allocations to foreign stocks. "I thought they would have been higher," he said of the foreign stock allocations. As he now puts it, "We have to come to grips with not how we think the world should be but with how the world works." And right now, he said, the close correlation of world stock markets to the United States is making diversification to reduce risks much less profitable. He does not recommend avoiding foreign stocks altogether, he said, "But we think it's prudent to make the change to a lower international exposure."

Other market strategists agree. Nicholas P. Sargen, the global market strategist for private clients at J. P. Morgan lowered his allocation guideline for foreign stocks to the 10 to 15 percent range at the end of 2000. "We overrode models that suggested more," he said. Rosemary Sagar, head of global investments at the United States Trust Company, said money managers there were lightening up on international stocks to reduce risks, the opposite of the common strategy before.

Even those who disagree are paying heed. James W. Paulsen, chief investment officer for Wells Capital Management, hasn't moved his foreign guideline, which is 21 percent. But he said the decline in risk reduction from diversifying abroad "has captured our attention," adding, "If it persists for a period, it will affect us."

This rising correlation of stock market performance results from common global economic policies and the diminished importance of a company's home base as businesses become more international. Since the 1980s, the economic policies of Western nations have been more aligned than ever. Global barriers against trade and capital flows have fallen. Central banks agree that inflation is the number one enemy, and they are determined to fight it. The introduction of the euro in 1999 has given Europe a homogeneity it never had. Telecommunication companies are the best example. Ericsson, Nokia and Vodafone move more and more to the rhythms of their global competitors than to those of the economies of Sweden, Finland and Great Britain, their home bases.

In the corporate world, mergers and acquisitions have given many more companies, in the United States and abroad, a global reach. Rapid communication, including the Internet, has also been a factor. Everybody around the world knows what happens to the Nasdaq composite index right away.

So when American stocks are falling, it is more likely foreign stocks are doing the same. "It is very comforting when there is a crash and you have something that isn't going down in another market," said Jeremy J. Siegel, author of *Stocks for the Long Run.* "But foreign equities won't give you that."

The world's markets have been so synchronized that Siegel has abandoned a strict allocation to international stocks. "Correlations have gone up and I don't think the returns from abroad have gone up enough to compensate for that," he said. The second edition of his now classic book, in 1998, recommended investing 25 percent of a stock portfolio outside the United States; Siegel now says that amount should be much less if one is investing by choosing countries.

Dumping foreign stocks based on the rising correlations is a gamble—and not every brokerage firm or analyst thinks it is a good idea. Some argue that lowered benefits of diversification may be temporary, more a product of the surge and fall in technology and Internet stocks, which rose and plunged in sync around the world, than a change in how a more global world is working. And just because you are clearly getting less risk reduction by diversifying abroad now does not mean you should turn your back. The correlations between domestic and foreign markets are not perfect. So there is still some benefit.

Roger G. Ibbotson, a professor of finance at the Yale School of Management, chairman of Ibbotson Associates and a longtime advocate of investing abroad, advises against cutting back—mostly because Americans have so little invested overseas to begin with. "Correlations have gone up, but nowhere to the extent that we should do less," he said.

Holding foreign shares will also allow investors to take advantage of those years, like 1993 and 1999, when foreign markets do better, as a whole, than the U.S. market.

The New Approach: Buying the Global Sectors

There is an alternative way to invest abroad. An American can have a handful of foreign stocks and reduce risks through diversification by using the relatively new global sector approach to investing. It is not an approach easy to do yourself, stock by stock. But more mutual fund groups are approaching the world this way. Some are offering sector funds. Others use sector biases to pick the stocks in their existing international or foreign stock funds. The growth of global sector indexes as new benchmarks to measure performance will produce more and more funds that follow these sectors.

The sector approach to investing was sparked by the switch to a single currency in Europe in 1999. The countries under the euro got one central bank, the European Central Bank, and one economic policy, significantly diminishing how much each country's economy affected its stock market. The single currency effectively broke down the barriers between stock markets, making analysts think about sectors, not countries. This shift was aided by the development of pan-

European stock indexes, which ignored borders, as new benchmarks for money managers.

"If all these countries are looking the same, I have to latch on to something else to differentiate between stocks," said Stefano Cavaglia, head of equity strategy at Brinson Partners in Chicago, an arm of UBS Asset Management. "We used to have all our analysts organized on a country line," he said. "That's gone. Everything is organized on an industry basis and all of the country directors have been reassigned." In 1999 Brinson began saying no when large institutions with money to manage said they wanted it handled on a country, or geographical, basis.

Putnam Investments, the Boston-based mutual fund, has also shifted its approach from one that concentrates on countries to one that focuses more and more on the performance of industries. "Sector is the biggest driving force," said Omid Kamshad, chief investment officer of international core equities there.

You don't pick Germany or Japan as this year's winner anymore and then get stocks in those markets. The winners now may be the energy sector or the drug sector, and you look globally for the best companies in those sectors, without regard to where they are based. "A company's market capitalization or the fact that it is part of the technology sector, for example, will become a more significant differentiator than whether the company is listed on the Norwegian or British stock exchange," said Sagar of United States Trust Company and another advocate of the sector approach.

New mutual funds based on sectors worldwide are popping up all over. There were twenty-four new global funds created in 2001 alone, most of them involving technology, telecommunications, the Internet and health care, according to Strategic Insight, a mutual fund research company. Another thirty were started in 2000 and nine more in 1998, totaling more than two-thirds of the global sector funds started since the first in 1985. Sargen said that J. P. Morgan began creating global technology, health care and financial sector funds for its private banking clients in 1999.

The index makers, like Morgan Stanley Capital International and Dow Jones Indexes, are creating new sector indexes as fast as they can. Morgan Stanley Capital International began creating sector indexes in 1994, and in 1999 established ten global indexes for developed countries, including utilities, telecommunications, information technology, financials, health care, consumer staples, consumer discretionary, industrials, materials and energy. At the beginning of 2000, Morgan Stanley announced a new group of sector indexes, which covers all countries, including emerging markets.

Dow Jones Indexes also started global sector indexes in 1994. "Nobody paid attention," Sheldon Gao, senior director for strategic development, said. But now interest is strong enough that in early 2000 Dow Jones released its Global Sector Titans, eighteen groups that each includes only the thirty biggest companies worldwide.

Merrill Lynch's advice to its private clients on what to do in this new environment is to lower the guideline for foreign stocks to zero percent for the least aggressive and most risk-averse investors. The guideline is 10 percent for the most aggressive investors. In the three risk categories in between the guideline is 5 percent to 10 percent.

Bowers, and his two colleagues, Douglas M. Wilde, a global investment strategist, and David A. Wilson, director of United States private client investment policy, are offering their clients two alternative ways of reducing risk. One is investing in the domestic bond market. Based on Ibbotson data, bonds are far less correlated to the moves of the American stock market than foreign stock markets. At end of 2001, that correlation had fallen to 0.02, with an average for the year of 0.15. A second alternative for Merrill Lynch is private equity funds, which involve a lot of venture capital investments. The correlations here are also very low, although this avenue of diversification is open to fewer individuals because of the high minimum investments required.

In practice, some investment advisers who remain more favorable to foreign investing like to combine the country and sector approaches. Though Cavaglia of Brinson Partners thinks the global sector approach offers a better way to choose stocks and diversify, he advises against switching entirely from choosing countries to choosing sectors. Besides giving up some of the remaining benefits of diversification by countries, a sector-only approach could, in some cases, leave investors' portfolios with a very large U.S. bias. So Cavaglia says that American investors should look for active money managers "who know that country and sector factors are important."

Putnam switched in 1997 to using a sector focus to pick stocks for its funds, but has not completely killed off country factors, Kamshad said. This is because investors can still profit from certain situations where country factors predominate. A company like a utility can still be tied closely to the performance of one country. Some retailers are in the same position. Because local factors can be important, Putnam uses sector analysis but does not offer many sector funds.

Another example of local opportunity can be found in Germany, where a broad reform of the tax code, approved in the summer of 2000, changed the landscape for a lot of companies and their stocks. The biggest change was the repeal of a capital gains tax on corporations that sell their shares in other German companies. This will revolutionize the structure of German business as big banks and insurance companies sell about $100 billion worth of shares in industrial companies like Siemens and DaimlerChrysler.

German cross-ownership, which the elimination of the capital gains tax should bring to an end, has impeded the kind of corporate restructuring that American companies began at the end of the 1980s. With that obstacle gone, there should be extra value in many German stocks, all from factors confined to Germany.

Katherine Schapiro, co–fund manager of the Wells Fargo International Equity Fund, said that country factors have the greatest impact on small and medium-size companies, which are not ready to be global, and on companies that do most of their business at home, like many basic materials or construction companies.

To many strategists now, however, sectors have the sway. "Sectors are more important as a diversifier and a driver of returns," Cavaglia said. Among those sectors that have developed to the global level are energy, pharmaceuticals, health care, technology and telecommunications.

Cavaglia and his colleagues concluded in an analysis that favoring companies based at home can be inefficient. In fact, Cavaglia's data show that spreading your investments across different sectors, rather than simply across different countries, provides stronger diversification, with reduced risks.

So do not be swept away by any tide against foreign stocks. Michigan State University professor Butler said that his own work, showing the higher correlations between world markets and the United States when Wall Street is in a tailspin, has not made him alter his portfolio, which is heavily weighted to foreign equities. He has held his ground because, he said, the closer correlation between the United States and world markets is due in large part to the rise in market volatility over the last few years. And if that volatility subsides with the bursting of the Internet bubble, then correlations may fall again.

Stan Kogelman, former head of private client research and strategy at Goldman Sachs, has seen nothing to persuade him to bring money home from foreign markets. "I am always cautious about taking too much from what has happened recently," he said. "I would be foolhardy to say that correlations will go down, but I also would be foolhardy to say that they will stay up. Let's think about it, but don't let's change our policy."

Even Bowers admits to some doubts, because he knows that market relationships can change quickly, just as they have in the past few years. "Is this the start of a new world order or is this just the time to get into international stocks?" he asks.

Proceeding, with Caution, in Emerging Markets

Emerging markets stretch from Asia to Africa and from Europe to Latin America. They are riskier than the world's developed country markets—yet still very alluring because of the huge gains they can provide.

Yet in the last few years, investors have had more anxiety than exhilaration and more big losses than huge gains. In fact, emerging markets, as a group, have not regained the peak they reached in September 1994, despite a huge rally that began in the fall of 2001.

They made a good run at it in 1997, but then the financial crisis in Asia proved how volatile and vulnerable these markets can be. Before its economy collapsed in 1998, Russia showed that a soaring emerging market can still attract investors who focus on giant returns and forget giant risks. Turkey's devaluation of its currency in early 2001 and Argentina's debt default, currency devaluation and subsequent economic collapse shortly after showed how instability persists.

What does this mix of risk and occasional big returns mean for investors? It means that emerging markets can be profitable but are not for the fainthearted. Don't get lured in, as many investors have been, by listening to stories of huge gains. One of the worst times to rush into emerging markets is just when they are doing their best.

You can approach these markets two ways. Many investors have bought the big-name telephone-company stocks, like Mexico's Telmex, and other stocks that are easy to purchase as American Depositary Receipts. Others get a broader range of stocks by investing in emerging markets mutual funds.

But in either case you must have a long-term view, longer than for American stocks and other foreign equities. At least five years is a good start.

This does not mean that once you put money into emerging markets you can't take it out. But it does mean that you need this type of commitment to increase your chance of coming out ahead, especially in view of recent performance. The five-year periods ending in 2001, 2000, 1999 and 1998 have had negative returns. In the periods before that, the returns are positive but have been declining since the 1993 peak for annual returns.

The risks also mean that you should limit what you invest in emerging markets. These markets are not for the money you hope to use to pay your child's college tuition. They are for that extra money that you can afford to lose. Several percentage points of all your stocks is a good beginning guideline. If the emerging markets go your way, this is a nice sweetener. But if they go against you, they do not sour your whole portfolio. Remember that while currency plays a role in all foreign investments, it can play a more volatile role in emerging markets. Sudden devaluations have produced big losses for investors.

After listing all these caveats, it is only fair to add that economic and financial reforms in emerging countries over the last two decades have made some of them less risky. The United States itself was an emerging market in the 1800s when Europeans invested in railroad stocks and bonds. At the turn of the nineteenth century, Russia was an emerging market, and is again today. Foreign investors put money into Argentina in the 1920s when it first shipped refrigerated meat to Europe.

After the 1929 crash and through World War II, emerging markets pretty much slipped off the investor radar screen. Then, in the 1950s, Sir John Templeton began investing in another emerging market—Japan. Despite its economic problems over the last decade, Japan proves, once again, that emerging markets can become fully developed.

The emerging market fad did not truly catch on until the 1980s, which is when they also got their current title. At the International Finance Corporation, an arm of the World Bank, Antoine Van Agtmael was promoting funds that would invest in what were then known as third world countries. At a conference in 1981, an investment banker told him that the name of one of his offerings, the Third World Equity Fund, was not very catchy. So Van Agtmael came up with Emerging Markets Growth Fund. And emerging markets stuck.

There is no precise definition of emerging markets. They tend to be countries whose economies are developing and, in many cases, growing much more rapidly than mature economies. Such rapid growth often produces soaring stock markets.

First World, Third World

Compared with American stocks, emerging markets are, as a group, more volatile. Stocks in other developed countries are no more volatile than American stocks, but neither did they enjoy as long a run of big gains in the bull market of the 1990s. Figures in the chart are for year-to-year price changes in dollar terms.

Emerging markets

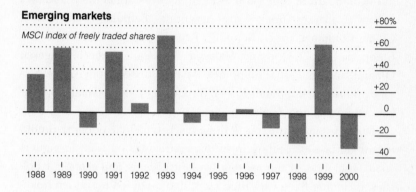

MSCI index of freely traded shares

Developed countries

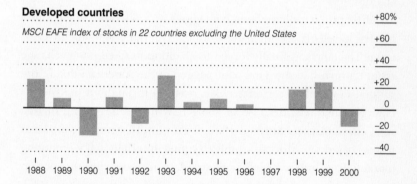

MSCI EAFE index of stocks in 22 countries excluding the United States

United States

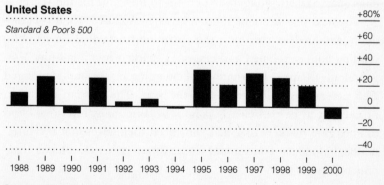

Standard & Poor's 500

Data source: Morgan Stanley Capital International

The emerging markets range from those whose exchanges are experimental to those with investment-grade credit ratings that are close to graduating from these ranks. Among the countries included in the Standard & Poor's and Morgan Stanley Capital International's emerging market indexes are Argentina, Bahrain, Brazil, Chile, China, Colombia, Czech Republic, Ecuador, Egypt, Hungary, India, Indonesia, Israel, Jordan, Malaysia, Mexico, Morocco, Nigeria, Oman, Pakistan, Peru, Philippines, Poland, Russia, Saudi Arabia, Slovakia, South Africa, South Korea, Sri Lanka, Taiwan, Thailand, Turkey, Venezuela and Zimbabwe.

The risks and drawbacks of these markets include political tumult, few or no laws protecting investors, restrictions on what foreigners could own, weak or nonexistent banking systems, and economic policies, including fixed exchange rates, that often led to sudden financial disasters.

Their problems have been contagious, so a sell-off in one country has led to sell-offs in other less-troubled emerging markets. In 1997, when Thailand was finally forced to abandon its fixed-rate exchange system, which had the Thai baht pegged to the American dollar, the sudden devaluation set off a chain reaction throughout the world's emerging markets. Because of a big rally in the beginning of that year, these markets finished 1997 down only 13.4 percent in dollar terms, based on Morgan Stanley Capital International's emerging markets free index, which is adjusted to include only the performance of stocks available to foreigners. But from the peak in 1997, emerging markets plunged 23 percent to their low for the year.

The next year brought another crisis. In August 1998, Russia suddenly devalued its currency, the ruble, and defaulted on its debt, sending both developed and emerging markets into a tailspin. Morgan Stanley Capital International's emerging market index plunged 27.5 percent in dollar terms for the year. The Russian downturn turned out to be particularly painful because many investors, blind to emerging market risks, had convinced themselves that the International Monetary Fund would rescue Russia rather than let its economy collapse.

Even with the 63.7 percent spurt in returns in 1999, in recent years emerging markets have been a lousy bet. After two fantastic years at the end of the 1980s and two in the early 1990s, these markets have spent more time plunging than climbing to new exhilarating heights. Since 1993, when these markets rose 71.3 percent, in dollar terms, they were down 41.2 percent through 2001, even with 1999's surge and a rally at the end of 2001.

Analysts at the International Monetary Fund, in a September 2000 report, concluded that the only allure for emerging markets is the potential for high returns. They said that emerging markets have become too closely correlated with Wall Street to provide the benefit of risk reduction through diversification, which had been an important argument for investing there.

Two other factors make investing in emerging markets difficult. One is that the performance can vary so sharply from one region to another that picking the right market can be crucial. Often, the star of one year falls the next while the previous year's laggard rallies. As the Securities and Exchange Commission requires Wall Street to remind investors, past performance does not predict future performance.

For example, in 1997 the Asian financial crisis pushed those emerging markets down more than 40 percent in dollar terms, while Latin American and European emerging markets rose nicely. But in 1998, when the crisis began in Russia and was expected to spread to Brazil, Latin American and European emerging markets dropped more than 30 percent while Asian markets limited their losses to 10 percent.

Another factor that investors have to remember is currency. The strength of the dollar and the weakness of emerging market currencies, whose value is often ravaged by inflation and devaluations, have slashed returns. When foreign currencies weaken against the dollar, the gains from those stock markets are reduced—or the losses increased—when they are translated back into dollars.

Based on the Morgan Stanley Capital International index, emerging markets have climbed 16,231 percent in local currencies from the end of 1987 to the end of 2001, but only 217 percent in dollar terms. Not too bad, but still only 60 percent of the return on the Standard & Poor's 500 stock index in the United States.

A falling currency, however, should not rule out an emerging market. It can signal a policy change that will benefit American investors. If the decline comes because the government is moving in the right direction on the economy, and the weaker currency makes the nation's companies more competitive abroad, then the results may drive stock prices higher. This was the case when Brazil was finally forced to devalue its currency, the real, in 1999. While the stock market jumped 141.4 percent that year in reals, the devaluation still left American investors with a gain of 61.6 percent in dollars.

Despite all the potential pitfalls, a small investment in emerging markets is still worth considering. For those with high risk tolerance, country funds or the new exchange traded funds that are indexes of a country's stock market could come in handy. These funds allow an investor to pick and choose, but require a lot of homework. Remember, the choosing may not add much in diversification benefits but will allow you to concentrate on the emerging markets or regions of your choice.

Investing in broader emerging markets mutual funds gives you the benefit of the money manager's expertise and is, therefore, easier, and could be less risky. But there you have to look closely at how the fund is invested, and how it has performed over at least five years. A fund could concentrate its money in telecommunications stocks, or in only a few countries. If that is the bet you want to make, you can buy American Depositary Receipts for foreign companies on American stock exchanges and have control over the buying and selling decisions. In looking at a fund's record, check 1997 and 1998, the bad years, and 1999, a good year, for clues about whether the managers can outperform the market in all conditions.

The big currency risk is harder to deal with. There are mutual funds that hedge against it and there are those that don't. It is probably easier to just accept currency as part of the volatility.

Despite their volatile history, some emerging markets are becoming less risky, especially when many others are in turmoil. Economic reforms and political changes over the last twenty years are pushing a few emerging markets close to developed market status and making others more stable. "Would I give them a clean bill of health?" asks Van Agtmael. "No. But have they fundamentally changed? Yes."

Hyperinflation has become rare. Turkey, with consumer prices rising at a 46 percent annual rate, and Venezuela, with prices up 18 percent, are at the high end. Mexico's annual inflation is around 5 percent.

After the financial crises of 1997 and 1998, the International Monetary Fund has assisted emerging market countries when economic problems have arisen, but, as seen in Argentina in 2001 and 2002, not always to success.

Emerging countries are moving to flexible exchange rates, opening their economies and lessening their vulnerability to nasty economic shocks like those in 1997 and 1998. The move away from fixed exchange rates makes it less likely that their currencies will suddenly collapse. In addition, the contagion factor, the spread of one country's or region's problems elsewhere, may be reduced. "The fact that you have flexible exchange rates means you will still have problems but they won't be the same nightmare as before," said Desmond Lachman, director of emerging markets economic research at Salomon Smith Barney. Turkey's devaluation of its currency, the lira, in early 2001 came with minimal fallout in the rest of the emerging markets.

Some of these emerging markets are likely to graduate into the developed category. "Poland, Hungary, Korea and the Czech Republic are further along the developed path," according to Lachman. Van Agtmael adds Israel and Taiwan to this list.

Mexico graduated when its debt denominated in dollars was raised to investment grade in February 2002, just eight years after the United States engineered a financial rescue. And South Korea already is investment grade, although it is still struggling with corporate and financial reforms.

But others could still fool you. In January 2001 Greece entered Euroland, the nickname for the countries now joined under the common currency, the euro. Greece was soon removed from popular emerging market indexes, but some analysts argue that it may still be more of an emerging market than not.

The lesson is that investors face more subtle decisions because emerging markets are no longer a generalized class that you can throw your money at. "One can fall into traps by overgeneralizing," Lachman warns. But with careful thought, either by picking countries and stocks yourself or by choosing good money managers, emerging markets, as a small portion of your portfolio, can offer you both added excitement and added profits over the long term.

- Emerging markets are risky, so keep your investment small.
- Annual returns are volatile, so keep your time horizon long.
- Compare fund records in poor performance years (1997 and 1998) and stronger years (1999) to see if managers are consistently outperforming the market.

Currency Risks

Most Americans think about currencies only when they are traveling. But if they are investing abroad, currency is the other moving part in their portfolios.

At home, stocks go up or down and at the end of the year the change is the simple gain or loss. In the rest of the world's markets—with few exceptions—there is another necessary calculation: how much the dollar has moved against the currencies of those foreign markets.

When a foreign currency falls in value against the dollar, it's negative for American investors. Put the other way, a rising dollar cuts into profits or increases losses from investing abroad.

These movements can have a major impact on your investment, sometimes overwhelming the performance in the foreign stock or bond market, for good or ill. A 9 percent drop in Japan's benchmark Nikkei 225 index in 1998 was turned into a 4 percent gain for American investors after the dollar fell in value against the yen that year.

Analysts sometimes make a lot of movements in currencies, using them as a reason to recommend investment abroad. If you can get a dollar trend right, it can be profitable. For most investors, however, it is better to first decide to invest abroad based on the stocks you want buy and the opportunities.

Hedging can take some or all of the risk out of currency movements by using futures contracts or other derivatives to lock in a set value for the dollar against a foreign currency. Hedging, however, can be expensive, sometimes costing several percentage points of return. It is not easy for an individual investor to do, so you have to choose a money manager or mutual fund that hedges. In addition, if an investor or fund hedges against a rising dollar (which means, for example, a falling euro) and the dollar falls instead, the investor does not get any benefit from a stronger foreign currency and still pays the cost of hedging.

For many mutual fund groups, hedging is the exception. Putnam Investments, a mutual fund company based in Boston, does hedge occasionally. "When we feel that any currency is very overvalued against the United States dollar, we would hedge it," according to Omid Kamshad, chief investment officer of international core equities at Putnam. A currency that is very overvalued against the dollar is likely to decline soon, he believes, cutting into returns for Americans. But Kamshad reports that, in the 1990s, currency was not a major factor in the performance of Putnam's International Growth Fund. Stock selection, sector selection and country selection, he said, accounted for more than 90 percent of the fund's performance.

David Antonelli, director of international equity research at MFS Investment Management, also based in Boston, said that he does not hedge, in part because he doubts he can get the currency direction right often enough to offset the cost of hedging. "When you hedge, you presume you know where the currency is going and we think that is a hard call to make," he said. "We want to rely on our stock-selecting abilities." In other words, while currency moves can rattle your portfolio, just picking the right stocks is hard enough.

Over both the long term and the short term the dollar's movement has been confounding. Since the dollar was taken off the gold standard and allowed to trade freely early in the 1970s, the value of the dollar has been in decline against two of the world's other major currencies, the Japanese yen and the German mark, which is being replaced by the euro. This decline has added to the returns from abroad for American investors.

The dollar's decline against the Japanese yen since 1973 has brought American investors more in gains than the Japanese stock market itself. The Nikkei 225 stock index is up 145 percent in yen terms, through 2001. In dollar terms, however, the Nikkei is up 421 percent, because during the same period the dollar fell 53 percent against the yen.

In Germany, the story is the same, although not as dramatic. Germany's DAX index of thirty stocks is up 1,202 percent in local currency from 1973 through 2001. With the 19 percent decline of the dollar figured in, it is up 1,502 percent.

Against the British pound, however, and other European currencies, like the French franc, the value of the dollar has been rising, cutting sharply into returns for Americans from those markets. During this period the dollar has jumped 60 percent against the British pound and 57 percent against the French franc. Many emerging market currencies, which have been trading freely for a shorter period of time, are also in a long-term downtrend against the dollar, reducing returns for Americans.

Shorter-term movements in major foreign currencies have also gone both ways, demonstrating again the risks of betting on direction.

Exchange Rate Effects

How are stocks faring overseas? The answer often depends on the currency in which an investor gauges returns. Benchmark stock indexes measure performance in local currency. But that currency's exchange rate may vary considerably, yielding a much different performance for an American investor who thinks in dollars.

The chart shows annual changes in the principal stock indexes for Japan and Germany in local currency and in dollars. In some years, the indexes rose by one measure but fell by the other because of shifting exchange rates.

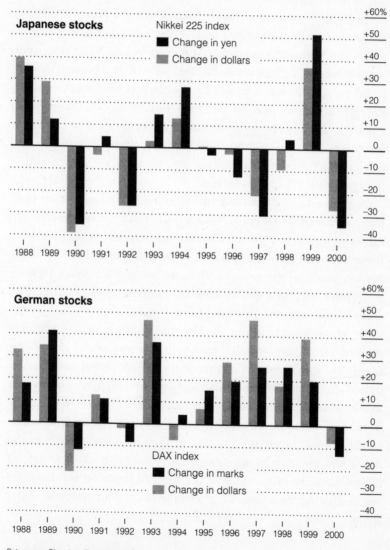

Data source: Bloomberg Financial Markets

The declining euro has been a drag on returns for Americans since it was introduced. In 1999 Germany's DAX stock index surged 39.1 percent in euro terms but climbed only 20 percent in dollar terms, after a decline of 13.8 percent in the euro. As a further example, in 2001 the 19.8 percent decline in the DAX index grew to 24.3 percent fall in dollar terms.

In Japan, on the other hand, Americans got a boost in 1999 as a dollar decline of 9.8 percent against the yen lifted a 36.8 percent rise in the Nikkei 225 index to a 51.6 percent gain. But a dollar rally in 2000 turned a 27.2 percent Nikkei loss to a 34.8 percent decline.

When you invest in a mutual fund or buy an American Depositary Receipt, a popular way to purchase foreign stocks, the currency impact just shows up in the dollar profits or losses. You can figure out the currency impact by checking the underlying currency and foreign stock movements. You can also translate the movements of foreign indexes into dollar terms.

At the end of 2000 a share of Volkswagen, the German car company, was worth 55.69 euros. That left the stock virtually unchanged for the year. But in 2000 the euro fell 6.3 percent against the dollar. It was worth 94.3 cents at the end of the year, down from $1.006 at the beginning of the year. So when an investor translates Volkswagen's stock back into dollars, its value declines, giving an American a negative return of 6.4 percent for the year.

To make this calculation, multiply the stock's value—or a foreign stock index's value—by the euro value to translate it into dollar terms. The euro's value, like that of the British pound and the Australian dollar, is quoted in the number of American dollars it is worth. Most other currencies, like the Japanese yen and the Swiss franc, are quoted in the number of yen or francs the dollar is worth. In these cases, divide the number of foreign currency units to the dollar into the value of the foreign stock or foreign index. Once you have figured the dollar value of the stock or index on the dates you are comparing, do a percentage change to get your return in dollar terms.

With the emergence of the euro, the difficulties of investing in Europe have diminished because there are fewer bouncing balls to watch. And there is intermittent talk of other currency unions in Asia and Latin America. For the time being, however, you can only accept the risk that currency adds to investing abroad and then choose how to live with it.

- Currency movements add risk, and can either improve or damage your returns. You can hedge to reduce currency risk, but the expenses can be high.
- Betting on the direction of international stocks is safer than betting on the direction of currencies.

How to Buy Foreign Stocks and Bonds

Picking stocks is a difficult game under any circumstances. But choosing foreign stocks is more difficult, given the differences between the United States and other countries in accounting, language and access to information.

That is why it is easiest to get your exposure to foreign stocks through mutual funds, where professionals do the choosing. Of course, you still have to look carefully for your mutual fund. This means checking a fund's record and where it has invested its money. You can be getting less foreign exposure or diversity than you think, or be in countries or regions that make you uncomfortable. You can also choose between actively managed funds and ones that just follow the stock indexes of countries, regions or the whole developing world. And you can find funds that hedge against currency fluctuations. As always, you have to consider the expenses of each fund you are interested in before deciding.

It is getting easier to pick foreign stocks yourself, and cheaper, if you are interested in only a few foreign stocks. There are well-known foreign companies whose stocks are traded in the United States, either as what are called American Depositary Receipts or as shares listed directly on an American exchange. Many of these are foreign telephone companies but they also include corporations like Nortel Networks and Royal Dutch Petroleum. Here, to help choose an avenue, is a closer look at how to invest abroad.

Some types of mutual funds give you more foreign exposure than others, so you have to be careful about what you choose. What are called foreign, or international, stock funds generally invest most of their money outside the United States. Along with regional mutual funds and single-country funds, they are a way to concentrate your exposure abroad.

Global funds, the other major category, have stocks from around the world including the United States. If they are your entire stock portfolio, they could give you more foreign exposure than you want. But if a global fund serves as only the foreign part of your portfolio, it could give you added domestic exposure that you do not want.

Unfortunately, there is no set percentage of foreign stocks that a foreign or global equity fund has to hold. So you have to check how much of a fund's money is invested overseas, and where. It can be concentrated in a few countries or even just a few stocks.

Morningstar (www.morningstar.com), which tracks mutual fund performance, counts as foreign stock funds those that have 90 percent or more of their money abroad. Of the 371 funds in this category, twenty-six are index funds, which means they just buy the stocks in a particular international index. The others are actively managed, with stocks and countries that can vary. According to Morningstar, foreign stock funds, at the end of 2001, had 65 percent of their money in Europe; 17 percent in Japan; 11 percent in the Pacific Rim excluding Japan; 2 percent in Latin America; and 5 percent in the United States and Canada. If you want to concentrate your international investments outside of Europe, you will therefore have to look at regional or even country funds.

Regional foreign funds concentrate their investments in Europe, Latin America, Asia excluding Japan, the Pacific (which includes

Japan) or some emerging markets. Check these carefully to see where the money is. Any of these funds might put more in the riskier emerging markets than you want. Or a Pacific mutual fund may put more in Japan than you want. Morningstar tracks several of these regional funds.

A new Securities and Exchange Commission truth-in-labeling rule requires that a fund put "at least 80 percent of its assets in investments that are tied economically to the particular country or geographic region suggested by its name." Mutual funds had to comply by July 31, 2002.

While their portfolio diversification benefits may not be big, single-country funds do allow an investor to choose very specific foreign exposure. New exchange traded funds, which are essentially single-country index funds, also offer such a choice.

A special category of country funds are among what are known as closed-end funds. Because shares in these funds are limited to a set number, their price can rise or fall both as investor demand for the shares shifts and as the stocks in the fund's portfolio go up or down. Because the performance of a closed-end country fund depends on investors' interest in that country's stocks, the shares usually trade at a premium or a discount to the value of the underlying stocks. A big discount means investors don't find the closed-end fund or the country—or both—very attractive. As investing in single-country funds has fallen in favor, the net asset value of closed-end country funds has dropped from a peak of $16.7 billion in 1996 to $8.2 billion in 2001, according to Michael T. Porter, director of global research at Clemente Capital. The number of these funds, meanwhile, has declined to sixty-three, representing twenty-seven countries, from eighty-four in 1995. But the key sign of investor disfavor is the discount. At the end of 2001, they were trading at an average discount of 15 percent.

Exchange traded funds offer a less complicated way to invest by countries. Most of these foreign E.T.F.s, which are priced in dollars, trade on the American Stock Exchange and are based on single-country indexes designed by Morgan Stanley Capital International.

Twenty countries are covered by E.T.F.s, which are called iShares. As with most other foreign funds and stocks traded here, investors still face currency risk. Lists of these funds can be found on the American Stock Exchange Web site (www.amex.com).

Global sector funds are becoming popular with some investors as a new approach to investing abroad. But beware, in some cases these funds offer much less foreign exposure than global or international funds, with more than 75 percent of their money in American and Canadian stocks. Many of these were technology sector funds.

While the global sector funds introduced so far are actively managed, aiming to pick the best companies in an industry, Barclays Global Investors launched five exchange traded funds based on global sector indexes late in 2001.

The broadest offerings are global or world stock funds, which invest everywhere, including the United States. Morningstar follows 113 of these. None are index funds. With these funds, you have to be especially aware of your exposure to foreign stocks, which can vary far more widely than with foreign or international funds. Morningstar defines a world fund as one that invests more than 10 percent outside of the United States. In 2001 the average U.S. and Canadian exposure in global funds was 51 percent, according to Morningstar. The rest of the major categories were Europe at 31 percent; Japan at 8 percent; the Pacific Rim excluding Japan at 6 percent; and Latin America at 2 percent. The emphasis on the United States and Canada could be more than you want if you already have enough money invested domestically.

In 2001, a year of sharp declines in stock markets around the world, actively managed foreign stock funds, according to Morningstar, fell 20.7 percent. The international funds based on indexes dropped 22.6 percent. Global funds dropped 15.9 percent.

In choosing among these mutual fund alternatives, you have to be clear about your foreign investing goals. With foreign and regional funds, unlike global funds, you can make fairly precise decisions about how much to invest abroad and, to a large extent, about where. You also leave yourself the opportunity to find different money managers or styles for your domestic investments. But remember that foreign and regional funds are more committed to foreign stocks than global funds and will, therefore, have more of their money abroad when those markets are falling. That means the decision on getting out is left to you.

If you use global funds, you are getting additional domestic exposure (though if all your money is in such a fund, you probably have far more foreign exposure than you want). While your money manager can move in and out of foreign markets based on the outlook, the nearly 50 percent invested abroad in 2001 in these global funds was a big bet.

You can also decide how much currency risk you want. Like the choice between a fixed-rate and an adjustable-rate mortgage, your strategy is determined by your risk tolerance. Some mutual funds hedge against currency fluctuations, or even try to profit from them. But fund managers who don't hedge say that the expense isn't worth it. Over the long run, many managers see that their returns depend much more on the performance of their stock picks than on the movements of currencies. But others say you have to try to profit from a decline in the dollar when you can.

Americans can buy foreign stocks individually, although this is not the best approach for most investors to assemble a diversified portfolio of stocks from abroad. Investors who prefer buying individual foreign stocks can choose either American Depositary Receipts or shares that are directly listed on American exchanges. Lists of these A.D.R.s and foreign stocks can be found on the exchange Web sites (the New York Stock Exchange, www.nyse.com; the Nasdaq, www.nasdaq.com; and the American Stock Exhange, www.amex.com).

However, the country variety is limited. Of the companies traded at the end of 2000 on the New York Stock Exchange, the Nasdaq and the American Stock Exchange as either A.D.R.s or direct listings, 24 percent were from Canada, 11 percent were from the United Kingdom and 10 percent were from Israel. About 40 percent of just the directly listed stocks are Canadian. And just because a foreign stock is listed here directly does not make it a good choice. There are some that are no better than penny stocks.

An American Depository Receipt is a certificate, issued by a bank, representing a share, or sometimes several shares, of a foreign stock. They are priced in dollars and trade like American stocks. Most of the best-known companies trading here—Allianz of Germany, LVMH Moet Hennessy Louis Vuitton of France and Nippon Telegraph and Telephone of Japan—are A.D.R.s listed on the main exchanges. Remember that A.D.R.s still pose a currency risk, with their value reflecting currency fluctuations in a company's home market. The A.D.R. can do better than the underlying stock if the dollar weakens, and worse if the dollar strengthens.

As of the end of 2001, there were depository receipts trading on the New York Stock Exchange, the American Stock Exchange and Nasdaq for more than five hundred foreign companies. Those traded on the exchanges conform to American accounting rules and send investors financial reports. In addition, there were nine hundred A.D.R.s that traded in the over-the-counter market. Unlisted A.D.R.s do not meet American accounting standards and are not required to send financial reports to investors. Their prices are not published in newspapers, but are supplied by traders, who determine them based on their perceptions of their own risks.

Most A.D.R.s are sponsored by the companies, while about 225 are not. Without such sponsorship, there can be more than one bank issuing an A.D.R. for the same foreign company. Except for A.D.R.s on the New York Stock Exchange, the investor is charged a fee for distribution of dividends. The Bank of New York has a Web site (www.adrbny.com) that answers many questions about A.D.R.s.

The number of foreign stocks listing directly on the New York Stock Exchange, Nasdaq and Amex is about 550 and growing. As with A.D.R.s, they trade in dollars and carry currency risks.

Another way some analysts recommend to get foreign exposure is buying American companies that do much of their business overseas. But this is a very limited approach, in part because you may own a lot of these companies already. As much as 40 percent of the earnings for the companies in the Standard & Poor's 500 index comes from abroad. There is still currency risk, if the company does not hedge, because earnings from abroad can shrink or grow based on the strength or weakness of the dollar. The plunge of the euro in 1999, 2000 and 2001 cut into the earnings of many of these multinational companies. For those interested, Morgan Stanley Capital International has an index of fifty American companies that get a substantial portion of their returns from abroad. Among them are Boeing, Cisco Systems, Coca-Cola, Exxon Mobil, General Electric, Merck and Procter & Gamble.

- Mutual funds can give you a diversified portfolio of foreign stocks, but be clear on what type of exposure your fund will give you. Always check how much and where your fund is investing abroad, especially since some funds might duplicate your domestic investments.
- Some well-known foreign companies can be bought on American exchanges. They meet American accounting standards, but beware of their currency risks.

7.

Taxes: How to
Protect Your Gains

DAVID CAY JOHNSTON

After doing all that hard work to pick winning investments, and learning to live with the ups and downs of the market, you face one more hurdle before reaping your rewards. You must minimize taxes on your investments. Even exceptional pretax returns can become just mediocre returns, or worse, unless you take care to pay as little tax as the law allows.

Congress has been friendly to investors in recent years, cutting taxes overall, lowering rates for those who hold on for the long haul and expanding opportunities to invest through Roth accounts, where capital gains, dividends, interest and royalties can all be tax-free if you follow the new rules. You can pay taxes on your gains at rates that, in 2002, ranged from 38.6 percent down to zero depending on what you invest in, how long you hold on to your winners and the type of investment account you choose.

These tax breaks have come at a price. Each has its own rules. And the rules are as harsh as they are specific. Sell a winning stock one day too soon and your tax bill can be nearly double. Indeed, you can even owe penalties that will confiscate an extra 10 percent of your gains above regular tax rates when you cash in a retirement account before reaching age 59½.

You also need to keep thorough records of your investments to prove what you paid and to determine your net gain. The Internal Revenue Service will often walk away from an initial inquiry when auditors encounter a taxpayer who can document every transaction. Those who keep their trading records in a shoe box, or throw them out, make themselves easy targets for the I.R.S.

While you need to think about taxes, and keep thorough records, you should not let taxes rule your investment decisions. Pay attention first and foremost to whether you have made the right investment choices. Then think about taxes. Holding a stock that has ballooned in value beyond any reasonable expectation just to avoid paying taxes can be disastrous. The law limits the percentage of your gains that can go to taxes to a maximum of 38.6 percent, the highest income tax rate, in 2002 and less in the future. A stock, however, can quickly lose a much larger percentage of its value, as investors learned in 2000 when some of the largest high-tech companies fell more than 90 percent from their peaks.

First, the Basics: Capital Gains

When you sell a stock that has risen in value you usually owe taxes on what are called capital gains. Starting in 1997, Congress enacted several new rules allowing significant breaks on these gains, and even an opportunity to completely avoid taxes on them. In general, you should hold winning investments longer than a year and a day to avoid paying taxes at the same rate as you do on your paycheck. And if you can find a winner worth keeping at least five years and a day, Congress gave most investors another 10 percent discount on their capital gains tax bill.

Capital gains taxes apply only to the increase in the value of the stock, bond or other property when it is sold. For example, if you bought 100 shares of stock, or shares in a mutual stock fund, for $10,000, including commissions, and sold them for $15,000, after commissions, then you would owe taxes on the $5,000 profit. If you bought a bond, or shares in a bond fund, for $10,000 and, because of falling interest rates, you sold for $11,000, you would owe taxes on the $1,000 gain. The price you paid for a security, plus commissions, is known as the "basis." When you sell, you deduct any commissions or sales charges to determine your net sales price.

To understand how to minimize your taxes, you need to know about the four categories of capital gains:

1. Short-Term Gains

You'll pay the top rate if you sell a winning investment in fewer than 366 days. The profits will be taxed just like your everyday income— at top rates that will remain between 30 and 40 percent even after the tax cuts enacted in 2001. A profit of $5,000 on a short-term gain could net Uncle Sam nearly $2,000. So don't sell winning stocks in the first year unless you fear a substantial loss, face only small gains or *really* need the money now.

2. Long-Term Gains

If you hold out for at least a year and a day, the tax laws smile on you with more favorable, long-term capital gains rates. Congress counts the day a trade is made, not when it settles. Moderate and middle-class wage earners, in the 15 percent income tax brackets or the new 10 percent bracket, will pay only 10 percent on their profits. Everyone in the higher brackets pays 20 percent. Someone in the 15 percent bracket who holds $10,000 of stock for at least a year and a day, and sells it for $15,000, would pay only $500 in taxes on the $5,000 gain. Those in higher tax brackets would pay $1,000. But that tax break may not be worth the wait if you think the market will take away a significant portion of your gains.

3. Special Long-Term Gains

For those great long-term growth stocks, Congress gave you another reason besides inertia to resist taking your profits. If you bought a stock after January 1, 2001, and hold it for five years and a day, you will be eligible for reduced long-term capital gains. The rates are 8 percent for those in the 10 or 15 percent income tax brackets, and 18 percent for those in the higher brackets. Imagine you bought $10,000 of stock after January 1, 2001, and hold it for at least five years and a day before selling it for $15,000. If you are in the 15 percent tax bracket you would pay just $400 in taxes on your $5,000 gain. Those in the higher brackets would all pay $900.

Those in the new 10 or 15 percent brackets can also apply the special 8 percent rate to any stock they sell after January 1, 2001, that they have held for five years and a day. This is especially advantageous if you give stock to children who sell at age fourteen or older, when they are no longer taxed at the parents' rate. Compared with selling at the usual 20 percent rate, the child's 8 percent rate cuts the tax bill by more than half.

4. Roth Gains

There is no tax on capital gains (or dividends, interest or other income) in a Roth retirement account if you observe all the rules, which will be discussed in the section in this chapter on retirement accounts. So if you want to do some short-term trading it may be best to do it in a Roth account because capital gains taxes will not take a bite out of your returns. Keep in mind, though, that transaction costs can also eat into your returns, and that, as numerous studies have shown, frequent traders seldom gain as much as those who stick with their stocks for long periods.

You can also trade in your individual retirement account and some 401(k)s and similar plans without incurring immediate taxes. (See the retirement plan investing section beginning on page 190 for the details.)

Capital Losses, or Deductible Mistakes

Of course, not all stocks will be winners. And bonds can sour, as well. Learning to sell losers, and knowing when, are important to taking full advantage of the tax laws and earning superior returns. Luckily, the law lets you deduct your losses, within limits, when you sell stocks, bonds or fund shares for less than you bought them.

If you have taken any capital gains during the year by selling winners, then you should look over your portfolio in the last two months of the year to see if you have any losers you may want to sell. Here, again, don't let tax strategy rule your investment decisions: don't sell a stock you think will rebound. But tax considerations can help you decide to admit a mistake and clear out of a stock whose recovery is in doubt. You can use your losses to avoid taxes on capital gains. Thus if you bought stock for $10,000 and sold it for $5,000, the resulting $5,000 loss could offset the $5,000 gain in the example above. With the right timing, you can control your capital gains tax exposure while systematically culling the losers from your portfolio.

But pay attention to the rules: Short-term losses offset short-term gains. Long-term losses offset long-term gains. Once you have fully offset corresponding gains, then any losses can eliminate taxes on any sort of gains. Given that short-term gains are taxed at the highest rates, they are the most worth balancing with losses.

If you have only capital losses, or if your losses exceed your gains, you can deduct these losses against earned income, such as wages, dividends, interest, rents and royalties. This deduction, however, is limited to $3,000 for an individual, head of household or married couple filing jointly and to $1,500 per spouse for married couples filing separately. Capital losses greater than $3,000 ($1,500 for those filing separately) are carried forward and can be taken as deductions against capital gains in future years or, if there are no gains, against future earned income. There is no adjustment for inflation, so the value of any deferred loss declines over time.

Thus, if you bought stock for $10,000, and the company went out of business, making your investment worthless, you can use this $10,000 loss to offset up to $10,000 of gains if both the loss and the gain are either long-term or short-term. If you had no capital gains then or for several more years, you could deduct only $3,000 against your earned income and would have to carry $7,000 forward, deducting $3,000 in the second and third years and $1,000 in the fourth year.

To time some of your worst losses, you'll want to consider selling a stock or bond before it becomes worthless. When a security is declared worthless, the tax laws construe your loss as happening on the last day of that year. A short-term loss you could use to avoid taxes on your most heavily taxed gains could therefore turn into a long-term loss.

The character of your capital loss remains the same each year that you carry it forward. A short-term capital loss is always treated as short-term loss, and a long-term capital loss is always treated as long-term.

Avoiding the Trading Trap

Frequent traders should be careful to avoid a "wash sale," which prevents you from taking a capital loss on your income tax return. If you buy securities within thirty days before or after you sell similar or identical securities at a loss, you cannot take the loss on your tax return until you have disposed of all of the securities. In the government's view, you haven't actually sold anything, and may have done all the transactions solely to avoid taxes. You can not buy until the thirty-first day after the losing sale.

The rule is broad enough so that if you own one mutual company's Standard & Poor's 500 index fund, you cannot sell it and then buy another 500 index. You could, however, sell a 500 index and buy a total stock market index. You also can sell a losing position in a company that has announced plans to merge with another company and buy shares of the other company, without creating a wash sale.

To minimize taxes, try to wait at least a year and a day to take your gains, or five years and a day if you can. Time the sale of your losers to avoid taxes on your gains, as well as on your ordinary income. But watch out: The rules are complicated. And never let tax strategy trump sound investment decisions.

Retirement Plans: Everybody's Tax Breaks

To encourage you to save for retirement, Congress has granted tax breaks that let you make tax-deductible contributions, as well as after-tax contributions where your investment gains are either taxed at withdrawal or never. While the opportunity to save now and be taxed later is usually understood to be the smartest tax strategy, one of the new rules is that an immediate tax deduction is sometimes a bad deal. If you defer taxes when you are in the bottom income tax bracket, for example, and then withdraw when you are in the highest bracket, you lose. Under the new rules, by paying taxes today you can often put more money in your pocket when you withdraw funds years or decades later.

Despite significant differences in how they work, all the retirement savings plans are such great deals that you should put as much money as you can into accounts that let your savings grow either tax-deferred or, even better, tax-free.

If your employer offers a 401(k) or similar retirement savings plan, your first priority should be to save as much money as your employer will match so that you capture that extra income. To avoid having to dip into these funds before retirement, and pay income taxes on your withdrawal plus a stiff 10 percent penalty, you should save enough cash outside your retirement accounts to tide you through the loss of a job or an illness. As discussed in chapter 2, make your goal at least three months of take-home pay at the early stages of your career, and six months later in your career.

Your second priority should be to put money into Roth accounts because your investment gains can be withdrawn free of income taxes. If you make too much money to qualify for a Roth I.R.A. (see the section below for the limits), a new rule taking effect in 2006 will extend this opportunity to you, by allowing Roth 401(k) plans on the same terms as traditional 401(k) plans. In all Roth plans, unlike traditional retirement savings plans, there are no required withdrawals, making Roths excellent vehicles to leave tax-free income to children, grandchildren and other heirs.

Your trading and investment strategies should be different for tax-deferred or tax-free accounts than for your taxable accounts. In general, use your tax-advantaged accounts for transactions and investments that would otherwise generate the highest tax bills. These accounts—which are also known as "qualified" plans because they qualify for favorable tax treatment—are the places to concentrate your trading. If you sell one stock that has run up in value to buy another with more potential in these accounts, you do not need to give a moment's thought to capital gains taxes.

You also do not need to worry that higher rates apply to dividends and interest than to capital gains. But make sure that you invest only in taxable investments to take advantage of tax deferrals. It would be foolish to buy tax-free municipal bonds in a retirement account. And remember that investment losses in these accounts are not deductible.

Traditionally, retirement accounts have been regarded as the best places for stocks that pay hefty dividends and for corporate bonds. Instead of being immediately taxed, the entire income from these investments can be reinvested. And the availability of tax-free income from municipal bonds has prompted some financial advisers to recommend buying these for your taxable accounts and concentrating stocks and stock funds of all sorts in your retirement account. For more tips on how to identify bonds with low or no tax burdens, see chapter 5.

If you invest in mutual funds, put any that trade frequently in your retirement accounts. High turnover can reduce the annual gains, before taxes, that the mutual fund companies advertise by 20 percent or more, creating a serious drag on your long-term after-tax returns. For stock index funds, which rarely trade, the annual tax cost is minimal, so buy them for both taxable and tax-deferred, or tax-free Roth, accounts. For more on mutual funds and your taxes, see chapter 4.

The rules for all retirement accounts apply to each worker, not to couples, because these are individually owned. If the maximum you and your spouse each can save a year in a tax-deferred retirement plan, like a 401(k), is $11,000, then together you can save $22,000.

Employer Savings Plans: 401(k)s and Their Siblings

Retirement savings plans can be divided into two types: those where money is deducted from your paycheck and those where you set aside the money yourself.

Much of your investing is likely to take place in accounts like 401(k)s, available to all workers; 403(b) plans for nonprofit sector workers; and 457 plans, usually for government workers. In all of these, your employer sets aside an amount you specify from your paycheck. Up to legal limits, contributions to these accounts can be made in pretax dollars, although Social Security and Medicare taxes still apply. Only 401(k) plans, though, can include a Roth feature, beginning in 2006, which requires after-tax contributions but also allows tax-free withdrawals.

Employers often match some of the money contributed to these plans. The first rule in using these payroll deduction plans is to collect every matching dollar you can. If your employer will contribute twenty-five cents on each dollar you save up to the first 6 percent of your pay, one of the most widely used formulas, you can have 7.5 percent of your pay working for you in your retirement plan. The matching contribution from your employer is like getting a 1.5 percent pay raise.

Think of the match as the employer paying your income taxes for you, instead of deducting them from your check. In the example above, the employer's match makes up one-fifth of your retirement plan savings. When you retire, every fifth dollar you withdraw will have come from the match by your employer, which is enough to pay much or all of the taxes on your withdrawals.

A warning: Some employers describe their match in ways that discourage employees from appreciating its value. Some companies tell workers that they will give them "three cents" in match money, suggesting to some workers that for each dollar saved the worker gets three cents. In fact, the employer probably is giving a match of up to 3 percent of salary—often a match that is dollar for dollar, or 100 percent, on the first 3 percent of their salaries that workers save in their retirement plans.

Starting in 2002, the amounts that can be saved pretax in 401(k), 403(b) and 457 plans each year will rise, to catch up and then keep pace with inflation. The maximum for 401(k)s was raised to $11,000 in 2002, plus an extra $1,000 for those age fifty and older. These limits will continue to rise by $1,000 annually until 2006 when they reach $15,000 plus $5,000 for those fifty and older. The amounts will then be adjusted annually for inflation.

It may be impossible to save exactly $11,000 in 2002 or the maximum in other years because most plans require you to designate a percentage of your pay. If you make more money, maybe because of commissions and overtime, than you anticipated, and therefore save more than $11,000, one of two things happens. Some employers will automatically stop your contributions from your paycheck when you reach the maximum allowed by law. Others will allow you to make after-tax contributions above the limits. (Some will even let workers choose a percentage of their pay that is certain to exceed the limits. In this case the extra money will go into your 401(k) plan, but you will owe income taxes on any amount above $11,000. Do this only if you would otherwise fall short of the maximum tax-deferred savings allowed.)

The extra, after-tax contribution should appear as a separate line on your annual retirement plan statement. Your money will grow tax-deferred until withdrawal. But just to be sure you are not taxed twice on these after-tax contributions, save your year-end reports. The law considers these after-tax dollars to be the last that are withdrawn from your retirement account. So unless you drain your retirement plan dry during your lifetime, whoever settles your estate is likely to be the one responsible for making sure these contributions are not taxed again.

Generally, it's not wise to contribute significantly above the tax deferral limit in your 401(k) plan. Unlike a standard, taxable account, the 401(k) won't give you access, without penalties, to the money until you retire.

Individual Retirement Accounts

Workers can also save through Individual Retirement Accounts, or I.R.A.s. Contributions can be made with pretax or after-tax dollars. The self-employed can also save through Keogh plans, named for the congressman who sponsored them.

I.R.A. contributions are limited to $2,500 per person in 2002, and will rise in stages to $5,000 in 2008. Those age fifty and older can save an extra $500 a year in 2002 through 2004 and then $1,000 a year. Anyone can create an I.R.A. with after-tax dollars, where the gains—but not the contributions—will be taxed at withdrawal. But not everyone can make tax-deductible contributions. You qualify automatically if you do not have either a pension plan or a retirement savings plan at any job you hold at any time during the year. For married couples where either spouse has such a plan, eligibility is rapidly phased out once they earn a total of $50,000; for a single person, eligibility is phased out at $30,000. The drawback of tax-deductible contributions to I.R.A.s is that all your withdrawals are taxed as ordinary income, with no preferential rates for capital gains.

No matter how much you earn and which retirement savings plans you have at work, you can make a nondeductible contribution to a traditional I.R.A. Such contributions only make sense for a very few people: those who cannot qualify for a Roth I.R.A. and those whose employers do not, beginning in 2006, offer the new Roth 401(k)s described below.

Roth I.R.A.s

For tax-smart saving, the best place to put your investments is a Roth I.R.A., which has been available to some investors, based on their income, since 1997. For those who qualify—most Americans—this is your one vehicle for keeping all your gains without ever paying any federal income taxes. Starting in 2006, though, you can qualify for a Roth, regardless of your income, if your employer offers a 401(k) plan with a new Roth option. Your after-tax contributions to your 401(k) will then grow and be withdrawn tax-free. You cannot, however, have a Roth at work if you save for retirement through a 403(b) plan for nonprofit workers or a 457 plan for government workers. Since both nonprofit and government employers can switch to, or create, 401(k) plans you may want to ask your employer about offering a 401(k) plan with a Roth option if you work for a nonprofit or government.

The benefits of Roths are not just in income taxes. They are especially flexible tools because there are no mandatory withdrawals under rigid schedules, as both traditional I.R.A.s and 401(k)-type plans require. In other retirement plans, withdrawals must begin no later than the calendar year after you turn 70½, regardless of whether you need the money, and you must withdraw the minimum under an I.R.S. formula or pay tax penalties. With a Roth you can just leave the money to continue growing untaxed. And when you die the money remaining in a Roth IRA can be passed on to future generations in ways that make it far more valuable to your heirs than any other retirement savings account.

Consider what happens if you make a single $2,000 contribution to a Roth I.R.A., and make your beneficiary a grandchild born that day. Assume that you die the day after you make the contribution, that your grandchild's life expectancy under actuarial charts used by the Internal Revenue Service is eighty-one years and that the Roth I.R.A. earns 11 percent annually, the historic long-term average for large company stocks. With proper planning, your grandchild can withdraw the money, starting the year after you die, over eighty years using tables published by the I.R.S. The Roth I.R.A. you created with that single $2,000 contribution will pay out nearly $1.3 million to your grandchild without a cent going to federal income taxes. Most of that money will come in the last few years of your grandchild's life, to be sure, but this is still an amazing transfer of wealth.

If you do not want your grandchild to have access to this money until adulthood, a lawyer can create a trust that will limit direct access to the money until a specific age. Or you can make the money available in stages, or for specific purposes, like college tuition. Not everyone is allowed to have a Roth I.R.A. The law limits eligibility for a full, $2,000-per-person annual contribution to spouses who together make less than $150,000. Smaller contributions are allowed for couples making up to $160,000. Single people can earn no more than $95,000 to qualify for the full $2,000 contribution, with smaller contributions allowed for those making up to $110,000.

Congress might decide to broaden eligibility or raise the allowed contributions. Still, these income boundaries encompass 95 percent of all taxpayers and are far more liberal than those for making tax-deductible contributions to traditional I.R.A.s.

The annual limit for individual retirement accounts applies to all accounts. If you open a traditional I.R.A. with the $2,500 savings limit in 2002, for example, you cannot put any money in a Roth. You can, however, split your savings and put part in a traditional I.R.A. and part in a Roth I.R.A. But you are best off putting all your money in

TABLE 7A

	Roth I.R.A.	Traditional I.R.A.	Taxable Account (Stock; No Dividend)
Contribution	$2,000	$2,000	$2,000
Tax Paid on Contribution	$778	$0	$778
Value at Withdrawal	$10,000	$10,000	$10,000
Tax Paid at Withdrawal	$0	$2,800	$1,440
Total Taxes Paid	$778	$2,800	$2,218
Spendable After-tax Funds	$10,000	$7,200	$8,560

Assumes a 28 percent tax bracket and 18 percent capital gains tax at all times. I.R.A. tax savings of $560 are spent, not invested.

a Roth. You can shield much more money from taxes and end up with much more in savings.

The ability to take money out of a Roth I.R.A. untaxed trumps the value of the immediate tax deduction for a traditional I.R.A. Consider the examples in table 7A, which compares the value, and tax effects, of three ways of investing $2,000 that grows over five or more years to $10,000. First, in a Roth I.R.A., where your initial contribution is taxable; second, in a traditional I.R.A., where the contribution is immediately tax deductible; third, in a taxable account, where you follow the tax-efficient strategy of buying a stock that pays no dividends, avoiding annual, taxable income—meaning that all gains would be taxed at the lower capital gains rate when the stock is sold.

Table 7A assumes a 28 percent federal income tax bracket, throughout your career and when you retire, and an 18 percent capital gains tax on the stock, for holding it more than five years, and that the investments are untouched until age 59½ or later. Note that putting $2,000 into a Roth I.R.A. or taxable account requires $2,778 before taxes.

Notice that the Roth I.R.A. produces the most money and incurs

	Roth	Traditional I.R.A.	I.R.A. Tax Savings	Traditional I.R.A. Total	Taxable Account
TABLE 7B					
Contribution	$2,000	$2,000	$560		$2,000
Tax Paid on Contribution	$778	$0			$778
Value at Withdrawal	$10,000	$10,000	$2,800		$9,000
Tax Paid at Withdrawal	$0	$2,800	$403		$1,260
Total Taxes Paid	$778	$2,800	$403		$2,038
Spendable After-tax Funds	**$10,000**	$7,200	$2,397	**$9,597**	**$7,740**

Assumes a 28 percent tax and 18 percent capital gains tax at all times. I.R.A. tax savings of $560 are invested.

the smallest tax cost. The traditional I.R.A. gives you a $560 tax break up front. Assuming you invest this in a taxable account, and that this money grew at the same rate as your I.R.A. investment, the $560 would grow to $2,800 (table 7B). If you paid capital gains taxes of $403, or 18 percent, you would have another $2,397 to spend. Add that to the after-tax value of your I.R.A. and your total spendable funds would be $9,597.

You are still better off with the Roth, because you can spend $10,000. The traditional I.R.A., where all withdrawals are taxed as standard income, still costs you nearly twice as much in taxes as the Roth I.R.A. If you paid the taxes up front and invested in a Roth I.R.A., you would have 4.2 percent more money to spend in retirement than if you opened a traditional I.R.A.

Let's say you expect your tax rate to drop to the 15 percent bracket in retirement, reducing your taxes on a traditional I.R.A. to $1,500 (table 7C). Looked at another way, the total cost of both the I.R.A. and the stock account is $2,778, the amount of the contribution plus the taxes paid. For the traditional I.R.A., the initial cost is only $2,000 because the taxes come out of the account at the end. But despite paying an extra $778 up front to cover the

TABLE 7C

	Roth I.R.A.	Traditional I.R.A.	Taxable Account (Stock; No Dividend)
Contribution	$2,000	$2,000	$2,000
Tax Paid at Contribution	$778	$0	$778
Value at Withdrawal	$10,000	$10,000	$10,000
Tax Paid at Withdrawal	$0	$1,500	$640
Total Taxes Paid	$778	$1,500	$1,418
Spendable After-tax funds	$10,000	$8,500	$9,360

Assumes a 28 percent tax bracket at time of contribution and 15 percent tax bracket at withdrawal, as well as an 8 percent capital gains tax.

taxes, the Roth I.R.A. puts more cash in your pocket in retirement.

There is another benefit to the Roth. In the fully taxable investment you will owe taxes if you sell one stock at a gain to buy another. But in the Roth, like the traditional I.R.A., there are no taxes owed on trades.

Even if you are just starting out, with low earnings that place you in the new 10 percent income tax bracket, and you expect to make so much more later that you will be in the highest tax bracket, you will be especially far ahead with a Roth. You have made the best tax deal available to workers.

In this case, if you invested $2,000 in a Roth I.R.A. you would pay just $222 in taxes on the $10,000 you could eventually spend, but in the traditional I.R.A. you would pay more than eigteen times as much in total taxes and net just $6,878.

But what if you are in the highest, 38.6 percent tax bracket in 2002, which applies only to the top 1 percent of earners, and expect to be in a much lower bracket when you retire? Few people in the top tax bracket are eligible to create a traditional I.R.A.; only those with no other pension plan for themselves or their spouse qualify. In this extreme case, whether you should put your money in a Roth or in a traditional I.R.A. depends on whether you have the discipline to invest your initial tax savings from the traditional I.R.A.

You still have the most money to spend with a Roth, but the initial cost of taxes is so high that you would be better off with a traditional I.R.A. Unless you invested your intial tax savings from the I.R.A., you would also have more cash to spend with a fully taxable investment than with a traditional I.R.A. In this case, the immediate tax deduction costs you more than twice as much as paying your entire tax bill up front with a Roth.

These examples also assume your investments in fully taxable accounts earned as much as your tax-deferred investments, a generous assumption given that annual taxes nibble away at the returns on fully taxable accounts. The only way to invest in stocks but avoid taxes, until you cash in, would be to buy and hold stocks, like Microsoft, that pay no dividends. For greater safety, you may prefer an index fund in your taxable account because it will incur only minimal income taxes, reducing your annual return by about one-third of 1 percent each year. But even optimistically projecting the likely returns from taxable accounts, Roth and traditional I.R.A. accounts generally give you a better return.

Clearly, the Roth I.R.A. produces the most money and incurs the smallest tax cost. The traditional I.R.A. gives you a $560 tax break up front, but that tax benefit comes at a substantial cost when the tax deferral ends—even if you invest your tax savings in a taxable account and add its earnings to the profits from your traditional I.R.A.

The traditional I.R.A., where all withdrawals are taxed as earned income, costs you more than four times as much in taxes as the Roth I.R.A. If you paid the taxes up front and invested in a Roth I.R.A., you would have more than 5 percent more money to spend in retirement than if you opened a traditional I.R.A., assuming that you invested your tax savings from the traditional I.R.A. If you just spend the tax savings, as most people do, then the Roth I.R.A. gives you almost 39 percent more money to spend.

In general, if your tax rate in retirement, when you are withdrawing, is not apt to fall by at least 10 percentage points from when you contributed, you will do better with a Roth I.R.A. than with a traditional I.R.A. But even if your tax rate falls by more, your doing better with a traditional I.R.A. depends heavily on your willingness to invest your initial tax savings.

What's more, the Roth offers a thrifty advantage if you have an unexpected need for cash in retirement to pay a big and unexpected bill, perhaps for a hospital visit or repairs to your home after a storm. With a Roth I.R.A. you can withdraw exactly the amount you need to pay these types of bills. But if you dip into your traditional I.R.A., you will need to take out enough extra to pay the income taxes. That, in turn, may push you into a higher tax bracket, cause you to lose some income tax deductions or make you ineligible for some government benefits.

So again, your first, last and best choice is, almost always, a Roth.

Conversions to Roth I.R.A.s

There is a second new rule if you are contemplating the conversion of an existing tax-deferred account into a Roth I.R.A. By rolling the money in a traditional account into a Roth, and paying the taxes now, you can enjoy the benefits of future tax-free growth in your retirement account. The longer you expect to live, or the longer you expect funds to stay in the Roth I.R.A. before your heirs withdraw them, the stronger the case for conversion. A Roth I.R.A. conversion becomes more and more advantageous over time for the same reasons that the Roth is a more tax-efficient vehicle than the traditional I.R.A., with its immediate tax deferral and later payment of taxes.

You should convert to a Roth only if you have a source of money outside your retirement account to pay the income taxes. If you take money from your retirement account to pay the taxes today, then there is no tax advantage. The amount of money you can spend from the reduced balance in the Roth account will be the same as the amount you could spend if you keep your traditional account and defer taxes until withdrawal. So convert only if you have extra cash with which to pay the taxes due at conversion.

- To minimize taxes, try to wait at least a year and a day to take your gains, or five years if you can.
- If you have taken any investment gains over the year by selling winners, look over your portfolio in the last two months of the year for losers you could sell to avoid taxes on those gains. But don't let tax strategy rule your investment decisions.
- Since short-term gains, those on investments you sell in fewer than 366 days, are taxed at the highest rates, they are the most worth balancing with losses.
- In saving for retirement, your first priority should be to save as much in your 401(k), or similar plan, as your employer will match.
- Your second priority should be to fully fund a Roth I.R.A. Although your contributions are taxable up front, these are the only accounts where your gains are tax-free forever.

Giving Gifts to Loved Ones and Charities (But Not the Government)

If you are successful at investing, or just plain generous, you will probably make gifts to family, friends and charities. Here, again, you should follow the rules to get the most in tax benefits—perhaps allowing you to be even more generous.

When making gifts to relatives or friends, keep in mind that if you give stock that has risen in value, rather than cash, you are also giving an obligation to pay a tax. Congress lets you give $11,000 ($22,000 for a married couple) to as many individuals as you want each year without incurring gift taxes. If you give more than this amount, you generally are required to file a gift tax return. (This will be true even in the year 2010, when, under current law, the estate tax is repealed for a single year.)

No tax is actually due until you have used up your lifetime exclusion, which rose to $1 million beginning in 2002. Once you have used up your lifetime exclusion, you owe a gift tax, at the same rate as the estate tax, on amounts above the annual exclusion.

You can give more than the $11,000 or $22,000 limits if you are paying someone's medical bills *directly* to their doctor, hospital or other health care provider, or if you are paying tuition *directly* to a recognized school on the recipient's behalf.

When you give securities, including mutual fund shares, to a family member or friend, the recipient will owe taxes on any gain over your purchase price when the securities are sold. You should therefore consider giving securities that have gained much in value only when the recipient has little or no income, or is a child fourteen or older, who, unlike younger children, is not taxed at the parents' rate. These recipients can take advantage of the 10 percent tax rate on capital gains held for at least a year and a day. Under the new law, these recipients can even take advantage of the 8 percent rate immediately, provided you bought the stock you are giving them at least five years and a day earlier.

You should also keep in mind when you make gifts to minors that the recipients can do as they please with the money once they reach adulthood under the laws of their states. Money that you thought would pay for college could end up paying for a fancy new convertible.

You cannot deduct gifts to family or friends on your tax return. You also cannot attach any strings to the gifts.

Recipients of your gifts owe no taxes unless you give them securities that have risen in value, and they sell them. When making gifts to charity, however, you should give highly appreciated stock because you can both avoid capital gains taxes and get the full income tax deduction. Say you and your spouse bought stock more than a year ago for $1,000 that is now worth $11,000. If you sell, you would owe $2,000 in capital gains taxes in the higher tax brackets, leaving $9,000 to give to the charity. But if you give the stock, you get to deduct $11,000 on your income tax return, saving you $3,080 if your last dollar of income is taxed at 28 percent. Instead of a $2,000 tax bill you receive a tax savings of more than $3,000.

The deduction for your gift of stock or bonds to a charity is the midpoint in the trading range on the day you make your donation. For example, if a stock trades at a low of $20 and a high of $30 on the day you give it away, then your income tax deduction is $25 regardless of the closing price. To make sure a volatile market does not rob you of some of your tax break, you may want to wait until the market closes to determine the trading range. Then either have your broker transfer the shares that day or rush to the post office with two letters, one with the stock certificates and another with a signed stock power giving the shares to the charity (your charity should have instructions for writing a stock power, but don't mail it with the certificates). Get a postal receipt for each letter to prove you mailed it that day.

You should also consider timing your tax break for maximum benefit by opening a fund at one of the more than six hundred community foundations. You can make a gift to a charitable fund these foundations can set up in your name, then arrange to have the money sent on to other charities later. This technique is especially valuable if you want to use a windfall in a stock to set aside a minimum of about $10,000 for years of charitable gifts, but could use the tax deduction immediately.

There are even more sophisticated devices for making gifts that maximize tax breaks, but they should be undertaken only with the advice of an estate tax lawyer. To demonstrate the possibilities you may want to discuss with a lawyer depending on the situation, consider this example: You can give highly appreciated stock, with a reasonable minimum of $100,000, to a charitable remainder trust set up by your lawyer. You get an immediate income tax deduction and the right to a stream of payments from the trust for the rest of your life. When you die the funds remaining in your trust can be used to establish a permanent charitable fund in your name at your local community foundation. During their lifetimes, your heirs can decide how to distribute these charitable funds, and then the foundation board will use them within the limits you specify. Meanwhile, with the money you saved on income taxes when you made your gift, you can buy life insurance that will replace, for your heirs, the investments you gave away.

That is, you can give investments away, get an immediate tax deduction, receive income for life, replace the value of your gift through insurance that benefits your heirs and create a permanent charitable fund in your name that your heirs will control, all with the same money. Remember that this kind of money magic, and all complex charitable arrangements, should be undertaken only with the advice of an estate tax lawyer.

Estate Taxes: New Laws Now, More Later

Congress made major changes to the estate tax laws in 2001 and more changes are certain in the years ahead. That is because Congress voted to repeal the tax, but only for people who die in the year 2010. Until then, the amount that a person can leave to heirs untaxed will rise from $1 million to $3.5 million, and the tax rates will drift downward from a high of 55 percent to 45 percent in 2009. Then, in a bizarre twist come 2011, the estate tax is to be resurrected with an exemption of only $1 million. Congress may extend the repeal, or repeal the repeal. More likely, it will continue with an exemption of $3.5 million ($7 million for married couples) or more, thus taxing only the largest estates.

Still, you must plan for uncertainty. You must review your will and related estate tax plan documents, and you might have to sign new ones.

If repeal actually takes effect, it will be important that you have carefully documented the price you paid for each investment you own. That's because, under repeal, your spouse would owe capital gains taxes on inherited gains greater than $3 million, and your other heirs would owe these taxes on gains greater than an additional $1.3 million. Until 2010, and again beginning in 2011, your spouse can inherit an unlimited amount, tax-free, when you die.

You also need to review your will to make sure that you do not unintentionally disinherit your surviving spouse or leave your spouse with less than you intend. Many wills contain a clause, designed to minimize estate taxes, that leaves a surviving spouse only as much as will escape estate taxes.

When you visit a lawyer who specializes in estates, ask him to divide his bill between advice on taxes and investing and advice on your will. The portion that you pay for tax and investment advice is deductible on your income tax return. For an experienced estate lawyer expect to pay at least one-tenth of 1 percent of your net worth, with a $2,000 minimum, and with half or more of the bill deductible. Thus, if you have a net worth of $3 million, your estate plan will cost at least $3,000, and perhaps $1,500 will be deductible. If your finances are complex, you will pay more.

The cost of a first-rate lawyer to write or revise your will and estate plan to conform with the new laws may seem burdensome. But spending a fraction of 1 percent of your net worth on sound legal advice can avoid litigation with the I.R.S. Fighting over your estate could leave your heirs broke or even in debt to the government, as well as mired in years of emotional turmoil.

The cardinal rules for tax planning are to document everything, to keep good records, and to be forthright. Being able to prove the original cost, known as the basis, for each asset you leave will be especially important if the estate tax is permanently repealed and your heirs therefore might have to pay taxes on capital gains. If you encounter a lawyer who suggests he can slip something past the I.R.S., walk out.

Other Tax Strategies

You can deduct a variety of fees and expenses for managing your investments, unless you invest solely in tax-exempt municipal bonds, in which case no deductions are allowed. These costs are reported as miscellaneous deductions on your tax return, deductible only to the extent that all miscellaneous deductions exceed 2 percent of your adjusted gross income. Adjusted gross income is the last line on the front page of your income tax return.

Deductible investment expenses include fees paid to accountants, lawyers and financial planners for tax and investment advice; custodial or trustee fees paid to the brokerage or mutual fund companies that hold your investments; telephone and postage expenses for managing your accounts; and the annual costs of a safe deposit box and of subscriptions to investment publications.

If you have miscellaneous itemized deductions greater than 2 percent of your income, then you should pay the annual custodial fees on your retirement accounts out of your own pocket instead of having the money deducted from your account.

There is one exception to this advice. If you are subject to the alternative minimum tax, explained below, your miscellaneous itemized deductions will be reduced or eliminated. So while you normally want to pay custodial fees out of current income, if you can't deduct these expenses you may want to have them taken directly from your retirement accounts.

In any year that you have large capital gains, you need to be careful to avoid two tax traps. The first trap is not having enough cash to pay your income taxes by April 15 of the following year. Putting 20 percent of your capital gains in a certificate of deposit that matures no later than April 15 will eliminate this problem. The second trap occurs in the year after you have realized large capital gains, when you might be penalized for not paying the extra taxes soon enough. Generally you must pay at least 90 percent of your total tax bill from the previous year by January 15 to avoid penalties.

You also avoid penalties if your payments and withholding fall less than $1,000 short, or if you pay as much as your actual income tax from the year before. Those making more than $150,000 have to pay slightly more than 100 percent, but the exact amount varies from year to year.

If you use software to do your own taxes, the tax planning feature will let you estimate what you will owe, so that you can adjust your withholding or your quarterly estimated payments to avoid penalties.

There is another technique you can use to avoid penalties in the year after you realized capital gains. This works best if your income and deductions are about the same as the previous year, and you have no capital gains in the current year. Subtract from your total tax bill for the previous year the amount you paid in capital gains taxes, usually 20 percent of the gain. Then make sure the amount of federal income tax withheld from your paycheck equals that result, plus whatever percentage increase you expect in your income over the tax on the prior year. If you find you are falling short, increase your withholding during the last few months of the year.

Another costly tax trap that investors should try to avoid is the alternative minimum tax, or A.M.T. You should be especially careful about selling investments with long-term gains greater than your losses if your other income, from all sources, risks triggering this tax. Generally, your gains can then be taxed at 27 percent instead of the usual 20 percent.

The A.M.T. is a parallel universe of taxes with its own rules and rates. By scaling back exemptions and deductions for the wealthy, it is intended to make sure they do not aggressively use deductions to pay little or no tax.

The 27 percent tax rate on long-term capital gains affects married couples with adjusted gross income before capital gains of between about $150,000 and $330,000, singles with about $75,000 to $165,000 and single parents with about $112,500 to about $247,500.

The only way to dodge the higher rate is to avoid taking long-term capital gains greater than your losses in any year until your income is above or below these ranges. Due to inflation and the new tax laws in 2001, the exposure will spread from about 1.5 million taxpayers who paid the A.M.T. in 2000 to more than 35 million taxpayers by 2010, according to official estimates.

Even so, you should always remember that you are investing to make money, not to avoid taxes. You should pay as little tax as the law allows, but never continue holding an investment just to avoid taxes.

- Investments that have gained in value make the best charitable gifts, because you get the full deductions and avoid any capital gains taxes.
- Check the changing terms for giving securities as gifts to family and friends to minimize their tax bills.
- Likewise, keeping up with changes in the estate tax laws, with a lawyer's advice, will allow you to pass your investments on to your heirs while limiting their taxes.
- If you are one of the increasing number of taxpayers subject to the alternative minimum tax, consider delaying long-term capital gains, or balancing them with losses.

8.

Let the Investor Beware:
Traps, Scams and Myths

GRETCHEN MORGENSON

Streaming into the stock market in recent years, many investors came to believe that with the help of financial news shows, Internet chat rooms and stacks of financial publications, they could invest successfully on their own. With all those facts at their fingertips, many felt that they had outgrown their need for professional guidance. Investors felt liberated from their brokers' bondage.

Many of these folks were forgetting, however, that a big part of an honest broker's job is keeping customers away from investment pitfalls, a task not even the smartest machine can manage.

Even though the do-it-yourself approach is the American way, investors are not as empowered as they may think. For all the technological advancements that have led individual investors to believe they are operating on the same level as professionals, even the smartest amateur remains at a distinct disadvantage.

For example, investors may like $5 commissions on stock trades, but behind these low prices often lurk excessive costs associated with getting the trade done. Even though brokerage firms like to recommend that investors borrow to maximize their potential gains, margin accounts carry greater risks than most investors should bear.

Investors must also be on guard against trusting reports written by research analysts at major Wall Street firms that are sales tools rather than objective advice. And investors should leave frequent trading, especially day trading, to the professionals. Don't count on the insurance fund financed by brokerage firms to help recoup losses, either, because this organization resists making payments.

While many of the risks of investing today seem to be peculiar to the Internet age, in truth they are similar to the perils that investors experienced in the past. It was ever thus: Wall Street's agenda and investors' goals are often flatly opposed.

Today, the stock market may be more accessible to investors, especially those with computers, than ever before, yet that ease of entry can carry significant but hidden costs. Investors must always stay alert if they want to protect themselves from highwaymen along the road to riches.

Online Investing

The terrain of the investing world has changed dramatically during the course of the 1990s and much of this change is the result of the embrace of new technology by Americans young and old. Nowhere did technology hold more promise than for investors, who took to the Internet in droves. Trading stocks by computer became as mesmerizing to investors as video games are to youngsters.

By the end of 2000, Americans controlled 23 million online brokerage accounts, up from 14 million at the end of 1999. Online volume grew from fewer than 100,000 trades a day in mid-1996 to more than 500,000 a day at the end of the decade, according to securities regulators.

This explosion in the popularity of online trading is largely the result of investors' view that the computer provides the same market access to novices that had been available only for professionals. It doesn't hurt that online trades carry commissions as low as $5 a trade.

While online investing appears to be low-cost, at least in terms of commissions, the accounts can be extremely expensive in other ways. Brokerage firms offering electronic trades often obscure the dangers of frequent trading just to keep their customers buying and selling and paying commissions. In addition, online brokerage firms often give their investors woeful prices on their trades—too high if they were buying, too low if they sold—notify them late about the status of their transactions and shrug off responsibility for other problems that customers encountered. All in all, online brokerage firms' practices made them treacherous access points for investors looking for a way to reap stock market gains.

Electronic investing does little to help individuals improve their chances. Indeed, an investigation in 2000 by the General Accounting Office into practices at the nation's best-known online brokers found that some of the firms are Wall Street's latest incarnation of the Wild West.

In 1999, among twelve major online firms, which accounted for 90 percent of the nation's electronic trades, delays and breakdowns were rampant, the GAO said. One firm encountered such problems so often that its management did not track their occurrences.

The study also found that online brokers provide little information to customers on the risks of borrowing money to buy stocks, known as trading on margin. Only a third of the firms posted information on their Web sites about the stocks they do not allow customers to buy on margin because they move too wildly in price. One investor found out that he had bought a stock the firm would not lend money on when he received a call from the firm demanding $75,000 to pay for the holding in full.

Regulators also found that many firms do not update customer account information regularly enough to let investors know when they are at risk of having the firm sell their holdings to pay down their margin loans. In some cases, these lapses allowed investors to buy stocks using money they thought was in their account when in fact they had no available cash. Also worrisome was the fact that online investors were able to buy stocks in their Individual Retirement Accounts that exceeded the value of their assets and borrowing capacity.

But these problems paled in comparison to the difficulties that online customers have in getting their trades executed in the market at the best possible prices. Every trader knows that poor execution can cost more than a $5 per trade commission.

The Securities and Exchange Commission found that more than half of the twenty-nine online firms it studied were not meeting their obligation to provide the best execution for their customers' trades. A major reason is that most online firms funnel their customers' trades to other brokerage firms to be completed. In exchange, the online firms receive payments of between one cent and two cents per share from the firms that complete the trades.

These payments determine where a customer's order is sent, even if another market or trader is offering a superior price. On a 1,000-share sale, for example, an investor would net $62.50 more if he got a price that was one-sixteenth above the prevailing market. The firms receiving payments for their customers' orders did not even try to assess current prices from firms other than those that were paying them. And most of the firms routed orders to traders whose execution quality was well below industry averages.

Another problem with investing by computer is that, unlike a human being, a machine will not stop an investor from making a mistake. It could be a simple one, like entering an incorrect stock symbol, or it could be more complex, like buying a stock that is inappropriately risky for the purchaser.

A top concern of regulators is that some online firms may try to escape their obligation to ensure that customers make investments suitable to their circumstances. The requirement that a brokerage firm ascertain appropriateness is a principal avenue of protection for investors under the securities laws. Almost a third of arbitration cases customers filed with the National Association of Securities Dealers between 1995 and 1999 involved their complaints of having been steered into unsuitable investments.

Some online firms have even tried to argue that because their customers make their own decisions—using the computer simply as an order taker—the firm need not consider suitability. But the Securities and Exchange Commission has said that any firm with published research should believe that the information is plausible and that the recommended investments are appropriate for at least some of its customers.

All in all, it seems, online investors stand to be at greater risk than customers of full-service firms. Until these firms improve their systems and practices, investors are better off dealing with a traditional and well-established brokerage firm and a representative of the firm who spends time assessing their needs, current financial position and future goals. Commissions may be higher at a full-service firm, but the extra service provided and the pitfall protection that an honest broker can give will more than cover the extra costs.

Before establishing a new brokerage account, investors should check with securities regulators about the firm's history and about any recent run-ins their specific broker may have had. These facts are available from the National Association of Securities Dealers (www.nasdr.com) in Washington, D.C.

- Poor trade execution and poor advice often make trading online far more expensive than the low commissions suggest.
- A trustworthy broker at a well-established, full-service firm can often give investors the extra help and protection against pitfalls that more than justify higher commissions.

Trading on Margin

Borrowing money from a brokerage firm to buy stocks became immensely popular among individual investors in the late 1990s and remains so today. Who can blame them? When stock prices go up, the biggest gains go to those who buy shares on borrowed money.

Unfortunately, stock prices do not always go up. And when they go sideways or down, margin becomes a knife with two sharp edges. As such, margin accounts should be avoided except by knowledgeable and practiced investors.

Most brokerage firms require customers who buy on margin to put up at least half of the purchase cost when they buy a stock. Not all stocks can be borrowed against; most firms do not lend on stocks that trade for $5 or less. And if a stock is exceedingly volatile, some brokerage firms restrict the ability of their customers to buy shares on margin.

Margin works beautifully when stocks rise. An investor who bought 1,000 shares of a $10 stock on margin would have to put up only $5,000 in cash or securities to make the purchase, not the $10,000 that would be required if he paid in full. If that stock rose to $15 and the investor on margin sold, he would have a $5,000 profit, or 100 percent of his original investment. Out of that profit, of course, he would have to pay the interest the broker charged on the loan. But compared with such gains, the interest costs, usually about a percentage point above the prime lending rate, can seem nominal. Meanwhile, for the investor who paid in full, the move to $15 would produce only a 50 percent gain.

But the mathematics stops working when the stock purchased on margin does not move up. If it stagnates, the investor is out the cost of borrowing, while the investor who paid for all the shares himself would be out nothing.

And when stocks actually decline? In a bear market, margin can be hazardous to investors' wealth. If a stock declines by even 10 percent, not a big move given the gyrations in recent years, an investor could receive an urgent call from his broker for more funds. Because the shares back the loan, if they decline below the loan's value, the investor has to put up more money.

Few warnings about the pitfalls of margin investing were made by the brokerage firms rushing to extend credit to their customers during the bull market of the late 1990s. These firms make big money lending to investors. One analyst of brokerage firms estimates that margin interest paid by investors can account for almost a quarter of the typical online brokerage firm's revenues. As a result, the collapse of Internet stocks in 2000 awakened many investors to margin's risks.

Prior to the collapse, many investors had seen only the sunny side of leverage. They took to the practice with a vengeance. Margin borrowings at firms that are members of the New York Stock Exchange almost tripled between 1995 and 2000. At the peak in the first quarter of 2000, borrowings exceeded $265 billion, a record. In February 2000 alone, a month that saw the final push skyward of Internet stocks, debt ballooned almost 9 percent. The biggest growth in margin debt was seen at electronic brokerage firms.

Especially worrisome was the rise of margin borrowings as a share of overall consumer debt. According to Sanford Bernstein, an investment research firm in New York, margin loans accounted for 16 percent of total consumer borrowings in March 2000, up from 7 percent in December 1995.

Securities regulators watched the growth in margin trading with alarm. Some feared that investors were also running up their credit cards or taking out second mortgages to buy stocks. As margin debt grew, the Securities and Exchange Commission saw a rise in investor complaints.

Lael Desmond, a medical school student in Indiana, learned the risks the hard way. At the age of twenty-six, Desmond opened an account at Ameritrade, a well-known electronic brokerage firm. By June 1998, he had roughly $30,000 in his account. New to investing, he began borrowing to buy such volatile companies as Amazon, Dell Computer, America Online and Yahoo.

Desmond did not fully understand what investing on margin meant. According to his lawyer, he thought that margin borrowing was like taking out a loan on a house or a car. He had no idea that he could wind up owing his broker more than the loan's amount.

In the late summer of 1998, stocks took a nosedive when Russia defaulted on its debt. Over three days, Desmond's portfolio had dipped $21,000 below what his margin loan required. This was money Desmond did not have, so he took out cash advances on credit cards for $13,000 and borrowed the rest from his brother.

Unfortunately, by the time he wired the money to his broker, the firm had already sold Desmond's holdings. That meant the $21,000 was completely lost; it could never be made up again by rising stock prices.

In a securities arbitration case decided in January 2000, Desmond won $40,453 from Ameritrade. Although none of the arbitrators commented, they clearly felt that Ameritrade had sold Desmond out of his stocks too quickly.

Novices were not the only ones hurt by aggressive leverage. After Internet shares began to tumble in April 2000, Baruch Israel Hertz, owner of a New York–based online brokerage firm called Track Data, found himself facing a $45 million call for more money from brokerage firms where he had been trading. It was a remarkable twist. Hertz had become ubiquitous in cable television advertisements for his stock-trading service, which he promised would make investing a breeze for anyone. "You don't have to be a pro to trade like one," he said in advertisements.

Hertz answered his brokers' calls by pledging 25 million shares in his own company, roughly half his holdings. But the irony of Hertz becoming the most public victim of the kind of investing he was promoting was not lost on many observers. Even in the wild and crazy Internet bubble, nobody had expected that the chief executive of an online trading company would generate one of the largest margin calls ever.

Unfortunately, excessive borrowing by some investors can even hurt others. When stock prices start to fall and brokerage firms have to ask their customers for additional funds to shore up their portfolios, many investors sell their stock rather than put in more money. Their sales can put further pressure on stocks that are already weak. Then a downward spiral begins exacerbating a stock's decline.

Margin debt levels, which are published monthly by the New York Stock Exchange, are figures all investors should look at. Excessively high margin borrowings may signal a coming downdraft in stocks, as they did in 2000.

- Only experienced investors able to tolerate high risks should borrow through margin accounts to buy stocks. Even they should avoid borrowing to buy the more risky stocks.
- Those wanting to invest on margin should be sure they understand the huge risks, which their brokers may not explain.

Investing Chat Rooms

One of the most amazing aspects of the mania for Internet and other technology stocks in the late 1990s was how many people bought because of upbeat messages in the Web's investing chat rooms. Since most of these messages were anonymous, buying stocks based on them was roughly equivalent to following investment advice from a total stranger. Yet droves of investors did just that, making investment chat rooms a powerful and sinister force in the markets.

While investors flocked to investing sites hoping to find hidden gems, many sites, in truth, were run by shadowy characters who used their followers to manipulate stocks, benefiting personally. Much of the information investors relied on turned out to be specious.

"The Internet, with its low cost, relative anonymity and unprecedented number of innocent investors, makes it ripe for out-and-out fraud," according to Arthur Levitt, former chairman of the Securities and Exchange Commission. And Levitt knows what he is talking about; fraudulent messages posted on investor Web sites have been the subject of many S.E.C. cases.

The civil case against a New Jersey teen named Jonathan Lebed shows how easily investors were gulled. According to prosecutors, Lebed attended high school by day and manipulated stocks on the Internet by night. Just before his sixteenth birthday, he was apprehended for masterminding a stock manipulation scheme on the Internet that earned him almost $273,000 in illegal gains, prosecutors said.

In August 1999, when he was fourteen, Lebed found he could push the prices of obscure, low-price stocks he had already bought by spewing out hundreds of optimistic messages, using many fictitious names, to investing chat rooms. As investors read his messages, about prospective 1,000 percent gains and a $2 stock soon to trade at $20, and bought, prosecutors said, Lebed sold his holdings at profits ranging from $11,000 to $74,000 a trade. At the same time that he bought shares, Lebed often placed orders to sell them at prices well above the prevailing market, the S.E.C. said, so that he could profit from jumps even if they came during his day at school. In September 2000, Lebed settled with the S.E.C., neither admitting nor denying the accusations but agreeing to pay the money he made plus interest, for a total of $285,000.

Some Internet stock pickers became investment gurus whose every word was watched by investors. Yet even some of these people used their followers to make personal gains.

In early 2000, the S.E.C. brought a high-profile fraud case against one of the Web's best-known stock pickers, a man known as Tokyo Joe, whose real name is Yun Soo Oh Park. An Internet celebrity who ran his own Web site that made stock picks, Tokyo Joe enriched himself at his customers' expense, overstated his past returns by as much as 2,000 percent and secretly accepted payment in exchange for recommending one company's stock, regulators said.

Between June 1998 and July 1999, prosecutors said, Park repeatedly recommended stocks and advised his almost four thousand customers to hold for several days or until the shares reached specific target prices. As investors rushed to buy, pushing up the prices, Park sold, even if they had not reached his targets, according to the government.

A year after he was charged, Park settled the S.E.C.'s charges. His lawyer had initially said he was simply exercising his First Amendment right of free speech. But his free speech proved costly to some investors who followed his advice only to see their stocks fall after the direction of the stampede reversed.

- Buying on a tip from an investing chat room is like buying based on bathroom graffiti.
- Assume that chat room tipsters have ulterior motives hidden from view.

Woeful Wall Street Research

Brokerage firm analysts gained fame and fortune in the great bull market of the 1990s. But when the hot stocks they had been promoting to prices never seen before began to fall, analysts showed their true colors. While the market sank in 2000 to its worst performance in more than a decade, many of those analysts kept right on smiling and saying "buy."

In the Nasdaq crash of 2000, investors found out that analysts are corporate cheerleaders whose top priority is to cement investment banking relationships and so fatten their paychecks. Their work for investors—especially providing advice about when to exit a stock—comes well down the priority list. Nowhere was this more evident to investors than with Internet stocks that were propelled by a gaggle of high-powered analysts, led by Mary Meeker at Morgan Stanley and Henry Blodget at Merrill Lynch.

In April 2002, almost exactly two years after the technology stock bubble burst, Eliot L. Spitzer, the New York attorney general, made it clear to investors just how compromised some Wall Street analysts had been. After conducting an investigation into analyst conflicts at brokerage firms, Spitzer released a series of internal e-mail messages among Merrill Lynch's Internet analysts in which Henry Blodget and others appeared to be deriding in private the same companies whose shares they were recommending to the public. The e-mails also illustrated that Merrill analysts in many cases had become marketers first, enlisted to help the firm attract investment banking fees. Analysis for the firm's individual investor clients took a distant second or third place.

After the e-mails were released, Merrill Lynch agreed to pay $100 million to settle the lawsuit brought by Spitzer. The firm neither admitted nor denied guilt in the matter, but the damage from the e-mails had been done. Spitzer then turned his sights on other Wall Street firms, focusing on Morgan Stanley and Salomon Smith Barney.

Having seen what Spitzer turned up in his investigation, the S.E.C. jumped on the bandwagon, opening its own investigation into analyst conflicts. And the self-regulatory organizations in the securities industry, the National Association of Securities Dealers and the New York Stock Exchange, launched multiple investigations into analyst conduct. At the same time, the regulators introduced new rules meant to prevent analysts from putting their own or their firms' interests ahead of investors'.

What few people realized, however, while the bull market was raging, was how analysts had morphed from green eyeshade types scrutinizing companies' financial statements to salesmen interested in procuring lucrative securities underwritings for their firms.

Although brokerage firm stock gurus are still called analysts, their day-to-day pursuits involve much less analysis and much more salesmanship than ever before. This explains why many who are paid so much to scrutinize companies blew it so spectacularly for their customers. A change in the way Wall Street analysts do their work—and how they are rewarded for it—brought riches and stardom to them, but cost investors billions in losses.

No one, of course, knows what stocks will do tomorrow, much less next year; but Wall Street's analysts are supposed to help investors judge the attractiveness of companies' shares. Investors look to analysts to advise them on whether to buy or sell a stock at its current price, given its near-term business prospects. Until the mid-1990s, that is how most analysts approached their work. But in 2000 there was virtually no such thing as a sell recommendation. At the end of that year, of the eight thousand recommendations made by analysts covering the companies in the Standard & Poor's 500 stock index, only twenty-nine were sells, according to Zacks Investment Research in Chicago. That's less than one-half of 1 percent.

Analysts have long been known for unrelenting optimism about the companies they cover. Yet during the great bull market of the late 1990s, the quality of Wall Street research sank to new lows. At work was the new economics of the brokerage business.

Lower trading commissions were one factor. These fees were much higher in the 1970s and 1980s, about ten cents a share, versus pennies per share in 2000. Because analysts' recommendations helped generate trades and commissions, research departments once paid for themselves. More important, an analyst who uncovered a time bomb ticking away within a company's financial statements and who advised customers to sell made an important contribution to his firm in commissions those sales generated. In short, analysts were rewarded for doing good, hard digging.

But as commissions declined, Wall Street firms looked elsewhere to cover the costs of research. The lucrative area of investment banking was an obvious choice. Analysts soon began going on sales calls for their firms, which were competing for stock underwritings, debt offerings and other investment banking deals. In this world, negative research reports carried a cost, not a benefit.

As a result, the traditional role of analyst as adviser to investors was severely compromised. The increasingly close relationships analysts have with corporate executives led many of them to be gulled by top executives intent on keeping the prices of their stocks up.

Consider Mary Meeker, the analyst at Morgan Stanley who became known as the Queen of the Internet for her prognostications on e-commerce companies like Amazon and Priceline. In 1999, as Internet stocks soared and new companies were taken public in droves, Meeker made $15 million, according to news reports. Two years later, when Internet stocks were in pieces on the ground, Meeker had become decidedly less vocal—but no less optimistic. At the end of 2000, she still rated all eleven Internet stocks she followed as "outperform" even though they were down an average of 83 percent. By comparison, the Interactive Week Internet index was down 60 percent from its recent peak at year-end. Of the eleven companies Meeker recommended, eight had their securities taken public by Morgan Stanley.

Ray O'Rourke, a Morgan Stanley spokesman, defended her, saying that she had warned investors in March 2000 that Internet stocks were volatile. Asked whether her nonstop optimism had anything to do with the fact that most of the companies had hired Morgan Stanley to take them public, O'Rourke said, "It is what it is. But you shouldn't be surprised necessarily to see 'outperforms' on the companies, because we've been very vigorous on the companies we've chosen to bring public."

And it's not just Mary Meeker. Anthony Noto, at Goldman Sachs, was another Internet analyst who remained upbeat on shares even when they were trading at a fraction of their former values. On December 18, 2000, he lowered the ratings to "market performer" on four of the nine stocks he followed, including the Webvan Group, an Internet grocer; Ashford and eToys, two troubled e-tailers; and PlanetRX.com, an online resource for medical products that was in danger of being thrown off the Nasdaq stock market. EToys filed for bankruptcy about two months later.

Noto downgraded these companies after they had dropped an average of 98.2 percent during the previous fifty-two weeks. Of the nine stocks Noto followed, seven, including the four above, had stock offerings underwritten by Goldman Sachs. "Our research is driven by fundamental analysis and is not influenced by anything else," Noto said.

It was not only the Internet analysts who steered investors wrong. Faces were also red—or should have been—at Salomon Smith Barney, where Jack Grubman, the highest-paid analyst at the firm and, perhaps, on Wall Street, reportedly made $20 million in 1999 covering the telecommunications industry. Investors who followed his picks did not do as well.

For example, Grubman began to advise caution on the eleven smallish telecom companies he covers only after the stocks had lost 77 percent of their value. All eleven had securities underwritten by Salomon. Grubman, who also covers the larger phone companies, declined to comment on his delayed caution. But in an article in *Business Week* in May 2000, he scoffed at the idea that his help peddling investment banking services to corporations put him in conflict with his firm's investor customers. "What used to be a conflict is now a synergy," Grubman said.

Mitch Zacks, vice president of Zacks Investment Research in Chicago, questions the claims of analysts who say they do not see freight trains bearing down on them. "It's not that they're oblivious to things getting worse," he said. "But the way an analyst can get fired is to damage an existing investment banking relationship with a company or sour a future investment banking relationship. The way you do that as an analyst is coming out and telling people to sell a stock."

Analysts must worry about angering not just corporate managers but also venture capitalists that send their firms companies to take public. If an analyst advises investors to sell a stock that venture capitalists still hold—as they often do for years—the likelihood of getting future deals will be slim.

Possibile fees also explain why analysts are loath to highlight a company's troubles even when it is on the brink of failure. The company could restructure or sell some operations, requiring aid from a brokerage firm.

Investors should know that the vocabulary of Wall Street analysts has different meanings from real-world definitions. At Merrill Lynch, before it changed its rating system in 2001, the word "accumulate" was not the strongest buy advice the firm gave. While Webster's defines "accumulate" as to collect, Merrill Lynch considers it a lukewarm recommendation. It could be considered to mean "sell."

Investors should also recognize that while the word "sell" is rarely uttered, when an analyst drops his rating from buy to accumulate, many investors will interpret the advice as negative and will sell. In addition, investors must be careful to read an analyst's entire report for negative news that could be included even though the analyst still rates the stock a buy.

Investors also should ignore outlandish price targets and new valuation methods. Price targets fanned the speculative fires in the bubble market and hurt a lot of investors.

Perhaps the most famous price target was the $1,000 given to Qualcomm by Walter P. Piecyk Jr., an analyst at PaineWebber, on December 29, 1999. It soared 30 percent, to $656, on the news and hit a high of $717.24, before splitting four for one, on January 3. The next year, it was all downhill. Qualcomm closed 2000 at $82.19 a share, 67 percent below Piecyk's price target.

Outlandish price targets also proved embarrassing for analysts who reduced them only well after the stocks had been crushed. For instance, on May 26, 2000, when Internet stocks were swooning, Jamie Kiggen, of Donaldson, Lufkin & Jenrette, rated GoTo.com a buy and set a $160 price target; it was then at $15.13. Only in early September 2000 did Kiggen lower his target. With the stock at $23.31, Kiggen said he expected it to reach $80 in the next twelve months. A month later, he reduced the target to $25. The stock closed the year at $7.31.

Kiggen, an analyst at Credit Suisse First Boston, said that the slowing economy was the surprise that made him ratchet down his targets. "Our price targets aren't arbitrary numbers," he said. But he added that investors also have to take responsibility for their mistakes, saying: "Using the fact of a price target as a substitute for analysis if you're an investor is dangerous."

Price targets have been just one of the methods analysts have used to persuade investors to keep buying. Equally pernicious were the new valuation methods analysts devised to justify rocketing prices. "Analysts no longer focus on tangible factors that make a stock worth what it's worth," said David Eidelman, a money manager at Eidelman, Finger & Harris in St. Louis who headed research departments at two regional brokerage firms in the 1970s. "For instance, analysts have valued Internet retailers based on how many customers they had. This may have nothing to do with earnings, but since they can't justify buying a stock based on its earnings, they justify it with some valuation method they invented."

Other money managers cited analysts' focus only on income statements, not balance sheets, as another flaw in many research reports. Balance sheets, which detail companies' assets (like cash, factories and so forth) and debts, are the place for investors to look for a company's net worth. Yet as companies loaded up on debt in the mid- to late 1990s, many analysts were silent on the potential for difficulties of paying interest costs. Many telecommunications companies got into such straits and had to file for bankruptcy when they could no longer borrow or sell stock.

As investors toted up the losses they have suffered at the hands of ebullient analysts, they may have decided to tune them out. Among fund managers, almost 40 percent spent less time reading brokerage firm research in 2000 than the year earlier, according to a study by Tempest Consultants for Reuters.

Clearly, the lesson of the Internet stock debacle of 2000 is that individual investors ought to bring a healthy dose of skepticism to brokerage firm analysts' views. While analysts can certainly help propel a stock during a bull market, they cannot keep prices up when stocks are in a downward trend. Investors should never rely on an analyst's recommendation when buying and selling shares. They should use research reports only for information about the industry and perhaps to help compare one company with another in the same sector. Analysts' earnings estimates should never be trusted and their recommendations—buy, accumulate, hold—should be ignored.

Because analysts have deep conflicts of interest, trying to attract business to their firms even as they purport to provide objective advice, their pronouncements have little value to investors.

The Dangers of Excessive Trading

In the 1990s, investors dumped the buy-and-hold strategy that had served them so well and embraced frequent stock trading. At the extreme, the sales pitch was oh so alluring: You, too, can learn how to trade your way to profits in the stock market. Quit your dreary day job and begin trading your own capital by computer from a day-trading firm. The potential profits are enormous. But novice investors who believed that they could quickly and easily learn how to trade soon found out how hard it is. It takes years of training for professionals to learn the ins and outs of securities trading. Such a pursuit is *not* for everyone.

Although it was never entirely clear how many investors traded enough to be considered day traders, the concept of trading in and out of stocks during the course of as little as a day or two did become an accepted strategy by otherwise intelligent people.

What do a manicurist, pizza delivery person, recent college graduate, registered nurse and professional dancer have in common? In recent years, they are among the people from all walks of life who lost thousands of dollars day trading. Some even lost their homes.

One state securities regulator even told of people who took up day trading in a pathetic, last-ditch attempt to excavate their way out of mountains of credit card debt. There were also people who had to borrow money from family members to trade stocks. Many of them wound up even worse off than they were before they began such frequent trading.

Day traders were hardly the only ones who traded too often. In the late 1990s, investors held stocks for just over eight months on average, well short of the two years that was typical a decade earlier, according to Sanford C. Bernstein, an investment research firm. For Nasdaq stocks, among the hottest when the market was roaring, the average holding period was five months, also down from roughly two years. The hypervolatile Nasdaq was turning over its shares at more than three times the pace of any major industrialized market in the world. The trading frenzy even infected the staid mutual fund world: investors are holding funds for less than four years on average. A decade ago, it was eleven years.

Online investors evidently traded some of their favorite Nasdaq stocks furiously. The entire share base of Doubleclick, which specializes in Internet advertising, turned over twenty-one times in 1998. That year, investors traded shares equal to sixteen times those available in CMGI, an incubator for Internet companies, and more than thirteen times the shares of Amazon, the online retailer. In the fifty Nasdaq stocks with the heaviest trading, investors hold their shares for just three weeks, on average.

Frequent trading is seductive, in part because interested investors can't look at the technique's past performance and judge their own chances of success. To beginners, day trading looked like a profitable enterprise because the only people who remained in the trading room were those who had not yet lost all their money, not the severe losers.

One of the most perplexing aspects of the craze was that the very investors who had learned not to trust stockbrokers looked at rapid-fire trading as a way to get rich quick and avoid becoming victims of any aggressive financial salespeople. But investors got these ideas from the firms peddling day-trading services, who do all they can to downplay the risks of what is an extremely risky venture.

Here's how day trading was described on the Web site for All-Tech Investments, one of the oldest day-trading concerns. In answer to the question "Can anyone day trade successfully?" All-Tech said: "People with at least an average intelligence and the traits of discipline, intensity and desire, have the potential to become a successful trader."

In another section of the Web site was this question and answer: "Do I have to know anything about the stock market?" Answer: "NO! As a matter of fact, in many instances, the less you know means the less baggage you have to discard when learning the new trading techniques taught by All-Tech."

Yet a look at All-Tech Investments' own financial statements revealed that, in one year, this company in the business of providing day-trading training courses, day-trading rooms and day-trading software actually lost money day trading with its own funds. All-Tech had almost $400,000 in losses from its own stock trading, something the company did not tell its prospective customers. If those losses aren't proof that trading stocks is difficult even for professionals, nothing is.

Day-trading operatives also like to push the notion that technological advancements alone can give investors all the edge they need. But while the companies peddling day-trading services to investors make money, the investors trading stocks in the rooms rarely do. Securities regulators estimate that nine out of ten day traders lose money.

Given the costs of day trading, these losses are not that surprising. At All-Tech, for example, customers were charged $25 a trade, awfully high when compared with other large brokerage firms that charge between $7 and $15 a trade. In addition, All-Tech charged $5,000 to investors who took its training course, which ran for a month. The fee for training could later be applied toward commissions, but it was an outlay nonetheless.

If you're paying $25 a trade, it is almost mathematically certain that you will lose money, maybe your shirt. Indeed, two professors of finance found that online traders in general, not just day traders, lose more money than they make, largely because they buy and sell too frequently rather than holding for the long term.

Terrance Odean and Brad Barber, professors of finance at the University of California at Davis's graduate school of management, analyzed data from sixty thousand households that traded shares through a discount broker from 1991 through 1997. They found that investors who moved from phone-based trading to online trading at discount brokerage houses fell behind the broad market by 3 percent a year. Before moving online, the investors beat the indexes by over 2 percent. The difference, the professors speculate, was more frequent trading and increased costs.

The truth about excessive trading started to dawn on some participants in 1999, even before the Nasdaq stock market collapse of 2000. Indeed, in the first nine months of 1999, online investors filed ten times as many complaints with the S.E.C. as they did in all of 1997. But the consequences of the rush to frequent trading will likely never be seen. Those who tried it and failed—losing perhaps their life savings or retirement accounts—are too embarrassed to come forward to tell their sad tales. Although there is no way to tally the losses amassed by people trading stocks too often, the number is certainly huge.

• Avoid excessive trading. Commissions will wipe out any gains.

Investors' Frayed Safety Net

Many investors believe their brokerage accounts are insured by an institution as secure and reliable as the Federal Deposit Insurance Corporation. They couldn't be more wrong.

The Securities Investor Protection Corporation, designed like the Federal Deposit Insurance Corporation to protect investors from theft of their stocks and bonds, provides little protection. Instead it operates like a private insurance company interested more in denying investors' claims than in returning money to investors victimized by theft or fraud. The list of what the corporation does not cover is lengthy, and many investors never get back their money when their brokerage firms fail.

Consider the travails of Kevin Heebner, the owner of a building supply store in Temple, Pennsylvania. In 1996 he got a call from his longtime stockbroker recommending an investment in short-term bonds. Assured the bonds were safe, Heebner invested $100,000. Three months later, Heebner received a stunning phone call. The broker told him the money he had put into the bonds was gone. The president of the broker's firm, Old Naples Securities, had stolen it.

With his wife about to deliver their third child, Heebner reeled at the thought of a $100,000 loss. Then he remembered with relief that his account was insured by the Securities Investor Protection Corporation, created by Congress in 1970 to protect investors' brokerage accounts from just the sort of theft he had been a victim of.

"I knew that if they didn't find the money from Old Naples Securities, I was insured through S.I.P.C.," Heebner recalled. The broker's "business card and letterhead all had S.I.P.C. logos on them; I figured S.I.P.C. would cover it."

Heebner figured wrong. For more than four years, the corporation maintained he was entitled to nothing—even though three federal courts ruled that the S.I.P.C. should pay him $87,000. Only after a reporter interviewed the lawyer representing the corporation about Heebner's situation did he receive a check for $87,000.

"I never got the sense that S.I.P.C. was in any way trying to help my client," said William P. Thornton Jr., a lawyer at Stevens & Lee in Reading, Pennsylvania, who represented Heebner. "They are very aggressive in attempting to prove that investors' claims do not come within certain legal definitions within the S.I.P.C. statute. And the loser is the investor."

At a time when millions of United States citizens have taken their money out of federally insured banks and put it into brokerage firms, the Securities Investor Protection Corporation's charge of protecting the investing public has never been more important.

Officials of the S.I.P.C. defend the corporation's record and say they must be vigilant in protecting against invalid claims by investors. A close look at this little-understood organization, however, shows that the safety net that investors believe the corporation offers is in fact full of holes.

Industry-financed but not government-backed, the corporation is a far cry from the agency on which it was loosely modeled, the Federal Deposit Insurance Corporation, which protects bank customers against losses.

Created three decades ago after a number of brokerage firm failures and securities thefts, the corporation is chartered to protect each investor for up to $500,000 in securities held at a major brokerage firm. Claims for cash held in a brokerage account are limited to $100,000 a customer, and subject to onerous restrictions. But convincing the corporation to pay can be extremely difficult. It requires investors to run a gauntlet of legal technicalities that would challenge even those knowledgeable about securities law. Some securities lawyers say this is because trustees overseeing the cases, rather than owing their allegiance to wronged investors, are chosen by, and paid by, the corporation. This differs from the independent trustees who are appointed by the courts to handle corporate and personal bankruptcy cases, and who work for the people owed money.

Indeed, the trustees working for the investor protection corporation—many of them from a coterie of lawyers who have made a lucrative specialty of such cases—have received far more from representing the corporation than the corporation itself has paid to investors. Their critics say that trustees wanting repeat business from the corporation have an incentive to minimize payouts to investors. One trustee is the former president of the corporation.

In Kevin Heebner's case, the corporation made several arguments. First, because the investor had sent his money not to Old Naples but to a subsidiary, his investment was not covered. In addition, because the corporation could find no proof that bonds had ever been bought with the $100,000, the organization assumed Heebner had given the money to the brokerage firm as a loan. Lenders are not covered by the corporation. "Although these legal arguments may follow the letter of the investor protection act, the S.I.P.C.'s reliance on them is reminiscent of a private insurance company trying to use every conceivable esoteric legal stratagem to avoid customer claims," said Lewis D. Lowenfels, a lawyer at Tolins & Lowenfels in New York and a leading authority in securities law.

The list of what the corporation does not cover is long. For one thing, $100,000 placed in a bank account insured by the Federal Deposit Insurance Corporation is covered regardless of why the bank failed. But investments lost in a failed brokerage firm are not covered if the loss is a result of most kinds of securities fraud, including a failure to execute a purchase or sale of securities or misrepresentation in the sale of a stock or bond. Losses from unauthorized trading, a large problem among small brokerage firms in the 1990s, are covered only if an investor can prove to the satisfaction of corporation representatives that he complained promptly to the firm.

In addition, because the act that created the corporation covers only securities held by a failed, or failing, brokerage firm, customers whose firms handle their trades through other brokerage firms may not have a claim for coverage by the corporation. Additionally, cash held in a brokerage account that is not earmarked for a securities purchase is not covered by the organization. Nor is an investment in gold, other commodities or a limited partnership.

"The bottom line is S.I.P.C. is outdated and needs to be reviewed," says Joseph P. Borg, securities commissioner for Alabama. "It's been around since 1970, when one in ten Americans were in the markets. Now everyone is in the markets. And everyone thinks that the S.I.P.C. logo reads F.D.I.C., but the protection is very limited."

The corporation started as an idea of Edmund S. Muskie, the former Democratic senator from Maine. He introduced a bill in 1969 to create a Federal Broker-Dealer Insurance Corporation to insure customers against losses, as the F.D.I.C. does with bank depositors. The securities industry countered with a proposal that it said would maintain public confidence in the markets without creating "a vast new governmental agency." The S.E.C. joined the group and drafted a proposal that lawmakers largely accepted.

The investor protection corporation and the F.D.I.C. are vastly different in many other respects. While the F.D.I.C., created in 1934, is an agency of the federal government and its insurance fund is backed by the full faith and credit of the government, the corporation is financed by the securities industry and can borrow from the government, with special approval, only in emergencies. It also maintains a $1 billion line of credit with a consortium of banks.

And while examiners employed by the F.D.I.C. routinely monitor risks at banks, the corporation steps in only when a brokerage firm has collapsed or is close to failure. Another difference is that a brokerage firm, no matter how large or troubled, pays just $150 a year to be an S.I.P.C. member, while payments into the F.D.I.C. insurance fund are based on a bank's size and financial health: the riskier the bank, the larger the fee.

Not long ago, brokerage firms paid much more to be members of the corporation. Between 1991 and 1995, levies were based on their net operating revenues. In 1995, for instance, members were required to pay 0.095 percent of their revenues and the organization received $43.9 million. But when the S.I.P.C. fund reached $1 billion, the corporation cut the levy to $150 a member. Last year, the corporation received $1.14 million in fees.

When a bank fails, the F.D.I.C. steps in to keep it operating or close it and return assets, up to $100,000 per depositor, to their rightful owners. The F.D.I.C. typically resolves bank failures by arranging for another institution to assume the crippled bank's deposits and other obligations. This has the effect of keeping most failed banks open and operating, if under new names.

When a brokerage firm fails, the wheels grind much more slowly. First, the S.I.P.C. applies to the appropriate court to issue a protective order. If it does, the corporation chooses a trustee to oversee the liquidation of the brokerage firm. The corporation has presided over the liquidation of 282 brokerage firms. In the 247 cases completed through the end of 1999, the corporation had returned $3.38 billion to customers in cash and securities. More than 90 percent of this money—$3.15 billion—came straight from the accounts of customers of the failed firms.

The corporation itself has paid investors the other $233 million over almost thirty years. But that amount is far less than the money received by the lawyers who act as trustees and the firms that help them shepherd the cases through the bankruptcy courts, trying to recover additional assets from the failed brokerage firms and assessing the validity of customer claims. Between 1971 and 1999, trustees and the allied firms have received $320 million, 37 percent more than has been paid to wronged investors.

As is typical in most bankruptcy cases, the corporation's trustees are paid first, customers second.

Most brokerage firm liquidations drag on for years. For instance, in 2000, the trustee was still billing for litigation in the 1985 failure of Donald Sheldon & Company, a New York brokerage firm. The corporation said that all the customers' claims it considered valid were paid early on, but that the trustee has been trying to recover assets from executives of the firm to defray the costs of administering the liquidations. Indeed, the trustee recently won $11 million from an insurance company that had covered the firm's officers and directors.

The corporation's president, Michael E. Don, disagrees with accusations that his organization does not put investors first. "Since 1970, S.I.P.C. has advanced $354 million in order to make possible the recovery of $3.3 billion in assets for an estimated 440,000 investors," he said. "S.I.P.C. estimates that more than 99 percent of eligible investors have been made whole in the failed brokerage firm cases that it has handled."

Yet it is impossible to say how many investors whom the corporation has considered ineligible over the years might have prevailed if they had had the money or tenacity to battle the corporation in various courts, as Kevin Heebner did. Some securities lawyers and regulators say that the corporation's arguments to justify the denial of Heebner's claim for more than four years are characteristic of its approach to investor protection. "It's part of the gauntlet to make it as difficult as possible for an investor to make a recovery," said Mark Maddox, a former Indiana securities commissioner who is now a lawyer representing victims in the failure of a fraudulent brokerage firm known as Stratton Oakmont.

One argument used to deny many investors' claims in that case, if applied to all brokerage firm failures, would disqualify millions of investors from S.I.P.C. coverage even though their brokerage firms are members of the organization. The trustee overseeing the Stratton case has successfully argued to the bankruptcy court that Stratton customers do not qualify for S.I.P.C. coverage because their assets were physically held not at Stratton but at the firm that cleared Stratton's trades. The law that created the corporation states that coverage extends only to customers of firms that hold their assets.

Customers of a failed broker that used another firm for clearing trades and administration do not qualify.

This wrinkle may have made sense in 1970, when most brokerage firms cleared their own trades. But today, most of the nation's brokerage houses use clearing firms to carry out their customers' transactions and administer their accounts. Using Stratton Oakmont's argument, customers of these firms, were they to fail, could get no satisfaction from the corporation. "The argument may be technically correct under the law," says Alabama securities commissioner Borg, "but it insulates a lot of people who sell stocks. It indicates even more reason why the S.I.P.C. has to be reexamined."

Until the S.I.P.C. is reassessed, as some in Congress want to do, investors cannot assume that their securities accounts are protected as reliably as their savings accounts. To be safer, investors should deal only with large, established firms, which are less likely to encounter financial problems than smaller firms. In addition, investors should not keep gold or cash in their brokerage firm accounts as they are not covered by the S.I.P.C. And investors who think that their broker is not following their directives must write promptly to the firm and keep records of all correspondence. Investors should be aware that the S.I.P.C., the institution set up to protect investors from losses due to brokerage theft and failure, often resists paying investors' claims.

• If a firm does fail, its customers should never assume that the S.I.P.C. will return what they are owed. When the S.I.P.C. steps in, investors must hire their own securities lawyers to make sure they are getting back from the S.I.P.C. what they are entitled to.

Index

About the Authors
and Editor

LESLIE EATON ("Stocks: How [and How Not] to Invest Directly") is the regional New York economics correspondent for *The New York Times*. Formerly a columnist and editor at *Barron's*, she joined the *Times* in 1994 to cover investing.

KURT EICHENWALD ("Investing for the Ages: Long-Term Strategies") is an investigative reporter for *The New York Times*, writing about business practices and personal finance for more than a decade. A two-time winner of the prestigious George Polk award for excellence in journalism and a finalist for the 2000 Pulitzer Prize, he has been repeatedly selected by *TJFR Business News Reporter* as one of the nation's most influential financial journalists. He is the author of *The Informant* and *Serpent on the Rock*.

DANNY HAKIM ("Mutual Funds: Leaving It to the Pros") is the Detroit bureau chief for *The New York Times*. He joined the *Times* in 2000 as a financial markets writer, specializing in mutual funds. Before joining the *Times*, he reported for *The Washington Post* and SmartMoney.com.

ROBERT D. HERSHEY JR. ("Bonds and Bond Funds: Why They Belong in Your Portfolio") was an economics correspondent for *The New York Times,* covering investment issues in Washington and London for twenty-two years until his retirement in 2001. He was a media fellow at Stanford's Hoover Institution in 1999.

JONATHAN FUERBRINGER ("International Investments: The New Landscape") is a financial writer for *The New York Times.* He was the economics and Congressional correspondent from 1981 to 1988. Since then he has covered financial markets, with an emphasis on foreign markets, currencies, commodities, and bonds.

DAVID CAY JOHNSTON ("Taxes: How to Protect Your Gains") is a financial writer for *The New York Times.* The winner of a Pulitzer Prize in 2001 for his reporting on the tax code, he has covered the I.R.S. and taxes for the *Times* since 1995. Previously, he was the assistant business editor for the *Los Angeles Times* and *The Philadelphia Inquirer.*

GRETCHEN MORGENSON ("Let the Investor Beware: Traps, Scams and Myths") is the market watch columnist for *The New York Times.* Before joining the *Times,* she was an assistant managing editor at *Forbes* magazine. She is the author of *Forbes Great Minds of Business* and *The Woman's Guide to the Stock Market.*

ALLEN R. MYERSON was the weekend editor of *The New York Times* and the editor of the *Times*'s Mutual Fund Quarterly. At the *Times,* he had also been a financial markets writer and Dallas bureau chief. Before he came to the *Times* in 1989, he worked for the *Dallas Morning News* and the *Lexington Herald* of Kentucky. The *Times*'s Sunday Money & Business section was inaugurated in 1995, when the *Times* broadened its business coverage in response to readers' increased interest in personal finance, and particularly in investing.

FLOYD NORRIS ("From Depressed to Delirious: Understanding Today's Market") is the chief financial correspondent for *The New*